Teacher Edition

Skills for RHETORIC

ENCOURAGING THOUGHTFUL CHRISTIANS TO BE WORLD CHANGERS

By James P. Stobaugh

10-Digit ISBN: 080545893X
13-Digit ISBN: 9780805458930

Published by Broadman & Holman Publishers
Nashville, Tennessee

DEWEY: 808
SUBHD: LITERATURE

Unless otherwise stated, scripture text is from The Holy Bible, *Holman Christian Standard Bible* ®,
Copyright © 1999, 2000, 2001, 2002, 2003 by Holman Bible Publishers. Other "Credits, Permissions,
and Sources" are listed at the back of the book.

Cover and interior design by Paul T. Gant, Art & Design—Nashville, TN

1 2 3 4 5   09 08 07 06 05

This Book is gratefully dedicated to
Karen
and
our four children:
Rachel, Jessica, Timothy, and Peter.

He has given us a ministry of reconciliation . . .
2 Corinthians 5:18

Students, to you 'tis given to scan the heights
Above, to traverse the ethereal space,
And mark the systems of revolving worlds.
Still more, ye sons of science ye receive
The blissful news by messengers from heav'n,
How Jesus blood for your redemption flows . . .

—Phillis Wheatley

ACKNOWLEDGMENTS

From the Broadman and Holman Home Education Division, I wish to thank Sheila Moss, whose editorial assistance and encouragement have been greatly appreciated; Matt Stewart, whose vision and perseverance have made this project possible; and Paul Gant and Mark Grover for their work with graphics and the DVD. Likewise, I thank my four children and my distance learning students who so graciously allowed me to use their essays. Finally, and most of all, I want to thank my best friend and lifelong editor, my wife, Karen. "Come, let us glorify the Lord and praise His name forever . . . ." (Psalm 34:3)

Contents

Preface

INTRODUCTION

The heart of *Skills for Rhetoric* is the ability to communicate effectively through the written and spoken word. Written and spoken are the crucial concepts of understanding rhetoric. We can communicate well enough by sending a photograph of something or a CD with music describing something, or painting a picture of something, but that is not rhetoric. Rhetoric is a discipline demanding that the reader dutifully follow laws of grammar, logic, and communication to explain and to describe something.

Quality rhetoric is important and necessary. I agree with Greek philosophers that a democracy demands a responsible, well-considered rhetoric. It is absolutely necessary that we participate in legitimate conversation about important issues. Rhetoric will help us do that.

Rhetoric demands that we reclaim the use of metaphor. A metaphor is a word picture. It describes one thing with a dissimilar thing. It demands discipline and control. A four-year-old cannot understand predestination, for instance, unless the communicator pulls out experiences and images that are familiar to the four-year-old. To describe predestination from the perspective of a seminary professor might be accurate, but it is not rhetoric for a four-year-old. We can take a picture of a sunset and send it to millions of people via e-mail, but that is not rhetoric either. *Rhetoric is the attempt to communicate [a sunset] by the use of the spoken or written word*. Thus, metaphor is at the heart of rhetoric, and rhetoric is at the heart of classical education.

Rhetoric is also at the heart of apologetics, a systematic argumentative discourse in defense of Christianity. It is my prayer that these courses will ultimately prepare your students to think apologetically.

To ignore rhetoric is to invite ourselves on a dangerous search for truth. Our mindless search for relevance and literalness has gotten us pretty lost in the cosmos. When something we seek is so easily obtained by computer chip or digital photograph, then we lazily refuse to engage ourselves in the discipline of metaphor, or even of thinking. For example, love is not easily photographed. Only the metaphor does it justice. Question: if we lose the written metaphor, will we also lose love? How can we understand 1 Cor.13 without first understanding metaphor? Metaphor, or comparison between two ostensibly dissimilar phenomena, is absolutely critical to understanding abstract theological concepts, and, for that matter, it is critical to creative problem solving.

The problems of this age demand a kind of thinking that is promoted and encouraged by rhetoric. The problems of this age will "literally" remain unsolved. However, rhetoric, through the power of metaphor, will invite this generation to look for more creative solutions. Immorality, for instance, will not be removed unless we look to the written Word, that is, the Bible, for answers. Nothing in our experience offers a solution. We will not understand the Bible unless we can employ metaphorical thinking. How else will we apply the Savior's ethical teachings spoken 2000 years ago? Metaphor, along with other mysteries, has become victim of 20th century pretension, pomposity, and obsequious thinking.

Loss of metaphor is only the beginning of the problem. Gertrude Himmelfarb (On Looking into the Abyss) laments that great literary works are no longer read—and if they are, there are no rules for interpreting them. In philosophy, indeed in all communication, truth and reality are considered relative. Without rules the rhetorician is invited to come to any kind of conclusion and is on shaky ground. Gordon Conwell's Seminary professor David Wells in *God in the Wastelands* argues that evangelical Christians, who believe in a personal relationship with God, as well as non-Christians, have both drunk from the trough of modernity. We have both embraced a sort of existential faith instead of a confessional faith. If it feels good do it and believe it. Unless evangelicals participate in serious apologetics, God will be "weightless."

The rise of relativism has had disastrous results. British historian Philip Johnson laments "the great vacuum" that has been filled with totalitarian regimes and superficial thinking. Rhetoric ferrets out truth. If there is no truth, can there be any sense of authority? And can a society survive if there is no authority? Without a legitimate, honest, well-considered rhetoric, will history be reduced to the "pleasure principle"? Literary Criticism, at least in the area of the written classics, forces us to dance with reality.

As I mentioned, in some ways American Evangelical Christianity's loss of rhetorical skills—and I think rhetoric is akin to apologetics—has presaged disaster in many arenas. Without rhetoric, we Christians have no tools to engage modern culture. In some ways we have lost mainline denominations to neo-orthodoxy, and we have lost universities to liberals. Where is a modern Jonathan Edwards? A modern C. S. Lewis? Good thinking and good talking may redeem the Church from both the Overzealous and the Skeptic. Rhetorical skills may help us regain the intellectual and spiritual high ground we so grievously surrendered without a fight (Alister McGrath, *Evangelicalism and the Future of Christianity*). George Marsden in *The Soul of the American University* and Leslie Newbigen in *Foolishness to the Greeks* both conclude that we Christians have conceded much of American culture to modernism by our inability to merge thought and communication in cogency and inspiration. We fail to persuade the modernist culture. Without the main tool to do battle—rhetoric—evangelicals allow orthodoxy to be sacrificed on the altar of relativism.

Basically, *Encouraging Thoughtful Christians to be World Changers: Skills for Rhetoric, Skills for Literary Analysis, American Literature, British Literature,* and *World Literature* are more than five challenging English courses; they are an attempt to equip this generation of students to participate in apologetics.

DESCRIPTION OF THE COURSE

Toward equipping this generation in apologetics, the *Skills for Rhetoric* and *Skills for Literary Analysis* courses are middle school or early high school courses. Both the most reluctant writer and speaker and the most gifted wordsmith will find these courses useful in establishing the necessary skills to analyze and to evaluate literature and to speak before an audience. Since these are skill-based courses, the student will need to complete the entire course.

The *American, British,* and *World Literature* books in the series are content-based. Each literary work is treated individually, much like a unit study. Therefore, each author or work, can be studied independently from the others. The literature critical thinking courses are primarily essay-based. Each lesson contains several critical thinking questions. Most students will write two or three essays per week. Students may answer the other questions orally or may outline their answers. Since the literature courses are *whole-book,* the entire book/literary piece must be read before the lesson begins. Finally, when writing essays, context is as important as content. In other words, *how* a writer says something is as important as *what* he says.

All courses in this series challenge students to think critically.

WHAT DOES IT MEAN "TO THINK CRITICALLY"?

If I show you a truck I am giving you knowledge of the truck. If I show you the parts of the truck, tell you their names, let you sit in the driver's seat and even play with the radio, I am increasing your comprehension of the truck. However, I have not allowed you to drive the truck yet. You know a lot about the truck, perhaps you even have pretended to drive it. You can now tell someone else the names of all the parts, and perhaps you learned how to work the radio. However, you haven't learned to drive it yet. You have passed from the knowledge phase, to the comprehension phase, and are now ready for the application phase. You know a lot about the truck, and you may even know something about how to drive it. However, the fact is you have not driven it yet.

When, if I allow you to drive the truck I am helping you apply your understanding about the truck to a specific task. Now all that you have learned is being used. It is at this point that this course begins. The student has learned information and hopefully understands it well. Now he needs to learn how to use this information.

Finally, if I wish you to know more about the truck, I could suggest that you take the truck apart, analyze each part, and discover how each part works together. You would be analyzing the truck at this point.

You would know the parts of the truck; you would know more about how to fix the truck if it breaks down. You could take the truck apart, put it back together again, and, what is more exciting, you could decide that you don't want a truck anymore. You could even build different things with the truck parts because you know what the truck parts are and do. This step is called synthesis.

Finally, you can decide if this is a good truck after all. Now that you know all about this truck, you can ask yourself, "Is this a good truck?" and "Can I make a better truck?" At this phase of knowledge acquisition, you are evaluating the truck

This is a crude analogy, and no doubt the metaphor breaks down at times, but you get the point. This course teaches students how to apply knowledge, how to analyze knowledge, how to synthesize knowledge, and finally how to evaluate knowledge.

All of the painstaking thinking is for one glorious purpose: to encourage our thoughtful students to be world changers for Christ.

GOALS AND OBJECTIVES

Learning how to write and to speak publicly will never be easy. Students will have to commit themselves to a year long, indeed, lifelong, discipline of learning. However, this course invites students to learn how to write specific essay types and how to effectively deliver speeches. In order to be an effective rhetorician or apologist, students will need to read and write. Therefore, there are is an assigned essay and speech each week throughout this course.

> Throughout *Skills for Rhetoric* students will
> write essay in all genres;
> compose and present various types of speeches;
> write a research paper.

Typically, the parent/educator will seek to inculcate several goals/objectives. Usually, these include:
cognitive or learning goals,
spiritual or affective goals,
behavioral goals.

Cognitive goals usually relate to the understanding of (a) concept(s) and/or the understanding or acceptance of a generalization. A concept is something understood from evidence or other information. It is an abstract or generic idea generalized from particular instances. The understanding of several concepts may lead to the acceptance and understanding of a generalization. A generalization is the act or process whereby a response is made to a stimulus similar to but not identical with a reference stimulus. A generalization will have application far beyond the original concept(s) introduced. For instance, a concept that students will study is "Puritanism." After the students read several literary pieces by and about Puritans, they should consider and hopefully accept this generalization: "Puritans were not dry, lifeless people as they are depicted in Hollywood films."

How will the parent/educator know when these goals have been fulfilled?

When the student is able to write cogent, inspired essays with minimal errors; to effectively present informative, well-argued speeches; to discuss the concepts with others.

Every lesson will include a suggested planning paradigm/format that the parent/educator may find helpful.

The following suggested planning paradigm will be helpful:

Goals/Objectives: What is the purpose of this lesson? Strategies to meet these goals: How will I obtain these goals/objectives? Evaluation: How will I know when I have met these goals/ objectives? As a result of this lesson students will learn a speech concept. (cognitive goal)

The parent/educator will engage students in discussions about ways to write and present speeches.

Students should compose an assigned speech and present it later in front of an audience.
Students will be able to write and to present an inspired speech.
A suggested evaluation tool:
Oratory Evaluation
I. Poise: How does the student present himself/herself? Is the oratory/dramatic reading memorized? (25 points)
II. Articulation: Does the student speak clearly, and slowly? (25 points)
III. Presentation: What is the overall effect of the speech? Does it accomplish its purpose? (50 points)

Improve writing skills. (cognitive goal) Students will write five warm-up essays/week. With minimal errors students will write these essays in 15-20 minutes. Increase vocabulary. (cognitive goal) Students will collect at least five new vocabulary words and use these words in their warm-up essays and assigned essay. Students will use five vocabulary words in conversation during the week as well as use the words in their essays.Experience reflective writing. (affective/spiritual goal)

Using the Journal Guide Questions in the Appendix, students will record at least three entries this week. Students will be given a suggested Scripture passage.Students will show evidence that they have reflected on this issue, including informed discussions and written responses.Increase knowledge through the assigned essay. (cognitive goal)Students will take the Lesson Test.Students will score at least 80% on the Lesson Test.Students will exhibit higher-level thinking as they write this essay. (cognitive goal).Students will write an essay assigned for this lesson. With minimal errors, students will clearly write this essay.Work in a group setting (behavioral goal). In a class, in a co-op experience, or during a family discussion, students will discuss in important issue/topic.Students will exhibit practical listening skills and will manifest understanding of opposing worldviews.Note: Completing a planning strategy for each lesson is optimum.

SPIRITUAL DEVELOPMENT OF THE STUDENT

The parent/educator should consciously stimulate spiritual/faith development in the student. Gone are the days, if they ever existed, that moral development can be separated from knowledge acquisition.

Moral decisions are made by:

1. factual information and
2. values and loyalties.

Other insights about morality include:

1. Morality is manifested in human relationships.
2. Moral/Faith growth only occurs when there is dissonance.
3. One goal is to participate in unselfish acts under authority of the Word of God in relationship with God (see Romans 12).
4. Risk is involved in moral/faith.
5. Learning to think critically can accelerate moral/faith development but does not guarantee its growth.

Students will mature in these approximate stages:

Age 0-4. Child decides what is sacred and important, usually determined by what the parent finds important.

Age 5-12. Family is primary but understands that "Johnny" has different beliefs; many children commit their lives to Christ at this age.

Age 12-17. Child understands faith, racial, and social classification.

Age 19-Adult Indigenous values inculcated in the young person are no longer accepted without question.

Adulthood. Individual learns from other individuals or knowledge bases and willingly changes.

Adulthood. Person is a living example of Galatians 2: 20—I have been crucified with Christ and I no longer live, but Christ lives in me. The life I live in the body, I live by faith in the Son of God, who loved me and gave himself for me.

Moral and spiritual formation of students will be under the direction of the parents and/or their designated authority figure. In *Skills for Rhetoric* moral and spiritual development is encouraged through discussions surrounding the speech topic, the essay topic, journal entries, and even the warm-up exercises.

SPECIAL NEEDS STRATEGIES

Skills for Rhetoric is an excellent course to use with students who learn differently. Students may complete the assignments according to your special instructions. The warm-up exercises, in particular, offer students an avenue to improve writing skills in an ungraded format. They can learn to express their thoughts without the added pressure of evaluation.

Additionally, the parent/educator may want to help the student read with supplemental readings by providing unabridged book tapes. Book tapes of most works can be obtained from www.forsuchatimeasthis.com.

Another strategy in working with students who learn differently is to share the reading and the speaking: students and parents enjoy literature and speaking topics by alternately reading and speaking to each other in a comfortable setting. This method is highly recommended by scholars who work with students who learn differently. Students can become more comfortable with public speaking by first experiencing intimate levels of speaking with parents and educators in a nurturing environment.

PARENT/EDUCATORS' ROLES AND RESPONSIBILITIES

It is the parent/educator's responsibility to:

1. Have students focus on the box in the right top corner of the first page of every lesson. The boxed information tells them the primary goal to be accomplished in the current lesson. It also cues them to "look ahead" to next week's lesson. Please note: The information given in the boxes at the start of every chapter refers directly to th eStudent Edition; therefore not all items mentioned in these boxes will apear, or will read exactly as stated, in this Teacher Edition.

2. Discuss the background material with students. Every lesson will highlight a particular academic/expository essay and a precise skill for developing the art of speaking. For example, in Lesson 1, students will learn how to write a descriptive essay. These writing tips will continue through Lesson 21. Student Final Portfolios are due in Lesson 22. Then, in Lesson 23, students will begin the step-by-step process of writing a research paper. For example, in Lesson 23, they will choose (or you will assign) and narrow their research topic. In Lesson 24, they will write their thesis statement. And so forth. (See the Scope and Sequence of Skills for Rhetoric below).

3. Review Writing Style with your students. Most students still struggle with grammar, effective sentences, diction, punctuation, mechanics, and even the larger elements of writing throughout their high school years. Students will need to review and to correct manifested grammar deficits. Parents/educators may provide worksheets or special assignments to address specific elements of writing. These reviews are additional to regular assignments.

If you or your students need more information, access an advanced composition handbook (*Warriner's, Hodges Harbrace College Handbook, Gregg's, Bedford's*, etc.)

Writing Style

Writing style concerns quality and substance, not content. Simply stated, writing style is the author's choice and arrangement of words, sentence structures, and ideas as well as such less- definable characteristics as cadence, harmony, and tone within the writing. An effective writing style might include focus, concreteness, vitality, originality, and intent.

Who is the audience? What is the task? How does the writer bring the reader to a point of enlightenment? Is the purpose to entertain? To inform? To describe? To clarify? To persuade? Answering these questions will help focus the paper and move the reader to a desired conclusion; without these answers, the reader can easily be confused. Is the focus clearly stated? Does the thesis statement cue the reader's expectations? Does it focus the reader or confuse the reader? Are the ideas totally relevant to the thesis, and are they fully developed? Is the paper logically organized?

Is the paper mechanically correct: spelling, capitals, italics, abbreviations, numbers, and design? Is the punctuation correct: commas, semicolons, apostrophes, quotation marks, periods and other marks? Is the diction appropriate to the topic: word usage, exactness, conciseness, clarity and completeness? Is the grammar correct: sentence sense, sentence fragments, comma splices and fused sentences, adjectives and adverbs, coherence (misplaced and dangling modifiers), pronouns, verbs, sentence unity, subordination and coordination, parallelism, emphasis, and variety?

4. Discuss with students the essay genre highlighted in the current lesson. The highlighted essay genre is defined in simple language and illustrated by a readable example.

5. Discuss with students the public speaking component for the lesson. Then, have students compose the assigned speech and present it in front of a live audience. You can access an Oratory Evaluation template in the Appendix.

6. Have students complete all assigned activities. Assign other work that you deem appropriate.

7. Have students complete one warm-up essay every day. The warm-up essay should be one page or less and should take no more than one-half hour to write. The warm-ups do not need to be edited or rewritten—they are for the purpose of easing students into expressing their thoughts on paper. Gradually, you should see improvement in their writing.

GUIDE FOR DESCRIPTIVE WARM-UP ESSAYS

	DAY 1	DAY 2	DAY 3	DAY 4	DAY 5
Descriptive	Describe a moment that changed your life.	Describe your best friend.	Describe the causes of World War I to a four-year old.	Describe the emotion of jealousy.	Describe the sunset.

WEEKLY IMPLEMENTATION SCHEDULE – SUGGESTIONS

If you follow this schedule, you will get all your work done in a timely way.

SUGGESTED Weekly Implementation

DAY 1	DAY 2	DAY 3	DAY 4	DAY 5
Write a Warm-up Essay. Read 35-50 pages/day. Reflect on the speech assignment for the week. Find five new vocabulary words. Write your assigned essay or complete your assigned tasks.	Make a journal entry. Write a Warm-up Essay. Read 35-50 pages/day. Compose a first draft of your speech. Find five new vocabulary words. Write your assigned essay or complete your assigned tasks.	Make a journal entry. Write a Warm-up Essay. Read 35-50 pages/day. Revise your speech and submit to your evaluator/guardian/parent. Find five new vocabulary words. Write your assigned essay or complete your assigned tasks.	Make a journal entry. Write a Warm-up Essay. Read 35-50 pages/day. Prepare to present your speech tomorrow. Find five new vocabulary words. Submit a copy of your paper to a peer for evaluation. Finish your assigned essay or complete your assigned tasks.	Make a journal entry. Write a Warm-up Essay. Read 35-50 pages/day. Present your speech to a live audience. Find five new vocabulary words. Submit your assignments to your evaluator/guardian/parent. Take Lesson Test.

8. Have students produce a Final Portfolio for Lessons 1-21; the research paper will be added last, at the end of lesson 35. See Appendix for more specific instructions. The Final Portfolio should include corrected essays, speeches, literary reviews, writing journal, vocabulary cards, pictures from field trips, and other pertinent material. In this teacher's edition, teachers will be prompted to engage students in progress discussions.

9. Guide students through the research paper process in Lessons 23-34. As students proceed through the process, teachers will be prompted on how to complete all requisite components of the research paper. At the end of each lesson, parent/educators will be prompted to engage students in progress discussions.

10. Choose other activities the student will complete during the assignment period. These activities include collecting vocabulary cards. Students will not be assigned particular works to read during this course; however, as time allows, students should read books from the Supplemental Reading List (Appendix) which is not meant to be exhaustive but is intended as a guide to good reading. Students should read many of the books in the list before graduating from high school. After reading a literary work, for this course or for any other reason, students should complete a literary reviews (Appendix) as a record of high school reading. Students are strongly encouraged to read 35-50 pages per night (or 200 pages per week), which includes any readings for this course.

Part of the reason students are asked to read so many challenging literary works is for increasing functional vocabulary. Studies show that within 24 hours most students forget new words given to them to learn every week if the words are not read in context. The best means of increasing students' vocabulary is through having them read a vast amount of classical, well-written literary works. While reading these works, students should harvest as many unknown words as possible. One way to have students remember vocabulary words is to have them use five new words in each essay they write.

Additionally, have students create three-by-five vocabulary cards.

The number of vocabulary card students will create will be determined by how many new words they encounter in their readings. Typically, students create more vocabulary words at the beginning of each course than later in the course. By the end of this course students will have collected between 350-500 vocabulary cards. Students may find this process tedious and frustrating, but the method is a valuable tool for learning.

11. Have students write in a prayer journal at least 3 times/week. If they don't have a prayer journal, have them use the template in the Appendix. Make 25-50 copies of this page and put it in a notebook. Students should fill out one of these sheets on a biblical passage as often as possible. Journal writing is one the best forms of reflection. The prayer journal should be a narrative of their spiritual journey. Encourage the entries to be mechanically correct, but the primary purpose is to pique creativity and spiritual formation. In *Skills for Rhetoric*, students are invited to journal through 1 & 2 Kings.

12. Make sure students submit the Final Portfolio and complete the Research Paper. The final portfolio should include corrected essays, speeches, literary reviews, writing journal, vocabulary cards, pictures from field trips, and other pertinent material. The research paper will include: a cover sheet, outline with thesis statement, the paper itself, a works cited (bibliography) page, and appropriate footnotes. Throughout the research process, you can collect and comment on the preliminary bibliography, preliminary outline with thesis statement, notes, revised outline, first draft with footnotes, rewrites, and works cited page. Working the research in stages tremendously aids the process for students, keeps parent/educators apprised of student progress and/or frustrations, and aids the final evaluation. Learning good strategies and techniques for research is a vital tool for future success in any writing program.

CREDITING THE COURSE

After students have satisfactorily completed the lessons, both writing and speaking, this course is a one year/one credit course.

SCOPE AND SEQUENCE
WORLD LITERATURE

LESSON	WRITING SKILL	STYLE (WRITING AND SPEAKING)	PUBLIC SPEAKING SKILL	JOURNAL PASSAGE
1	Overview (A)	Overview Components of Writing and Planning	Overview (A) Types and Purposes of Speeches Outline	1 Kings 1:1-53 The Adonijah Factor
2	Overview (B)	Paragraph (A) Topic Sentence/Thesis	Overview (B) Selecting your Topic Researching Your Topic Knowing your Audience	1 Kings 1:41-53 The Solomon Factor
3	Eyewitness Account	Paragraph (B) Introduction	Introduction Converting the Eye-Witness Account to a Speech	1 Kings 3 Solomon Asks for Wisdom
4	Firsthand Experience	Paragraph (C) Main Body	Main Body Converting the Firsthand Experience to a Speech	1 Kings Overview
5	Descriptive Essay	Paragraph (D) Conclusion	Conclusion Converting the Descriptive Essay to a Speech	1 Kings 8: 22-53 1 Kings 10: 1-14
6	Persuasive vs. Coercive Essay	Paragraph (E) Unity and Coherence	Delivery (A) and Converting the Persuasive Essay to a Speech	Queen of Sheba
7	Persuasive Advertisement Essay	Coherence Paragraph (F) Transitional Devices	Delivery (B) and Converting the Persuasive Advertisement Essay to a Speech	1 Kings 11 Foreign Wives
8	Summary Report	Sentences (A) Overview	Overcoming Fear and Converting Summary Essay to a Speech	1 Kings 11: 14-24 Solomon's Enemies

9	Précis	Sentences (B) Emphasis	Presentation Aids (A) Converting a Précis to a Speech	1 Kings Themes
10	Character Profile	Sentences (C) Expanding Sentences	Presentation Aids (B) Converting a Character Profile to a Speech	1 Kings 1-17 Life's Lessons
11	General Analysis Essay	Sentences (D) Writing Complete Sentences	Converting a General Analysis Essay to a Speech	1 Kings 16 Evil King Ahab
12	General Synthesis Essay	Sentences (E) Writing Clear Sentences	Converting a General Synthesis Essay to a Speech	1 Kings 18:9 Obadiah
13	Literary Analysis Essay	Sentences (F) Sentence Variety	Converting a Literary Analysis to a Speech	1 Kings 18 Elijah
14	Evaluation Essay	Words (A) Using the Dictionary vs. the Thesaurus	Converting the evaluation Essay to a Speech	1 Kings 16-19 The Evil Jezebel
15	Cause/Effect	Words (B) Connotation vs. Denotation	Converting the Cause/Effect Essay to a Speech	1 Kings 19 Down and Out
16	Comparison/Contrast	Words (C) Standard and Substandard English	Converting the Comparison/Contrast Essay to a Speech	1Kings 19:10-18 In the Cleft of the Rock
17	Problem/Solution	Words (D) Idioms	Converting the Problem/Solution Essay to a Speech	1 Kings 19:19-21 Call of Elisha
18	Definition	Words (E) Adjectives and Adverbs in Comparative and Superlative Cases	Converting the Definition Essay to a Speech	1 Kings 20 Using Donkeys and Apostates
19	Explanatory	Words (F) Precise Language	Converting the Explanatory Essay to a Speech	1 Kings 20: 35-41
20	Fact, Inference, and Opinion	Usage (A) Pronoun and Subject/Verb Agreement	Converting the Fact, Inference, and Opinion Essay to a Speech	1 Kings 21
21	Historical Profile	Usage (B) Pronoun Usage	Converting the Historical Profile to a Speech	1 Kings Overview
22	Final Portfolio Due	Final Portfolio Due	Final Portfolio Due	Final Project Due

23	Research Paper: Pre-writing	Usage (C) *Fewer/Less, Good/Well, and Double Negatives*	Speech: Effective Listening	1 Kings 21:29
24	Research Paper: Thesis Statement	Usage (D) *Who* vs. *Whom*	Speech: Oratory	1 Kings 22
25	Research Paper: Preliminary Bibliography	Usage (E) *Further/ Farther; Than/ As.*	Speech: Dramatic Readings	1 Kings 22
26	Research Paper: Taking Notes (A)	Usage (F) *There, And/Nor/Or, There/Their*	Speech: Poetry Reading	1 Kings 22
27	Research Paper: Taking Notes (B) and Preliminary Outline	Usage (G) Use of Comparatives and Superlatives	Debate (A)	1 Kings 22
28	Research Paper: Designing a Working Plan	Punctuation – Quotation Marks	Debate (B)	2 Kings 1 Ahaziah's bad choices
29	Research Paper: Introduction (A)	Introductory Words and Phrases	The Spoken Introduction	2 Kings 2 Chariots of Fire
30	Research Paper: Introduction (B)	Using the Right Word: Being Specific	Speech: Impromptu	2 Kings 2: 23 Mocking God's authority
31	Research Paper: Body	Avoid Sexist Language	Didactic Speech	2 Kings 3 The Moabite Revolt
32	Research Paper: Body	Avoid Pretentious Language, Evasive Language, and Euphemisms, Footnotes and Endnotes	Summary	2 Kings 4 The Shunammite's Son
33	Research Paper: Conclusion	Mixed Metaphors	Enunciation	2 King 5 Namaan Healed of Leprosy
34	Research Paper: Rewriting and Submission	Summary	Summary	2 Kings 6

Audio presentations of most of the readings in the book may be obtained from Blackstoneaudio.com

My prayer for you is

"For this reason I bow my knees before the Father from whom every family in heaven and on earth is named. I pray that He may grant you, according to the riches of His glory, to be strengthened with power through His Spirit in the inner man, and that the Messiah may dwell in your hearts through faith. I pray that you, being rooted and firmly established in love, may be able to comprehend with all the saints what is the length and width, height and depth of God's love, and to know the Messiah's love that surpasses knowledge, so you may be filled with all the fullness of God. Now to Him who is able to do above and beyond all that we ask or think — according to the power that works in you — to Him be glory in the church and in Christ Jesus to all generations, forever and ever. Amen."
(Ephs. 3:14-21)

James Stobaugh

From the Editor

Developing appropriate curricula for a specific audience is a major and intricate endeavor. Doing so for the homeschool and Christian communities is perhaps even more difficult: homeschool approaches, methodology, and content are as diverse as traditional educational trends have ever dared to be. Homeschooling is complex—from unschooling to the Classical approach, there are myriads of opinions of what to teach, when to teach it, and how to teach it to whom at what age and at what level of development. Perhaps you struggle with choices between a *whole-book* approach to literature study or a more traditional and inclusive canon. Perhaps you are still wading through myriads of questions associated with homeschooling teenagers. However, perhaps your decision is final and you merely need a solid literature-and-writing-based English curriculum. Keep reading.

In one-year literature/writing-based courses, including all the quality literature that has ever been published is impossible—there is simply too much good literature and not enough space to include it; neither is there time enough to read it all. Regrettably, many selections of quality literature have not been included in this course—not because they are unworthy, but because they all cannot fit into the designated framework. The author and I have done our best to include whole-book or whole-work selections from the major genres of literature (prose, poetry, and drama). In the *Literary Analysis, Rhetoric*, and *American, British*, and *World Literature* courses in this series, literary selections incorporate many ethnicities from both male and female writers. We believe our selections inform the purpose of the curricula: *Encouraging Thoughtful Christians to be World Changers.*

According to a well-known author, homeschool conference speaker, and long-time homeschooling mom, two of the greatest needs in the homeschool community reside in curricula for high school and for special needs. These English curricula consider those needs; they were conceived in prayer, deliberated through educational experience, and nurtured with inspiration. We are providing unique five-year curricula for required English studies for the multifarious Christian community. Canonical and Classical literature is emphasized; students are meticulously guided through carefully honed steps of *critical thinking, biblical challenge for spiritual growth*, and even additional *enrichment* motivators. A major key to the successful completion of these courses falls in the statements, "Teachers and students will decide on required essays for this lesson, choosing two or three essays. All other essays may be outlined, discussed, or omitted." These statements, repeated in every lesson, allow tremendous flexibility for various levels of student maturity and interests. Since each lesson may offer 10-15 essays, choosing essays each week is vital.

In any literature course offered to Christian audiences there will be differences in opinions regarding acceptable and appropriate content, authors, poets, and playwrights. Some educators may object to specific works or specific authors, poets, or playwrights included in these curricula *even though we have been very conscientious with selections*. For that reason we highly encourage educators and students to confab—choose units according to students' maturity, ability, age, sensitivity, interests, educational intentions, and according to family goals. Educators decide how much they want to shelter their students or to sanction certain works or authors, poets, and playwrights.

On a broader note, our goal in this series is to provide parent educators and Christian schools with educationally sound, rigorous literature courses that equip students

1. to think critically about their world and their participation in it;
2. to write their thoughts, primarily through essays;
3. to articulate their thoughts through small group discussions with peers, families, broader communities, and through occasional formal speeches;
4. to enhance vocabulary through reading and studying quality literature;
5. to converse about the major worldviews of authors of literature, past and present;
6. to develop and refine their own worldviews through participating in biblical application and Christian principles in weekly studies.

Additionally, we provide educators with an instructional CD in the back of each teacher edition. Narrated by the author, the CD is designed to provide extra commentary on the unit studies.

Ideally, students will complete these entire curricula; however, parent educators and teachers are free to choose literary selections that best fit their goals with students. Regardless of the choices, I pray that students come away from studying *Skills for Literary Analysis, Skills for Rhetoric, American Literature, British Literature*, and *World Literature* not only highly educated but also equipped to participate in and contribute to their earthly home while preparing for their heavenly home.

Enjoy!
Sheila Moss

Introduction

I am profoundly enthusiastic about the future. Not only do I trust in our Mighty God, I am greatly encouraged by what I see in this generation. God is doing great things in the midst of students.

There is much need in our physical world. In his seminal work *The Dust of Death* (Downers Grove, Illinois: Intervarsity Press, 1973), social critic Os Guinness prophetically argues that "western culture is marked . . . by a distinct slowing of momentum . . . a decline in purposefulness. . . . Guinness implies that ideals and traditions that have been central to American civilization are losing their compelling cultural authority. In short, there is no corpus of universally accepted morality that Americans follow. As Dallas Willard in *The Divine Conspiracy* (San Francisco: HarperCollins Publishers, 1997) states, ". . . there is no recognized moral knowledge upon which projects of fostering moral development could be based."

In his poem "The Second Coming" William Butler Yeats writes

The best lack all conviction, while the worst
Are full of passionate intensity
Turning and turning in the widening gyre;
The falcon cannot hear the falconer.

In the beginning of the twenty-first century, America is spinning out of control. She is stretching her wings adventurously but is drifting farther away from her God. America is in trouble. How do we know?

You are America's first generation to grow up when wholesale murder is legal; the first generation to access 130 channels and at the same time to access almost nothing of value. In 1993 in their book *The Day America Told the Truth* (NY: Simon & Schuster Publishers, Inc.), James Patterson and Peter Kim warned that 87% of Americans do not believe that the Ten Commandments should be obeyed and 91% of them tell at least one lie a day. Unfortunately, I doubt things are any better today than they were over 10 years ago. The challenge, the bad news, is that this is a time when outrage is dead. Whatever needs to be done, you and your friends are probably going to have to do it.

I think the good news is that we are turning a corner. I believe that in the near future Americans will be looking to places of stability and strength for direction. Besides, by default, those people whose lives are in reasonably good shape, who have some reason to live beyond the next paycheck, will have an almost inexorable appeal. Those who walk in the Light will draw others into the very-same Light. My prayer is that these curricula will help you walk in the Light in a modest way.

I believe that God is raising a mighty generation at the very time that many twenty-first century Americans are searching for truth—at the very time they are hungry for things of the Lord. You will be the culture-creators of the next century. You are a special generation, a special people.

Young people, I strongly believe that you are the generation God has called *for such a time as this* to bring a Spirit-inspired revival. God is stirring the water again at the beginning of this century. He is offering a new beginning for a new nation. I believe you are the personification of that new beginning.

You are part of one of the most critical generations in the history of Western culture. Indeed, only Augustine's generation comes close in importance to your generation. In both cases—today and during the life of Augustine, Bishop of Hippo—civilizations were in decline. Young Augustine lived through the decline of the Roman world; you are living through the decline of American cultural superiority. Even though the barbarians conquered Rome, the Christians conquered the barbarians.

Similar to Anne Bradstreet and other young Puritans who settled in 1630 Boston, you will need to replace this old, reprobate culture with a new God-centered, God-breathed society, or our nation may not survive another century.

While I was a graduate student at Harvard University in the mid-1970s, I attended a chapel service where the presenter self-righteously proclaimed that we Harvard students were the next generation of culture creators. Indeed. Perhaps he was right—look at the moral mess my generation created!

Evangelical scholars Nathan Hatch and George Marsden argue, and I think persuasively, that you young people will be the next generation of elites: important politicians, inspired playwrights, and presidents of Fortune 500 companies.

I profoundly believe and fervently hope that you young people will also be the new elite of culture creators. I define "elitism" as the ability and propensity of an individual or a group to assume leadership and culture-creation in a given society. In his essay "Blessed Are the History-Makers," theologian Walter Bruggemann reminds us that culture is created and history is made by those who are radically committed to obeying God at all costs.

Will you be counted among those who are radically committed—being smart, but above all, loving, worshipping, and being obedient to the Word of God? In your generation and for the first time in 300 years of American cultural history, the marriage of smart minds and born-again hearts is becoming visible. This combination is potent indeed and has revolutionary implications for twenty-first century cultural America. Now, as in the Puritan era, a spirit-filled elite with all its ramifications is exciting to behold.

This book is dedicated to the ambitious goal of preparing you to be a twenty-first century world changer for the Christ whom John Milton in *Paradise Lost* called "the countenance too severe to be beheld." (VI, 825)

James Stobaugh

LESSON 1

Writing Skill: Overview (A)

Style (Writing and Speaking): Overview (A): Components of Writing and Planning

Public Speaking Skill: Overview (A): Types and Purposes of Speeches and The Outline

Looking Ahead: Determining the purpose and plan of the Composition (Writing), Knowing your Audience (Speaking), and Researching Your Topic (Speaking)

Goals/Objectives: What is the purpose of this lesson?	Strategies to meet these goals: How will I obtain these goals/objectives?	Evaluation: How will I know when I have met these goals/objectives?
Concept: A one-minute speech on "My Many Virtues" (cognitive goal)	The parent/educator will engage students in discussions about ways to write and present speeches. Students should compose, practice, and later present in front of an audience a one minute speech on the topic "My Many Virtues."	Students will be able to write and to present an inspired speech. Suggested evaluation sheet includes: Oratory Evaluation I. Poise: Calm presentation? Appropriate word inflections? Familiarity with oratory/dramatic reading? Cue cards used appropriately? (20 points) II. Articulation: Distinct enunciation? Appropriate tone? Appropriate volume? (30 points) III. Organization: Introduction? Thesis stated? Points supported? Conclusion effective? Accomplish the stated purpose? (50 points)
Concept: Promote ease with spontaneous writing (cognitive goal)	Students will write five warm-up essays/week.	With minimal errors, students will write these essays in 15-20 minutes.
Concept: Vocabulary (cognitive goal)	Students will collect at least five new vocabulary words and use these words in their warm-up essays.	Students will use five vocabulary words in conversation during the week as well as use the words in their essays.

Goals/Objectives: What is the purpose of this lesson?	Strategies to meet these goals: How will I obtain these goals/objectives?	Evaluation: How will I know when I have met these goals/objectives?
Concept: Reflective writing (affective/spiritual goal)	Using the Journal Guide Questions in the Appendices, students will record at least three entries this week. Suggested Scripture: 1 Kings 1:1-53	Students will show evidence that they have reflected on this issue, including informed discussions and written responses.
Concept: Evaluating writing (cognitive goal)	Students will take Lesson 1 Test.	Students will score at least 80% on the Lesson 1 Test.
Concepts: Thesis statement, introduction, body, and conclusion (cognitive goal).	Students will write an essay of their choice, then underline the thesis statement, italicize the introduction, put in bold letters a transition, and, finally, type/write in capital letters the conclusion.	With minimal errors students will be able to identify the thesis statement, introduction, body, and conclusion.
Concept: Working in a group setting (behavioral goal).	In a class, in a co-op experience, or during a family discussion, students will determine the most colorful relative in the family.	Students will exhibit practical listening skills and will manifest understanding of opposing worldviews.

SUGGESTED
Weekly *Implementation*

DAY 1	DAY 2	DAY 3	DAY 4	DAY 5
Write a Warm-up Essay.	Write a Warm-up Essay.	Write a Warm-up Essay.	Write a Warm-up Essay.	Write a Warm-up Essay.
Read 35-50 pages/day.	Read 35-50 pages/day.	Read 35-50 pages/day.	Read 35-50 pages/day.	Read 35-50 pages/day.
Find five new vocabulary words.	Find five new vocabulary words.	Find five new vocabulary words.	Find five new vocabulary words.	Find five new vocabulary words.
Reflect on the speech assignment for the week.	Compose a first draft of your speech.	Revise your speech and submit to your evaluator/ parent.	Prepare to present your speech tomorrow.	Present your speech to a live audience.
Write an outline and thesis for your essay.	Write the first draft of your essay.	Revise the first draft of your essay.	Finish the final copy of your essay.	Submit your assignments to your evaluator/ guardian/parent.
Make a journal entry.	Make a journal entry.	Make a journal entry.	Make a journal entry.	Submit a copy of your paper to a peer for evaluation.
				Make a journal entry.
				Take Lesson 1 Test

ENRICHMENT ACTIVITIES/PROJECTS

Students should play a word game such as *Charades*.

Students should try to describe complicated machinery in language that a four-year-old can understand.

SPEECH ASSIGNMENT

Students should compose and practice a one-minute speech on the topic "My Many Virtues" and then present it in front of an audience. The speech should entice and earn the audience's interest through the introduction, fulfill the promise that is made in the introduction, and then present the audience with a final conclu-

sion(s). Evaluator should complete an oratory evaluation form. (Appendix)

ANSWER: *Suggested Outline*
I. Introduction
Among my many virtues are . . .

II. Body
A. Virtue 1
Example
B. Virtue 2
Example

III. Conclusion

WRITING ASSIGNMENTS

1. Write a one-two page essay of your choice or an essay on the topic "My Many Virtues." Next, underline the thesis statement, *italicize the introduction*, put in **bold letters the transitions**, and, finally, type/write the CONCLUSION IN CAPITAL LETTERS.

Emphasize the following elements of essays: Starting Point, Purpose, Form, Audience, Voice, and Point of View.

This essay should include an outline with thesis statement, a rough draft, several revisions, a final copy, and five new (circled) vocabulary words. Your essay must pay particular attention to style (focus, content, organization).

Give a copy to a peer/friend to complete a peer evaluation form (Appendix) and to instructor to evaluate.

ANSWER: *Sample Essay taken from Henry David Thoreau (note the differences in the English language, in the structuring of sentences, and in punctuation between Thoreau's writing and current writing standards):*

(Introduction)

I wish to speak a word for Nature, for absolute freedom and wildness, as contrasted with a freedom and culture merely civil—to regard man as an inhabitant, or a part and parcel of Nature, rather than a member of society. *I wish to make an extreme statement, if so I may make an emphatic one, for there are enough champions of civilization: the minister and the school committee and every one of you will take care of that.*

(Body)

I have met with but one or two persons in the course of my life who understood the art of Walking, that is, of taking walks—who had a genius, so to speak, for sauntering, which word is beautifully derived "from idle people who roved about the country, in the Middle Ages, and asked charity, under pretense of going a la Sainte Terre," to the Holy Land, till the children exclaimed, "There goes a Sainte-Terrer," a Saunterer, a Holy-Lander. They who never go to the Holy Land in their walks, as they pretend, are indeed mere idlers and vagabonds; but they who do go there are saunterers in the good sense, such as I mean. Some, however, would derive the word from sans terre without land or a home, which, therefore, in the good sense, will mean, having no particular home, but equally at home everywhere. For this is the secret of successful sauntering. He who sits still in a house all the time may be the greatest vagrant of all; but the saunterer, in the good sense, is no more vagrant than the meandering river, which is all the while sedulously seeking the shortest course to the sea. But I

prefer the first, which, indeed, is the most probable derivation. For every walk is a sort of crusade, preached by some Peter the Hermit in us, to go forth and reconquer this Holy Land from the hands of the Infidels.

(Conclusion)

It is true, we are but faint-hearted crusaders, even the walkers, nowadays, who undertake no persevering, never-ending enterprises. Our expeditions are but tours, and come round again at evening to the old hearth-side from which we set out. Half the walk is but retracing our steps. WE SHOULD GO FORTH ON THE SHORTEST WALK, PERCHANCE, IN THE SPIRIT OF UNDYING ADVENTURE, NEVER TO RETURN—PREPARED TO SEND BACK OUR EMBALMED HEARTS ONLY AS RELICS TO OUR DESOLATE KINGDOMS. IF YOU ARE READY TO LEAVE FATHER AND MOTHER, AND BROTHER AND SISTER, AND WIFE AND CHILD AND FRIENDS, AND NEVER SEE THEM AGAIN—YOU HAVE PAID YOUR DEBTS, AND MADE YOUR WILL, AND SETTLED ALL YOUR AFFAIRS AND ARE A FREE MAN—THEN YOU ARE READY FOR A WALK. *("Walking," Henry David Thoreau)*

2. Read a book from the reading list or a book assigned in your literature and/or history elective (or another approved book). Read at least 35/50 pages/day. Make vocabulary cards from words in your reading.

3. Write and present your speech and have a teacher evaluate it with a speech evaluation form. (Appendix)

4. Concentrate on writing *style* this week. Pay particular attention to the way you organize and write your papers.

5. Using the devotional questions as a guide (Appendix), write at least three journal entries. Reflect on the biblical characters in 1 Kings 1:1-53. Compare the collapse of intellectual and political Israel with the moral and cultural demise of America in the last 150 years. What choices does King David make that may lead the nation into a generation of apostasy? Speculate on what King David is thinking as he chooses Solomon over Adonijah. Write in essay form. This journal is meant to be private, but you are invited to share reflections with others.

6. Complete one warm-up essay every day. The warm-up essay should be one page or less; it should not take more than one-half hour. The warm-ups do not need to be edited or rewritten. Every day will build progress with writing ease, and over time you will experience improvement.

FINAL PROJECT

Students should correct and rewrite all essays and place
them in their Final Portfolio.

WARM-UP ESSAYS:

	DAY 1	DAY 2	DAY 3	DAY 4	DAY 5
Elements of Writing	Create a thesis for an essay entitled "My favorite pencil."	Create an introduction for the same essay.	Create a three-point body for the same essay.	Create a conclusion for the same essay.	Rewrite the same essay.

LESSON 1 TEST

ESSAY (100 POINTS)

Read the following essay several times in preparation for critiquing it. Evaluate the effectiveness of the introduction, the thesis, the transitions, and the conclusion.

How can we react to rejection? Hopefully, we keep our eyes focused on Jerusalem and do not allow rejection to sidetrack us. We may be tempted to stop and annihilate a few Samaritans, but remaining firm in our resolve to possess the land, to journey to the end of our quest, and to reach Jerusalem will be far more rewarding. Refusing to allow rejection to destroy us and choosing not to react in hatred will ease our journey toward our "Jerusalem."

Ruth Graham in the *Christian Herald* relates a story about a jellyfish attack. "Suddenly I was struck. It was as if my right arm had touched a high voltage wire," she exclaimed. "It wasn't long before ugly welts rose around my right forearm and a vivid red line crossed my back. By dinner time the pain had subsided to bone-deep ache...but it hurt for weeks." Many weeks later she naturally found that she had a well-deserved aversion to the ocean. However, she knew she had to return to the sea. The longer she waited the more difficult it became. She loved the ocean, but she knew that as long as she swam, there would be a chance that she would experience the same pain again. She returned to the ocean.

Life is a lot like the sea—full of unseen hazards and venomous creatures. Hurting and fearful after undeserved rejection, we are tempted to call it quits, to stay out of the ocean altogether. However, life is in the ocean, and the road to our spiritual Jerusalem leads through treacherous waters. Returning to the ocean can help us face our hurts and fears.

Perhaps the most common form of rejection we experience is self-rejection. Self-rejection is very dangerous because it negates the work of the cross in our lives. In many churches there is so much emphasis on humility that we pretend to be humble by practicing self-rejection. However, true humility evokes love, kindness, and self-control. Self-rejection evokes sadness, depression, anger, and perhaps even violence. We fall into the trap of self-rejection when we listen to the voices that call us worthless and unlovable. We can then fall into the traps of success, popularity, power, or excessive work as antidotes. There is no antidote to poor self-esteem but a profound realization that God loves us.

LESSON 1 TEST ANSWER

ESSAY (100 POINTS)

Read the following essay several times in preparation for critiquing it. Evaluate the effectiveness of the introduction, the thesis, the transitions, and the conclusion.

ANSWER:

The use of a rhetorical question in the introduction is an effective tool for inviting the reader into a problem that needs a solution. The introduction is the place to explain references to "Jerusalem" and "Samaritans" for readers who are not familiar with the author's use of symbolism.

In the body, the author effectively develops his exposition by using the metaphor of a jellyfish and the ocean.

Lack of effective transitions is a problem in this paper: There is no clear transition between the author's introductory paragraph and the first paragraph of the body. At the end of the first paragraph, the author could have stated something like, "Often we can follow the lead of others when we are faced with rejection. Ruth Graham is one such person." To transition to the second body paragraph the author could have concluded the first with something like, "Ruth refused to allow the ocean's rejection, through the jellyfish, to prevent her from returning to it." The second body paragraph could have begun with, "Similarly, life is ..." as a transition and could have ended with, "There is another kind of rejection that we will encounter in our journey." Then, the last paragraph could have begun with "Another form of rejection...."

Even though there is a lack of transitions, the author does keep the main theme alive by repeating the emphasis on "rejection."

Finally, the conclusion is weak because it offers no closure and because it is not properly set up with a transition; it leaves the reader hanging—wondering if the author was clear about the purpose of the essay.

LESSON 2

Writing Skill: Overview (B)

Style (Writing and Speaking): Paragraph (A) Topic Sentence/Thesis

Public Speaking Skill: Overview (B) Selecting Your Topic, Researching Your Topic, and Knowing Your Audience

Looking Ahead: Eyewitness Account (Writing), The Speech Outline (Speaking)

Goals/Objectives: What is the purpose of this lesson?	Strategies to meet these goals: How will I obtain these goals/objectives?	Evaluation: How will I know when I have met these goals/objectives?
Concept: In front of two different audiences, present a speech on the topic, "the importance of finishing my chores before I go to soccer/ballet/practice." (cognitive goal)	The parent/educator will engage students in discussions about ways to write and present speeches. In front of an audience, students should present a 3-5 minute eye-witness account of how my family eats dinner.	Students will be able to write and to present an original speech. Suggested evaluation sheet includes: Oratory Evaluation I. Poise: Calm presentation? Appropriate word inflections? Familiarity with oratory/dramatic reading? Cue cards used appropriately? (20 points) II. Articulation: Distinct enunciation? Appropriate tone? Appropriate volume? (30 points) III. Organization: Introduction? Thesis stated? Points supported? Conclusion effective? Accomplish the stated purpose? (50 points)
Concept: Improve writing skills (cognitive goal)	Students will write five warm-up essays/week.	With minimal errors students will write these essays in 15-20 minutes.

Goals/Objectives: What is the purpose of this lesson?	Strategies to meet these goals: How will I obtain these goals/objectives?	Evaluation: How will I know when I have met these goals/ objectives?
Concept: increase vocabulary (cognitive goal).	Students will collect at least five new vocabulary words and use these words in their warm up essays.	Students will use five vocabulary words in conversation during the week, as well as use the words in their essays.
Concept: reflective writing (affective/spiritual goal).	Using the Journal Guide Questions in the Appendices, students will record at least three entries this week. Suggested Scripture: on 1 Kings 1:41-53.	Students will show evidence that they have reflected on this issue including informed discussions and written responses.
Concept: increased knowledge essay writing (cognitive goal)	Students will take Lesson 2 Test.	Students will score at least 80% on Lesson 2 Test.
Concept: overview of writing process (cognitive goal)	Students will write two 75-word essays on the topic, "the importance of finishing my chores before I go to soccer practice." The first essay is written for the team. The second essay is written for parents.	With minimal errors students will clearly write two well-organized essays.
Concept: working in a group setting (behavioral goal).	In a class, in a co-op experience, or during a family discussion, students discuss strategies that they employ to share the Gospel in an inhospitable setting.	Students will exhibit practical listening skills and will manifest understanding of opposing worldviews.

SUGGESTED
Weekly *Implementation*

DAY 1	DAY 2	DAY 3	DAY 4	DAY 5
Write a Warm-up Essay.	Write a Warm-up Essay.	Write a Warm-up Essay.	Write a Warm-up Essay.	Write a Warm-up Essay.
Read 35-50 pages/day.	Read 35-50 pages/day.	Read 35-50 pages/day.	Read 35-50 pages/day.	Read 35-50 pages/day.
Find five new vocabulary words.	Find five new vocabulary words.	Find five new vocabulary words.	Find five new vocabulary words.	Find five new vocabulary words.
Reflect on the speech assignment for the week.	Outline and compose first draft of speech.	Revise speech and submit to evaluator/ parent.	Prepare to present speech tomorrow.	Present speech to a live audience.
Write an outline and thesis for your essay.	Complete first draft for essay.		Finish final copy of essay.	Submit assignments to evaluator/ parent.
Make a journal entry.	Make a journal entry.	Finish first draft of essay.	Make a journal entry.	Submit a copy of essay to a peer for evaluation.
		Make a journal entry.		Make a journal entry.
				Take Lesson 2 Test

ENRICHMENT ACTIVITIES/PROJECTS

Students should reflect on how their pastor's sermons would be presented differently to a crowd on the beach or at a sporting event. For example, would their pastors discuss Predestination at a NASCAR race? If so, how?

SPEECH ASSIGNMENT

Present a speech on the topic, "the importance of finishing my chores before I go to soccer/ballet/practice." The first speech is presented to the team/troop. The second speech is presented to parents. This essay should include an outline with thesis, rough draft, several revisions, final copy with five new (circled) vocabulary words, cue cards (index cards) and oral practice. Give a copy to a peer/friend to complete a peer evaluation form (Appendix) and to instructor for evaluation.

ANSWER: *The speech to the parents would hopefully exhibit deferential commitment to the worthy task of finishing all chores. The speech to the team might emphasize the commitment to finishing the chores in order to fulfill the commitment to the team.*

WRITING ASSIGNMENTS

1. Write two 75-word essays on the topic, "the importance of finishing my chores before I go to soccer/ballet/practice." The first essay is written for your

team/troop. The second essay is written for your parents. Write as precisely as possible. This essay should include an outline with thesis, rough draft, final copy containing five new (circled) vocabulary words, and cue cards (index cards). Give a copy to a peer/friend to complete a peer evaluation form (Appendix) and to your instructor to evaluate.

ANSWER: Sample tone: *For My Team/Troop: Hey guys! It is 2pm and 2 hours til practice! I am looking forward to the touch of the pig skin, the feel of my Adidas ©, the smell of sweat! Yet, between then and now, I have to finish my schooling and chores. No problem. I would not enjoy practice knowing my chores were not finished! I can't attend practice unless I finish my chores, but I know you depend on me to finish my chores and be at practice on time. For my parents: It is 2pm and 2 hours to soccer practice! I am looking forward to the touch of the pig skin, the feel of my Adidas ©, the smell of sweat! Yet, before then and now, I have to finish my schooling and chores. No problem. I would not enjoy practice knowing my chores were not finished! My family depends on me to finish my chores.*

2. Read a book from the reading list or a book assigned in your literature and/or history elective (or another approved book). Read at least 35/50 pages/day. Make vocabulary cards from words in your reading.

3. Present your speech and have a teacher evaluate it with a speech evaluation form (Appendix).

4. Consider writing and speech style this week. Be sure to create a precise but inspiring thesis statement.

5. Using the devotional questions as a guide (Appendix), write at least three journal entries. Reflect on 1 Kings 1:41-53. Relate the incident first from the viewpoint of Solomon and then from Adonijah. Again, record your reflections in essay form. This journal is meant to be private although you are invited to share your reflections with others.

6. Complete one warm-up essay every day. The warm-up essay should be one page or less; it should not take more than one-half hour to write. The warm-ups do not need to be edited or rewritten. With time you will see a difference with your writing comfort and improvement in your writing.

FINAL PROJECT

Students should correct and rewrite all essays and place them in their Final Portfolio.

WARM-UP ESSAYS:

	DAY 1	DAY 2	DAY 3	DAY 4	DAY 5
Speaking/ Writing to an Audience	Write an essay defending the Atkins Diet. Audience: Wheat Growers Association.	Write an essay defending the Atkins Diet. Audience: Atkins Diet Support Group.	Write an essay arguing for a vegetarian diet. Audience: National Beef Growers Association.	Write an essay arguing for a vegetarian diet. Audience: Vegetarian Diet Support Group.	Write an essay arguing for classical music. Audience: Rolling Stone Magazine Board of Directors.

LESSON 2 TEST

ESSAY (100 POINTS)

You have been hired by a consulting firm to edit a speech written by a politician to be presented at an American Agricultural Convention. Help him out.

Mr. Secretary, Delegates, and esteemed visitors, welcome. I am very grateful to be here! Only yesterday morning, while eating my Coco Puffs ©, Pop-Tarts ©, and drinking a Pepsi ©, I was suddenly so grateful for the farmers in America! What a great job you do! Papaya fruits, mustard, figs and dates, corn—they are all provided to the American consumer, thanks to you! Day in and day out, you walk behind those plows, spreading those seeds, hoeing those weeds. Thank you!

I know how hard you work and that is why I am going to introduce a bill to remove price supports for milk products. It is vital that you are rewarded for your hard work.

And those dangerous chemicals! If I have my way, I will push through legislation that will remove all those life-threatening chemicals. Why, in a year or so, you will only have ladybugs to protect you from pests and critters!

Finally, my good friends, let's limit exports. Yes, why should American consumers suffer for us to feed people overseas? Prices for American consumers will drop, too, with fewer grain exports. There will be supply and less demand.

LESSON 2 TEST ANSWERS

ESSAY (100 POINTS)

You have been hired by a consulting firm to edit a speech written by a politician to be presented at an American Agricultural Convention. Help him out.

ANSWER: *The speech writer shows that he is totally unfamiliar with the audience; he would probably get booed off the platform. First, the politician should not mention that he ate processed food yesterday—it would be different if he ate eggs, bacon, and toast—all products raised by American farmers. Next, American farmers do not grow papaya fruits or mustard and they grow very few figs and dates. Also, modern farmers do not walk behind plows—they use high-tech machinery to perform all those agricultural tasks. Next, farmers are in favor of price support for products like milk but not in favor of chemical controls (within reason) because chemicals help them kill bugs and pests who eat their crops. Finally, farmers are not in favor of limiting exports—they make a lot of money exporting grain to countries around the world.*

LESSON 3

Writing Skill: Eyewitness Account

Style (Writing and Speaking): Paragraph (B) Introduction

Public Speaking Skill: The Speech Introduction and Converting the Eyewitness Account to a Speech

Looking Ahead: The Firsthand Experience Essay (Writing) and the Speech Main Body (Speaking)

Goals/Objectives: What is the purpose of this lesson?	Strategies to meet these goals: How will I obtain these goals/objectives?	Evaluation: How will I know when I have met these goals/objectives?
Concept: In front of an audience, present a 3-5 minute eyewitness account of how your family eats dinner. (cognitive goal)	The parent/educator will engage students in discussions about ways to write and present speeches. In front of an audience, students should present a 3-5 minute eyewitness account of how their family eats dinner.	Students will be able to write and to present an original speech. Suggested evaluation sheet includes: Oratory Evaluation I. Poise: Calm presentation? Appropriate word inflections? Familiarity with oratory/dramatic reading? Cue cards used appropriately? (20 points) II. Articulation: Distinct enunciation? Appropriate tone? Appropriate volume? (30 points) III. Organization: Introduction? Thesis stated? Points supported? Conclusion effective? Accomplish the stated purpose? (50 points)
Concept: writing skills (cognitive goal) Concept: increase vocabulary (cognitive goal).	Students will write five warm-up essays/week. Students will collect at least five new vocabulary words and use these words in their warm up essays and eyewitness account.	With minimal errors students will write these essays in 15-20 minutes. Students will use five vocabulary words in conversation during the week, as well as use the words in their essays.

Goals/Objectives: What is the purpose of this lesson?	Strategies to meet these goals: How will I obtain these goals/objectives?	Evaluation: How will I know when I have met these goals/ objectives?
Concept: reflective writing (affective/spiritual goal).	Using the Journal Guide Questions in the Appendices, students will record at least three entries this week. Suggested Scripture: on 1 Kings 3.	Students will show evidence that they have reflected on this issue, including informed discussions and written responses.
Concept: increased knowledge of the assigned essay (cognitive goal)	Students will take Lesson 3 Test.	Students will score at least 80% on Lesson 3 Test.
Concept: Eyewitness Account (cognitive goal)	Students will write a one-page eyewitness account of their family eating dinner.	With minimal errors students will clearly write two well-organized essays.
Concept: working in a group setting (behavioral goal).	In a class, in a co-op experience, or during a family discussion, students will give an eyewitness account of what happened in Sunday school last week.	Students will exhibit practical listening skills and will manifest understanding of opposing worldviews.

SUGGESTED
Weekly *Implementation*

DAY 1	DAY 2	DAY 3	DAY 4	DAY 5
Write a Warm-up Essay.	Write a Warm-up Essay.	Write a Warm-up Essay.	Write a Warm-up Essay.	Write a Warm-up Essay.
Read 35-50 pages/day.	Read 35-50 pages/day.	Read 35-50 pages/day.	Read 35-50 pages/day.	Read 35-50 pages/day.
Find five new vocabulary words.	Find five new vocabulary words.	Find five new vocabulary words.	Find five new vocabulary words.	Find five new vocabulary words.
Reflect on the speech assignment for the week.	Compose a first draft of your speech.	Revise your speech and submit to your evaluator/ parent.	Prepare to present your speech tomorrow.	Present your speech to a live audience.
Write an outline and thesis for your eyewitness account.	Compose the first draft for your eyewitness account.	Finish the first draft of your eyewitness account.	Finish the final copy of your eyewitness account.	Submit your assignments to your evaluator/ parent.
Make a journal entry.	Make a journal entry.	Make a journal entry.	Make a journal entry.	Submit a copy of your paper to a peer for evaluation.
				Make a journal entry.
				Take Lesson 3 Test

ENRICHMENT ACTIVITIES/PROJECTS

Carefully approach a veteran of the Vietnam War and ask if you may have an interview; record his eyewitness account of one of the struggles.

SPEECH ASSIGNMENT

In front of an audience, present a 3-5 minute eyewitness account of how your family eats dinner.

> **ANSWER:**
> *Suggested Outline*
> *I. Introduction*
>   *Overview of incident*
> *II. Body*
>   *A. Example 1*
>   *B. Example 2*
> *III. Conclusion*

WRITING ASSIGNMENTS

Write a one-page eyewitness account of "How My Family Eats Dinner." Using vivid imagery and precise language, recreate this event in your essay. This essay should include an outline with thesis statements, rough draft, several revisions, and final copy with five new (circled) vocabulary words. Give a copy to a peer/friend to complete a peer evaluation form (Appendix) and to your instructor for evaluation.

ANSWER: *See outline for speech above.*

2. Read a book from the reading list or a book assigned in your literature and/or history elective (or another book approved by his parents). Read at least 35/50 pages/day. Make vocabulary cards from words in your reading.

3. Present your speech and have a teacher evaluate it with a speech evaluation (Appendix).

4. Pay particular attention to the introduction that you write for your essay and speech.

5. Using the devotional questions as a guide, write at least three journal entries. This week reflect on 1 Kings 3, where Solomon asks for wisdom. Answer this question: How does Solomon change between chapters 3 and 11? By chapter 11 Solomon has married foreign wives and led Israel into apostasy. Record your reflections in essay form.

6. Complete one warm-up essay every day. The warm-up essay should be one page or less; it should not take more than one-half hour to write. The warm-ups do not need to be edited or rewritten. Over time you will experience greater with writing and will see improvement in your writing if you carefully attend to the evaluation and revisions.

FINAL PROJECT

Students should correct and rewrite all essays and place them in their Final Portfolio.

WARM-UP ESSAYS:

	DAY 1	DAY 2	DAY 3	DAY 4	DAY 5
Eyewitness	Imagine that you are a dog, sleeping in the rain.	Imagine that you have one hour to share Jesus Christ with 19-year-old Adolf Hitler.	Imagine that you were never born.	Imagine that no one came to your birthday party.	Imagine that you were adopted by someone of another race.

LESSON 3 TEST

ESSAY (100 POINTS)

Based on the picture below, write a one-page eyewitness account of Abraham Lincoln's assassination.

LESSON 3 TEST ANSWER

ESSAY (100 POINTS)

Based on the picture below, write a one-page eyewitness account of Abraham Lincoln's assassination.

    ANSWER: *The student should describe the play itself, the stage, and Lincoln's box. Then, after setting the scene, the student should describe—as if he was there—the assassination itself. All aspects of an essay should be present. Careful evaluation will aid the student's progress as a writer.*

LESSON 4

Goals/Objectives: What is the purpose of this lesson?	Strategies to meet these goals: How will I obtain these goals/objectives?	Evaluation: How will I know when I have met these goals/objectives?
Concept: persuasive speech (cognitive goal)	The parent/educator will engage students in discussions about ways to write and present speeches. In front of an audience, students will present a firsthand experience speech.	Students will be able to write and to present an inspired speech. Suggested evaluation sheet includes: Oratory Evaluation I. Poise: Calm presentation? Appropriate word inflections? Familiarity with oratory/dramatic reading? Cue cards used appropriately? (20 points) II. Articulation: Distinct enunciation? Appropriate tone? Appropriate volume? (30 points) III. Organization: Introduction? Thesis stated? Points supported? Conclusion effective? Accomplish the stated purpose? (50 points)
Concept: improved writing skills (cognitive goal)	Students will write five warm-up essays/week.	With minimal errors students will write these essays in 15-20 minutes.
Concept: increased vocabulary (cognitive goal)	Students will collect at least five new vocabulary words and use these words in their warm-up essays and firsthand experience essay.	Students will use five vocabulary words in conversation during the week, as well as use the words in their essays.

Goals/Objectives: What is the purpose of this lesson?	Strategies to meet these goals: How will I obtain these goals/objectives?	Evaluation: How will I know when I have met these goals/objectives?
Concept: reflective writing (affective/spiritual goal)	Using the Journal Guide Questions in the Appendices, students will record at least three entries this week. Suggested Scripture: 1 Kings in general.	Students will show evidence that they have reflected on this issue, including informed discussions and written responses.
Concept: increased knowledge of the assigned essay. (cognitive goal)	Students will take Lesson 4 Test.	Students will score at least 80% on Lesson 4 Test.
Concept: firsthand experience essay (cognitive goal)	Students will write a firsthand experience of a life-changing event.	Students, with minimal errors, will clearly write a firsthand experience essay of a life-changing event.
Concept: working in a group setting (behavioral goal)	In a class, in a co-op experience, or during a family discussion, students will discuss how to clean their room in 15 minutes.	Students will exhibit practical listening skills and will manifest understanding of opposing worldviews.

SUGGESTED
Weekly *Implementation*

DAY 1	DAY 2	DAY 3	DAY 4	DAY 5
Write a Warm-up Essay.	Write a Warm-up Essay.	Write a Warm-up Essay.	Write a Warm-up Essay.	Write a Warm-up Essay.
Read 35-50 pages/day.	Read 35-50 pages/day.	Read 35-50 pages/day.	Read 35-50 pages/day.	Read 35-50 pages/day.
Find five new vocabulary words.	Find five new vocabulary words.	Find five new vocabulary words.	Find five new vocabulary words.	Find five new vocabulary words.
Reflect on the speech assignment for the week.	Compose a first draft of your speech. Work on the first draft for your first-hand experience essay.	Revise your speech and submit to your evaluator/ parent.	Prepare to present your speech tomorrow.	Present your speech to a live audience.
Write an outline and thesis for your first hand experience essay.	Make a journal entry.	Finish the first draft of your first hand experience essay.	Revise and finish the final copy of your first hand experience essay.	Submit your assignments to your evaluator/ parent.
Make a journal entry.		Make a journal entry.	Make a journal entry.	Submit a copy of your paper to a peer for evaluation.
				Make a journal entry.
				Take Lesson 4 Test

ENRICHMENT ACTIVITIES/PROJECTS

Students should discuss the most embarrassing moment in their lives.

SPEECH ASSIGNMENT

Present a two-three minute firsthand experience speech on some experience that changed your life.

WRITING ASSIGNMENTS

1. Write a firsthand experience of a life-changing event. This subject essay/oration should be on two pages and include an outline with thesis statement, rough draft, revisions, and final copy with five new (circled) vocabulary words. Give one copy to teacher/guardian/parent and one to peer evaluator.

ANSWERS: (Compare the differences between standard writing during this era and current standards of writing.)

Dear son:

I have ever had pleasure in obtaining any little anecdotes of my ancestors. You may remember the inquiries I made among the remains of my relations when you were with me in England, and the journey I undertook for that purpose. Imagining it may be equally agreeable to you to know the circumstances of my life, many of which you are yet unacquainted with, and expecting the enjoyment of a week's uninterrupted leisure in my present country retirement, I sit down to write them for you. To which I have besides some other inducements. Having emerged from the poverty and obscurity in which I was born and bred, to a state of affluence and some degree of reputation in the world, and having gone so far through life with a considerable share of felicity, the conducing means I made use of, which with the blessing of God so well succeeded, my posterity may like to know, as they may find some of them suitable to their own situations, and therefore fit to be imitated.

That felicity, when I reflected on it, has induced me sometimes to say, that were it offered to my choice, I should have no objection to a repetition of the same life from its beginning, only asking the advantages authors have in a second edition to correct some faults of the first. So I might, besides correcting the faults, change some sinister accidents and events of it for others more favorable. But though this was denied, I should still accept the offer. Since such a repetition is not to be expected, the next thing most like living one's life over again seems to be a recollection of that life, and to make that recollection as durable as possible by putting it down in writing.

Hereby, too, I shall indulge the inclination so natural in old men, to be talking of themselves and their own past actions; and I shall indulge it without being tiresome to others, who, through respect to age, might conceive themselves obliged to give me a hearing, since this may be read or not as any one pleases. And, lastly (I may as well confess it, since my denial of it will be believed by nobody), perhaps I shall a good deal gratify my own vanity. Indeed, I scarce ever heard or saw the introductory words, "Without vanity I may say," &c., but some vain thing immediately followed. Most people dislike vanity in others, whatever share they have of it themselves; but I give it fair quarter wherever I meet with it, being persuaded that it is often productive of good to the possessor, and to others that are within his sphere of action; and therefore, in many cases, it would not be altogether absurd if a man were to thank God for his vanity among the other comforts of life.

And now I speak of thanking God, I desire with all humility to acknowledge that I owe the mentioned happiness of my past life to His kind providence, which lead me to the means I used and gave them success. My belief of this induces me to hope,

though I must not presume, that the same goodness will still be exercised toward me, in continuing that happiness, or enabling me to bear a fatal reverse, which I may experience as others have done: the complexion of my future fortune being known to Him only in whose power it is to bless to us even our afflictions. (*Autobiography*, Ben Franklin, http://www.bartleby.com/1/1/)

2. Read 35 to 50 pages each day and keep vocabulary cards.

3. Complete the speech assignment and have a teacher complete a speech evaluation form (Appendix).

4. Pay attention to your writing style this week. Consider the main body of your essay and speech.

5. Using the devotional questions as a guide, write at least three journal entries this week. Reflect on 1 Kings in general. Pastor Ray Stedman argues, (The Ray Stedman Library, www.pbc.org/dp/stedman/).

The book of 1 Kings holds the secret of success in reigning over the kingdom of your life. It is the secret of learning to be submissive to the authority and dominion of God in your own life. In other words, man can never exercise dominion over his life unless he first subjects himself to the dominion of God.

Evaluate this statement and find evidence for your view from 1 Kings. Record your reflections in essay form.

6. Complete one warm-up essay every day.

FINAL PROJECT

Students should correct and rewrite all essays and place them in their Final Portfolio.

WARM-UP ESSAYS:

	DAY 1	DAY 2	DAY 3	DAY 4	DAY 5
Firsthand Experience Essays	Describe your mother's reaction to your bedroom.	Describe your first day of schooling.	Describe your dad's reaction to your statement, "I lost control of the car and hit a tree because I was stung by a bee."	Describe what your dad sounds like in the shower.	Describe your mom's reaction when she discovers that you used her favorite formal silverware knife to filet a goldfish.

LESSON 4 TEST

ESSAY (100 POINTS)

Write a one-page firsthand-experience essay describing the first time you rode a bicycle without training wheels.

LESSON 4 TEST ANSWERS

ESSAY (100 POINTS)

Write a one-page firsthand-experience essay describing the first time you rode a bicycle without training wheels.

    ANSWER: *Answers will vary. Evaluator: Please carefully evaluate students' essays in order to aid writing development.*

LESSON 5

Writing Skill: Descriptive Essay

Style (Writing and Speaking): Paragraph—Conclusion

Public Speaking Skill: The Speech Conclusion and Converting the Descriptive Essay to a Speech

Looking Ahead: The Persuasive Essay (Writing) and the Speech Delivery (Speaking)

Goals/Objectives: What is the purpose of this lesson?	Strategies to meet these goals: How will I obtain these goals/objectives?	Evaluation: How will I know when I have met these goals/objectives?
Concept: descriptive speech (cognitive goal)	The parent/educator will engage students in discussions about ways to write and present speeches. In front of an audience, students will present a descriptive speech.	Students will be able to write and to present an inspired speech. Suggested evaluation sheet includes: Oratory Evaluation I. Poise: Calm presentation? Appropriate word inflections? Familiarity with oratory/dramatic reading? Cue cards used appropriately? (20 points) II. Articulation: Distinct enunciation? Appropriate tone? Appropriate volume? (30 points) III. Organization: Introduction? Thesis stated? Points supported? Conclusion effective? Accomplish the stated purpose? (50 points)
Concept: improved writing comfort (cognitive goal)	Students will write five warm-up essays/week.	With minimal errors students will write these essays in 15-20 minutes.
Concept: increased vocabulary (cognitive goal)	Students will collect at least five new vocabulary words and use these words in their warm-up essays and descriptive essay.	Students will use five vocabulary words in conversation during the week, as well as use the words in their essays.

Goals/Objectives: What is the purpose of this lesson?	Strategies to meet these goals: How will I obtain these goals/objectives?	Evaluation: How will I know when I have met these goals/objectives?
Concept: reflective writing (affective/spiritual goal)	Using the Journal Guide Questions in the Appendices, students will record at least three entries this week. Suggested Scripture: 1 Kings 8:22–53.	Students will show evidence that they have reflected on this issue, including informed discussions and written responses.
Concept: essay processing (cognitive goal)	Students will take Lesson 5 Test.	Students will score at least 80% on Lesson 5 Test.
Concept: descriptive essay (cognitive goal)	Students will write a descriptive essay of a person who changed their lives.	Students, with minimal errors, will clearly write a descriptive essay of a person who changed their lives.
Concept: working in a group setting (behavioral goal)	In a class, in a co-op experience, or during a family discussion, students will describe the perfect car.	Students will exhibit practical listening skills and will manifest understanding of opposing worldviews.

SUGGESTED
Weekly *Implementation*

DAY 1	DAY 2	DAY 3	DAY 4	DAY 5
Write a Warm-up Essay.	Write a Warm-up Essay.	Write a Warm-up Essay.	Write a Warm-up Essay.	Write a Warm-up Essay.
Read 35-50 pages/day.	Read 35-50 pages/day.	Read 35-50 pages/day.	Read 35-50 pages/day.	Read 35-50 pages/day.
Find five new vocabulary words.	Find five new vocabulary words.	Find five new vocabulary words.	Find five new vocabulary words.	Find five new vocabulary words.
Reflect on the speech assignment for the week.	Compose a first draft of your speech.	Revise your speech and submit to your evaluator/ parent.	Prepare to present your speech tomorrow.	Present your speech to a live audience.
Write an outline and thesis for your descriptive essay.	Work on the first draft for your descriptive essay.	Revise and finish the first draft of your descriptive essay.	Finish the final copy of your descriptive essay.	Submit your assignments to your evaluator/ guardian/parent.
Make a journal entry.	Make a journal entry.	Make a journal entry.	Make a journal entry.	Submit a copy of your paper to a peer for evaluation.
				Make a journal entry.
				Take Lesson 5 Test

ENRICHMENT ACTIVITIES/PROJECTS

Turn off the television for 2 weeks and discuss with students how their lives have changed.

SPEECH ASSIGNMENT: THE DESCRIPTIVE SPEECH

Present a two-three minute descriptive speech of a person who had a great impact on your maturation as a Christian. A descriptive speech must by definition be full of numerous and of well-constructed descriptions. A descriptive speech normally describes its subject *ad nauseum*. Look for numerous ways, with multiple metaphors, to help your reader grasp what you are describing.

ANSWER: *In the following essay note the descriptives with the young boy fishing with his father:*

Fishing in King Tut Lake was the manliest fishing possible. King Tut was no manmade lake with Augustine grass, manicured seashores and smooth welcoming docks launching the angler into a viscous realm. King Tut, only a mile in length, coiled around like a horseshoe through a swamp. It was difficult to know, at some places along its circumference, where the swamp ended and King Tut began. Within its environs were a plethora of vicious water snakes, venomous moccasins — euphemistically called cotton mouths — and huge snapping turtles. The intrepid aggression of these wild animals was encouraged by the dirth of human contact.

The most salient feature of King Tut Lake, however, was huge cypress trees, some older than the Republic. Over the years, dry seasons had teased huge cypress knees out of the shallow transplanted bayou water, until, by 1965, the cypress trees squatted in the tepid lake, only a few years from being a swamp, like squatting sumo wrestlers. At 5pm on this July evening in the middle of the 1960s my dad and I pushed our little 14 footer into the mossy King Tut Lake. It felt a lot like the way the French explorer Marquette must have felt when he eased his canoe from the relative safety of backwater streams into the Mississippi River.

We were immediately attacked by a disoriented or terribly brave three-foot water snake which skillfully circled our Duracraft and then went in for the kill. For three successive attacks, the water snake bit our aluminum boat. I had been told that snakes do not bite in the water—but don't believe it—this one surely did. While I found the whole thing unnerving, my dad merely laughed. While I lobbied strenuously to shoot the awful thing with the 22 caliber pistol in our boat, my dad gently pushed the vicious serpent away with his paddle—even as the serpent continued to attack his paddle! 'What courage!' my dad muttered, as I was thinking 'What stupidity!' But Dad was like that. He liked lost causes, felt compassion for those who failed in pursuit of a great cause.

Finally, after the water snake was sufficiently satisfied that the big old floating monster in his lake was dead or knew his position in the cosmos or was not going to bother him again or whatever water snakes think when they attack big things, it withdrew with obvious satisfaction and quietly slid on top of a cypress knee from which it unceremoniously drove a snapping turtle and glared at us as we slid by in our boat. (James Stobaugh)

WRITING ASSIGNMENTS

1. In a two-page essay, describe a person who had a great impact on your maturation as a Christian.

Emphasize the following elements of descriptive essays: Starting Point, Purpose, Form, Audience, Voice, and Point of View. This description essay should include an outline with thesis statement, rough draft, several revisions, and a final copy with five new (circled) vocabulary words. Your essay must pay particular attention to style (focus, content, organization). Give a copy to your peer/friend to complete a peer evaluation form (Appendix) and to your instructor for evaluation.

ANSWER: *See speech discussion above.*

2. Read a book from the reading list or a book assigned in your literature and/or history elective (or another approved book). Read at least 35/50 pages/day. Make vocabulary cards from words in your reading.

3. Present your speech and have a teacher evaluate it with a speech evaluation form (Appendix).

4. Using the devotional questions as a guide, write at least three journal entries. This week meditate on 1 Kings 8:22–53. Record your reflections in essay form.

5. Complete one warm-up essay every day. The warm-up essay should be one page or less; it should not take more than one-half hour. The warm-ups do not need to be edited or rewritten. With time you will notice greater comfort with writing and will see improvement in your writing if you carefully attend to revisions following evaluations.

FINAL PROJECT

Students should correct and rewrite all essays and place them in their Final Portfolio.

WARM-UP ESSAYS:

	DAY 1	DAY 2	DAY 3	DAY 4	DAY 5
Descriptive	Describe a moment that changed your life.	Describe your best friend.	Describe the causes of World War I to a four-year old.	Describe the emotion *jealousy*.	Describe the sunset.

LESSON 5 TEST

ESSAY (100 POINTS)

In a one-page essay, describe the following strange invention and speculate upon its use(s).

© clipart.com

LESSON 1 TEST ANSWERS

ESSAY (100 POINTS)

In a one-page essay, describe the following strange invention and speculate upon its use(s).

ANSWER: *Answers will vary, but students will write an expository essay offering metaphors and other figurative language to describe the object. Check for proper essay form. As evaluator, what you do with student writing is crucial to the student's development as a writer.*

LESSON 6

Writing Skill: Persuasive vs. Coercive Essay

Style (Writing and Speaking): Paragraph—Unity and Coherence

Public Speaking Skill: Delivery (A) and Converting the Persuasive Essay to a Speech

Looking Ahead: The Persuasive Advertisement Essay (Writing) and the Speech Delivery (B) (Speaking).

Goals/Objectives: What is the purpose of this lesson?	Strategies to meet these goals: How will I obtain these goals/objectives?	Evaluation: How will I know when I have met these goals/objectives?
Concept: persuasive speech (cognitive goal)	The parent/educator will engage students in discussions about ways to write and present speeches. In front of an audience, students will present a persuasive speech.	Students will be able to write and to present an original speech. Suggested evaluation sheet includes: Oratory Evaluation I. Poise: Calm presentation? Appropriate word inflections? Familiarity with oratory/dramatic reading? Cue cards used appropriately? (20 points) II. Articulation: Distinct enunciation? Appropriate tone? Appropriate volume? (30 points) III. Organization: Introduction? Thesis stated? Points supported? Conclusion effective? Accomplish the stated purpose? (50 points)
Concept: improved writing skills (cognitive goal)	Students will write five warm-up essays/week.	With minimal errors students will write these essays in 15-20 minutes.
Concept: increased vocabulary (cognitive goal)	Students will collect at least five new vocabulary words and use these words in their warm-up essays and persuasive essay.	Students will use five vocabulary words in conversation during the week, as well as use the words in their essays.

Goals/Objectives: What is the purpose of this lesson?	Strategies to meet these goals: How will I obtain these goals/objectives?	Evaluation: How will I know when I have met these goals/objectives?
Concept: reflective writing (affective/spiritual goal)	Using the Journal Guide Questions in the Appendices, students will record at least three entries this week. Suggested Scripture: 1 Kings 10.	Students will show evidence that they have reflected on this issue, including informed discussions and written responses.
Concept: increased knowledge of the assigned essay (cognitive goal)	Students will take Lesson 6 Test.	Students will score at least 80% on Lesson 6 Test.
Concept: persuasive essay (cognitive goal)	Students will write a persuasive essay on the pledge of allegiance.	Students, with minimal errors, will clearly write a persuasive essay.
Concept: working in a group setting (behavioral goal)	In a class, in a co-op experience, or during a family discussion, students will argue persuasively that they should be allowed to take the garbage out every week.	Students will exhibit practical listening skills and will manifest understanding of opposing worldviews.

SUGGESTED
Weekly *Implementation*

DAY 1	DAY 2	DAY 3	DAY 4	DAY 5
Write a Warm-up Essay. Read 35-50 pages/day. Find five new vocabulary words. Reflect on the speech assignment for the week. Write an outline and thesis for your persuasive essay. Make a journal entry.	Write a Warm-up Essay. Read 35-50 pages/day. Find five new vocabulary words. Compose a first draft of your speech. Work on the first draft for your persuasive essay. Make a journal entry.	Write a Warm-up Essay. Read 35-50 pages/day. Find five new vocabulary words. Revise your speech and submit to your evaluator/ parent. Revise and finish the first draft of your persuasive essay. Make a journal entry.	Write a Warm-up Essay. Read 35-50 pages/day. Find five new vocabulary words. Prepare to present your speech tomorrow. Finish the final copy of your persuasive essay. Make a journal entry.	Write a Warm-up Essay. Read 35-50 pages/day. Find five new vocabulary words. Present your speech to a live audience. Submit your assignments to your evaluator/ parent. Submit a copy of your paper to a peer for evaluation. Make a journal entry. Take Lesson 6 Test

ENRICHMENT ACTIVITIES/PROJECTS

Students should join a local debate club and participate in its activities.

SPEECH ASSIGNMENT: THE PERSUASIVE SPEECH VS. COERCIVE SPEECH

Present a three-minute coercive speech and persuasive speech on the same topic.

ANSWER: *The persuasive speech would state facts and persuade the reader. The coercive speech would state a position and would imply a veiled threat if the hearer did not comply.*

WRITING ASSIGNMENTS

1. In current American society there is much discussion about the separation of church and state. The First Amendment to the Constitution of the United States of America reads: "Congress shall make no law respecting an establishment of religion, or prohibiting the free exercise thereof." Some people argue that "under God" in the Pledge of Allegiance is a violation of the First Amendment. They argue that this phrase moves beyond persuasiveness and becomes coercion. Write a one-two page essay arguing a position concerning this debate. This essay should include an outline with thesis statement, rough draft, several revisions, and final copy with five new (circled) vocabulary words. The essay must pay particular attention to style (focus, content, organization). Give a copy to a peer/friend to complete a peer evaluation form (Appendix) and to the instructor for evaluation.

ANSWER: *The intention of adding "under God" to the Pledge in 1954 was to create unity and nationalism; there was no religious persuasion attached. Thus, one opinion is that* *to argue that "under God" violates the First Amendment is spurious.*

2. Read 200-250 pages/week and make vocabulary cards.

3. Complete the speech assignment and have a teacher complete a speech evaluation (Appendix).

4. Pay particular attention to your writing style this week.

5. With the devotional questions as a guide, write at least three journal entries. Reflect on the story of Solomon and the Queen of Sheba (1 Kings 10:1–14).

Consider appropriate and inappropriate ways to interact with nonbelievers. Record your reflections in essay form. This journal is meant to be private, but you are invited to share your reflections with others.

6. Write a warm-up essay every day.

FINAL PROJECT

Students should correct and rewrite all essays and place them in their Final Portfolio.

WARM-UP ESSAYS:

	DAY 1	DAY 2	DAY 3	DAY 4	DAY 5
Persuasive Essay	Persuade a friend to commit his life to Christ.	Persuade your parents to give you a BMW for your birthday.	Persuade your parents to release you from doing homework.	Persuade a tollbooth operator to forgive the toll because you dropped your last quarter down the back of the seat.	Persuade your parents to let you move into your college-bound older brother's room.

LESSON 6 TEST

ESSAY (100 POINTS)

In a one-page essay: even though the student already has four pairs of soccer shoes, the student should persuade his parents to give him money to purchase the latest, kangaroo leather, soccer shoes costing $189.

LESSON 6 TEST ANSWER

ESSAY (100 POINTS)

In a one-page essay: even though the student already has four pairs of soccer shoes, the student should persuade his parents to give him money to purchase the latest, kangaroo leather, soccer shoes costing $189.

ANSWER: *A persuasive paper inevitably begins with an argument in favor of a position and then offers arguments to support it. The following is an essay vilifying unscriptural decisions being promoted in the Unites States court system. The essay compares the contemporary situation in the United States to Lewis Carroll's* Alice in Wonderland. *Its intention is to persuade the reader to rethink this unhappy situation.*

Last week, as I listened to the debate concerning same-sex marriages, it seemed, at times, that I had fallen into Alice's rabbit hole described by Lewis Carroll in his classic <u>Alice in Wonderland</u>. Wonderland was full of improbabilities: the rules of time, space, and orderly sequence, and cause and effect were reversed. In such a world, consciousness is adrift, unable to anchor itself to any universal ground of justice, truth, or reason. Consciousness itself is thus <u>decentered</u>: no longer an agent of action in the world but a function through which impersonal forces pass and intersect. When our justice system is committed to serving political agendas and when it becomes the instrument of per-sonal gain, our nation is in trouble. We have fallen into the rabbit hole and lost our way.

As I listened to CNN, I felt I had entered the Caterpillar's living room. "Who are you?" the Caterpillar asked Alice. "I hardly know she said. . . . I know who I was when I woke up this morning, but I think I must have been changed several times since then."

As I watched sincere, but sincerely wrong, people of the same sex saying marriage vows, I felt that I was following the white rabbit into a surrealistic rabbit hole of unreality. But it was too real, unfortunately.

What is real, and bizarre, is that some people think they can break God's laws. We most assuredly cannot. "Please tell me," Alice asked the Duchess, "why does your cat always grin?" "He is a Cheshire cat and Cheshire cats always grin!" the Duchess answered. We in our society violate God's law, but the Cheshire cat still grins. What kind of world is it when a man of peace and of honor is perceived as an aberration because of calumny and rascally lies?

I may not like this rabbit hole I am in, but I am awfully glad I am in the hole with other followers of Jesus Christ. Many who follow inequity persecute the righteous. To those who threaten, who bully, who malign the innocent, let me remind you of a truth that will never change, a truth as painful as the squeaking of the Lizard's slate pencil, "Don't be deceived: God is not mocked. For whatever a man sows he will also reap." (Gals. 6:7) Think of that, shrill Queen, as you rule in the rabbit hole. (James P. Stobaugh)

LESSON 7

Writing Skill: Persuasive Advertisement Essay

Style (Writing and Speaking): Paragraph—Transitional Devices

Public Speaking Skill: Delivery (B) and Converting the Persuasive Advertisement Essay to a Speech

Looking Ahead: The Summary Essay (Writing) and Overcoming Fear (Speaking)

Goals/Objectives: What is the purpose of this lesson?	Strategies to meet these goals: How will I obtain these goals/objectives?	Evaluation: How will I know when I have met these goals/objectives?
Concept: persuasive advertisement speech (cognitive goal)	The parent/educator will engage students in discussions about ways to write and present speeches. In front of an audience, students will present a persuasive speech.	Students will be able to write and to present an inspired speech. Suggested evaluation sheet includes: Oratory Evaluation I. Poise: Calm presentation? Appropriate word inflections? Familiarity with oratory/dramatic reading? Cue cards used appropriately? (20 points) II. Articulation: Distinct enunciation? Appropriate tone? Appropriate volume? (30 points) III. Organization: Introduction? Thesis stated? Points supported? Conclusion effective? Accomplish the stated purpose? (50 points)
Concept: improved writing skills (cognitive goal)	Students will write five warm-up essays/week.	With minimal errors students will write these essays in 15-20 minutes.
Concept: increased vocabulary (cognitive goal)	Students will collect at least five new vocabulary words and use these words in their warm-up essays and persuasive essay.	Students will use five vocabulary words in conversation during the week, as well as use the words in their essays.

Goals/Objectives: What is the purpose of this lesson?	Strategies to meet these goals: How will I obtain these goals/objectives?	Evaluation: How will I know when I have met these goals/ objectives?
Concept: reflective writing (affective/spiritual goal)	Using the Journal Guide Questions in the Appendices, students will record at least three entries this week. Suggested Scripture: 1 Kings 11.	Students will show evidence that they have reflected on this issue, including informed discussions and written responses.
Concept: increased knowledge of the assigned essay (cognitive goal)	Students will take Lesson 7 Test.	Students will score at least 80% on Lesson 7 Test.
Concept: persuasive advertisement essay (cognitive goal)	Students will write a persuasive advertisement essay.	Students, with minimal errors, will clearly write a persuasive essay.
Concept: working in a group setting (behavioral goal)	In a class, in a co-op experience, or during a family discussion, students will argue persuasively the liver and onions meal selection for dinner.	Students will exhibit practical listening skills and will manifest understanding of opposing worldviews.

SUGGESTED
Weekly *Implementation*

DAY 1	DAY 2	DAY 3	DAY 4	DAY 5
Write a Warm-up Essay.	Write a Warm-up Essay.	Write a Warm-up Essay.	Write a Warm-up Essay.	Write a Warm-up Essay.
Read 35-50 pages/day.	Read 35-50 pages/day.	Read 35-50 pages/day.	Read 35-50 pages/day.	Read 35-50 pages/day.
Find five new vocabulary words.	Find five new vocabulary words.	Find five new vocabulary words.	Find five new vocabulary words.	Find five new vocabulary words.
Reflect on the speech assignment for the week.	Compose a first draft of your speech.	Revise your speech and submit to your evaluator/ parent.	Prepare to present your speech tomorrow.	Present your speech to a live audience.
Write an outline and thesis for your persuasive essay.	Work on the first draft for your persuasive essay.	Revise and finish the first draft of your persuasive essay.	Finish the final copy of your persuasive essay.	Submit your assignments to your evaluator/ parent.
Make a journal entry.	Make a journal entry.	Make a journal entry.	Make a journal entry.	Submit a copy of your paper to a peer for evaluation.
				Make a journal entry.
				Take Lesson 7 Test

ENRICHMENT ACTIVITIES/PROJECTS

Students should join a local debate club and participate in its activities.

SPEECH ASSIGNMENT: THE PERSUASIVE ADVERTISEMENT SPEECH

Create a persuasive advertisement speech for your favorite vacation spot.

ANSWER: Sample skeleton of a speech's elements: *Maine is the coolest place (temperature) (logos) in the coolest section of the country (pathos) —Northeast —at the most frequented vacation spot in the North (ethos).*

WRITING ASSIGNMENTS

1. Write a one-page persuasive advertisement essay for your favorite vacation spot. This essay should include an outline with thesis statement, rough draft, several revisions, final copy with five new (circled) vocabulary words. The essay must pay particular attention to style (focus, content, organization). Give a copy to a peer/friend to complete a peer evaluation form (Appendix) and to your instructor for evaluation.

ANSWER: *See speech assignment above.*

2. Read 200-250 pages/week and make vocabulary cards.

3. Complete the speech assignment and have a teacher complete a speech evaluation form (Appendix).

4. Pay particular attention to your writing style this week.

5. Using the devotional questions as a guide, write at least three journal entries. Meditate on 1 Kings 11. Consider the consequences of Solomon's choice to marry many foreign, unbelieving wives. The purpose of many of these marriages was to create political alliances. The effect on his walk with God, however, was devastating. Record your reflections in essay form.

6. Write a warm-up essay every day.

WARM-UP ESSAYS:

	DAY 1	DAY 2	DAY 3	DAY 4	DAY 5
Persuasive Advertisement	Create an advertisement for your favorite meal.	Create an advertisement for your favorite line of clothing.	Create an advertisement for your favorite sport.	Create an advertisement for your favorite musician.	Create an advertisement for your favorite novel.

LESSON 7 TEST

ESSAY (100 POINTS)

In a one-page essay, analyze your favorite advertisement being careful to discuss the logos, pathos, and ethos of the ad.

LESSON 7 TEST ANSWER

ESSAY (100 POINTS)

In a one-page essay, analyze your favorite advertisement being careful to discuss the logos, pathos, and ethos of the ad.

    ANSWER: *Answers will vary. A typical soft drink commercial, for example, will appeal more to the emotions (pathos) than to the mind (logos) or to credibility (ethos). This is the reason advertisers use images and rhetoric that may have nothing directly to do with the product.*

LESSON 8

Writing Skill: Summary Report

Style (Writing and Speaking): Sentences—Overview

Public Speaking Skill: Overcoming Fear and Converting Summary Essay to a Speech

Looking Ahead: Précis (Writing) and Converting the Précis Essay to a Speech

Goals/Objectives: What is the purpose of this lesson?	Strategies to meet these goals: How will I obtain these goals/objectives?	Evaluation: How will I know when I have met these goals/objectives?
Concept: a one-minute summary speech of your favorite book (cognitive goal)	The parent/educator will engage students in discussions about ways to write and present speeches. In front of an audience, students should present a summary speech.	Students will be able to write and to present an inspired speech. Suggested evaluation sheet includes: Oratory Evaluation I. Poise: Calm presentation? Appropriate word inflections? Familiarity with oratory/dramatic reading? Cue cards used appropriately? (20 points) II. Articulation: Distinct enunciation? Appropriate tone? Appropriate volume? (30 points) III. Organization: Introduction? Thesis stated? Points supported? Conclusion effective? Accomplish the stated purpose? (50 points)
Concept: Improve writing skills (cognitive goal)	Students will write five warm-up essays/week.	With minimal errors students will write these essays in 15-20 minutes.
Concept: increase vocabulary (cognitive goal)	Students will collect at least five new vocabulary words and use these words in their warm-up essays and summary report.	Students will use five vocabulary words in conversation during the week, as well as use the words in their essays.

Goals/Objectives: What is the purpose of this lesson?	Strategies to meet these goals: How will I obtain these goals/objectives?	Evaluation: How will I know when I have met these goals/objectives?
Concept: reflective writing (affective/spiritual goal)	Using the Journal Guide Questions in the Appendices, students will record at least three entries this week. Suggested Scripture 1 Kings 11:14-24.	Students will show evidence that they have reflected on this issue, including informed discussions and written responses.
Concept: increased knowledge of the assigned essay (cognitive goal)	Students will take Lesson 8 Test.	Students will score at least 80% on Lesson 8 Test.
Concept: summary (cognitive goal)	Students will a summary of their favorite book.	Students, with minimal errors, will clearly write a summary of their favorite book.
Concept: working in a group setting (behavioral goal)	In a class, in a co-op experience, or during a family discussion, students will give a summary of Sunday school last week.	Students will exhibit practical listening skills and will manifest understanding of opposing worldviews.

SUGGESTED
Weekly *Implementation*

DAY 1	DAY 2	DAY 3	DAY 4	DAY 5
Write a Warm-up Essay.	Write a Warm-up Essay.	Write a Warm-up Essay.	Write a Warm-up Essay.	Write a Warm-up Essay.
Read 35-50 pages/day.	Read 35-50 pages/day.	Read 35-50 pages/day.	Read 35-50 pages/day.	Read 35-50 pages/day.
Find five new vocabulary words.	Find five new vocabulary words.	Find five new vocabulary words.	Find five new vocabulary words.	Find five new vocabulary words.
Reflect on the speech assignment for the week.	Compose a first draft of your speech.	Revise your speech and submit to your evaluator/ parent.	Prepare to present your speech tomorrow.	Present your speech to a live audience.
Write an outline and thesis for your summary report.	Work on the first draft for your summary report.	Revise and finish the first draft of your summary report.	Finish the final copy of your summary report.	Submit your assignments to your evaluator/ parent.
Make a journal entry.	Make a journal entry.	Make a journal entry.	Make a journal entry.	Submit a copy of your paper to a peer for evaluation.
				Make a journal entry.
				Take Lesson 8 Test

ENRICHMENT ACTIVITIES/PROJECTS

Students should summarize their favorite movie.

SPEECH TASK: SUMMARY SPEECH

In front of an audience, present a one-minute summary of your favorite book. A summary speech has an introduction, body, and a conclusion. It carefully highlights salient components of the book that make it a good book, or, in this case, your favorite book. Remember: a summary is an overview—not an analysis—of something. Your speech will include the following literary elements (Appendix): Plot, Theme, Characters, Setting, and Tone.

ANSWER: *The Divine Comedy by Dante is not funny at all. Dante so called this literary piece in order to contrast it with* a tragedy. However, the long poem is not a tragedy. It is the story of a character who understands and then accepts first the reality of his sin and, secondly, the redemption of his soul.

Why would it be my favorite book? First, the very fact I read and understood it is a source of pride and accomplishment! Dante's narrator, Virgil, is a suave guy who constantly surprises the reader with new insights. At the same time, Dante's veiled, ironic statements about his Italian society could easily be a statement about the foibles of contemporary politics.

The setting is superb, the characters are well developed, the theme is universally important, and the plot flows along very well.

WRITING ASSIGNMENTS

1. Summarize your favorite book, being sure to include all aspects of a good summary. Remember: a summary is an overview—not an analysis—of

something. Your essay will include the following literary elements (Appendix): Plot, Theme, Characters, Setting, and Tone. This expository essay should be a two-page essay and should include an outline, rough draft, thesis statement, final copy, and five new (circled) vocabulary words. Give one copy of the paper to the teacher/parent/guardian and one copy to the peer evaluator.

ANSWER: *The Divine Comedy was entitled by Dante himself merely Commedia, meaning a poetic composition in a style intermediate between the sustained nobility of tragedy and the popular tone of elegy. The word had no dramatic implication at that time, though it did involve a happy ending. The poem is the narrative of a journey down through Hell, up the mountain of Purgatory, and through the revolving heavens into the presence of God. In this aspect it belongs to the two familiar medieval literary types of the Journey and the Vision. It is also an allegory, representing under the symbolism of the stages and experiences of the journey, the history of a human soul, painfully struggling from sin through purification to the Beatific Vision. Other schemes of interpretation have been worked out and were probably intended, for Dante granted the medieval demand for a threefold and even fourfold signification in this type of writing.*

However, the "Divine Comedy" belongs to still other literary forms than those mentioned. Professor Grandgent has pointed out that it is also an encyclopedia, a poem in praise of Woman, and an autobiography. It contains much of what Dante knew of theology and philosophy, of astronomy and cosmography, and fragments of a number of other branches of learning so that its encyclopedia character is obvious. In making it a monument to Beatrice, he surpassed infinitely all the poetry devoted to the praise of women in an age when the deification of women was the commonplace of poetry. And finally he made it an autobiography—not a narrative of the external events of his life but of the agony of his soul.

Thus, in an altogether unique way, Dante summarizes the literature, the philosophy, the science, and the religion of the Middle Ages. Through the intensity of his capacity for experience, the splendor of his power of expression, and the depth of his spiritual and philosophic insight, he at once sums up and transcends a whole era of human history. (http://www.bartleby.com/20/1001.html)

2. Read a book from the reading list or a book assigned in your literature and/or history elective (or another approved book). Read at least 35/50 pages/day. Make vocabulary cards from words in your reading.

3. Present your speech and have a teacher evaluate it with a speech evaluation form (Appendix).

4. Pay attention to your stylistic tendencies this week. Make a special effort to write precisely.

5. Using the devotional questions as a guide, write at least three journal entries. Reflect on 1 Kings 11:14-24. In this passage, God causes enemies to come against Solomon. Reflect on this fact and ask yourself, "Why?" Record your reflections in your prayer journal. This journal is meant to be private, but you are invited to share your reflections with others.

6. Complete one warm-up essay every day.

FINAL PROJECT

Students should correct and rewrite all essays and place them in their Final Portfolio.

WARM-UP ESSAYS:

	DAY 1	DAY 2	DAY 3	DAY 4	DAY 5
Summary Report	Summarize a favorite book.	Summarize a recent sporting event.	Summarize a typical family Christmas.	Summarize a boring book.	Summarize your reaction to this course.

LESSON 8 TEST

ESSAY (100 POINTS)

In a one-page essay, *summarize* the Book of Esther (in the Bible).

LESSON 8 TEST ANSWER

ESSAY (100 POINTS)

In a one-page essay, *summarize* the Book of Esther (in the Bible).

ANSWER SAMPLE: *Among other things, the book of Esther is a story of justice. Justice fell on Mordecai who was a Jew working in the king's palace. Esther received justice for being faithful to God.*

Jewish captive, Mordecai, a righteous relative of Queen Esther, heard two guards planning to assassinate the king of Babylon. He had two hard choices. He could let the king who conquered his country die or he could inform him of this evil plot and save him. Mordecai told the king of the guard's plan. The king hanged the guards on the gallows. Mordecai was praised and was promised further rewards, but the king forgot his promise.

An acquaintance of Mordecai, the Babylonian Haman hated the Jews, and most of all he hated Mordecai. Haman was on his way home from a party when he saw Mordecai sitting by a gate. Haman noticed that Mordecai was not afraid of this Babylonian overlord, which infuriated Haman. He plotted to kill Mordecai by persuading the king to kill all Jewish people, including Mordecai. However, the king, with the help of Esther his queen, saw through Haman's evil plan and hanged him on the gallows on which Haman had planned to hang Mordecai. As a reward Mordecai was placed on top of the royal horse, clothed in royal garments, and lead through the streets while being praised. Again, justice fell on the wicked and the righteous. Out of Haman's own personal hatred, he sought to destroy Mordecai. However, it was not steadfast Mordecai who was destroyed. Instead it was Haman. (Peter Stobaugh)

LESSON 9

Goals/Objectives: What is the purpose of this lesson?	Strategies to meet these goals: How will I obtain these goals/objectives?	Evaluation: How will I know when I have met these goals/objectives?
Concept: précis speech (cognitive goal)	The parent/educator will engage students in discussions about ways to write and present speeches. In front of an audience, students will present a 3-5 minute précis speech on their favorite book.	Students will be able to write and to present an inspired speech. Suggested evaluation sheet includes: Oratory Evaluation I. Poise: How does the student present himself/herself? Is the oratory/dramatic reading memorized? (25 points) II. Articulation: Does the student speak clearly, and slowly? (25 points) III. Presentation: What is the overall effect of the speech? Does it accomplish its purpose? (50 points)
Concept: improved writing skills (cognitive goal)	Students will write five warm-up essays/week.	With minimal errors students will write these essays in 15-20 minutes.
Concept: increased vocabulary (cognitive goal)	Students will collect at least five new vocabulary words and use these words in their warm-up essays and précis.	Students will use five vocabulary words in conversation during the week, as well as use the words in their essays.

Goals/Objectives: What is the purpose of this lesson?	Strategies to meet these goals: How will I obtain these goals/objectives?	Evaluation: How will I know when I have met these goals/objectives?
Concept: reflective writing (affective/spiritual goal)	Using the Journal Guide Questions in the Appendices, students will record at least three entries this week. Suggested Scripture: 1 Kings.	Students will show evidence that they have reflected on this issue, including informed discussions and written responses.
Concept: increased knowledge of the assigned essay (cognitive goal)	Students will take Lesson 9 Test.	Students will score at least 80% on Lesson 9 Test.
Concept: précis (cognitive goal)	Students will write a précis of their favorite book.	Students, with minimal errors, will clearly write a précis of their favorite book.
Concept: working in a group setting (behavioral goal)	In a class, in a co-op experience, or during a family discussion, students will give a précis of their last week's Sunday school lesson.	Students will exhibit practical listening skills and will manifest understanding of opposing worldviews.

SUGGESTED
Weekly *Implementation*

DAY 1	DAY 2	DAY 3	DAY 4	DAY 5
Write a Warm-up Essay.	Write a Warm-up Essay.	Write a Warm-up Essay.	Write a Warm-up Essay.	Write a Warm-up Essay.
Read 35-50 pages/day.	Read 35-50 pages/day.	Read 35-50 pages/day.	Read 35-50 pages/day.	Read 35-50 pages/day.
Find five new vocabulary words.	Find five new vocabulary words.	Find five new vocabulary words.	Find five new vocabulary words.	Find five new vocabulary words.
Reflect on the speech assignment for the week.	Compose a first draft of your speech.	Revise your speech and submit to your evaluator/ parent.	Prepare to present your speech tomorrow.	Present your speech to a live audience.
Write an outline and thesis for your précis.	Work on the first draft for your précis.	Revise and finish the first draft of your précis.	Finish the final copy of your précis.	Submit your assignments to your evaluator/ parent.
Make a journal entry.	Make a journal entry.	Make a journal entry.	Make a journal entry.	Submit a copy of your paper to a peer for evaluation.
				Make a journal entry.
				Take Lesson 9 Test

ENRICHMENT ACTIVITIES/PROJECTS

Students should write a précis of their favorite movie.

SPEECH ASSIGNMENT: CONVERTING THE PRÉCIS ESSAY TO A SPEECH

Convert a précis speech of your favorite book. Remember, in your speech, you will need to follow the same guidelines established in the "Writing Skills" section of this lesson. A précis speech is based on a précis manuscript. It is important that you identify the salient points of your favorite book and emphasize them. For example, if you were presenting a précis speech on "Charge of the Light Brigade," you would be wise to memorize the refrain and maintain eye contact with your audience as you repeat phrases numerous times. It

would also allow you to catch your thoughts as you progress through the speech.

WRITING ASSIGNMENTS

1. Write a précis of your favorite book, being sure to include all aspects of a good précis. This subject essay should be on two pages and include an outline, rough draft, thesis statement, final copy, and five new (circled) vocabulary words. Give one copy of your paper to your teacher/parent/guardian and one copy to your peer evaluator.

ANSWER: *It need hardly be said that Goethe's Faust does not derive its greatness from its conformity to the traditional standards of what a tragedy should be. He himself was accustomed to referring to it cynically as a monstrosity, and yet* *he put himself into it as intensely as Dante put himself into The Divine Comedy. A partial explanation of this apparent contradiction in the author's attitude is found in its manner of composition. Goethe began it in his romantic youth, and availed himself recklessly of the supernatural elements in the legend, with the disregard of reason and plausibility characteristic of the romantic mood. When he returned to it in the beginning of the new century, his artistic standards had changed, and the supernaturalism could now be tolerated only by being made symbolic.* (Charles Eliot, Harvard Classics, www.bartleby.com)

2. Read 35–50 pages each day and keep vocabulary cards. Finish reading your first literary work.

3. Complete the speech assignment and have a teacher complete a speech evaluation form (Appendix).

4. Pay attention to sentence emphasis in your essay and speech.

5. Using the devotional questions as a guide, write at least three journal entries. This week reflect on 1 Kings in general. Man can never exercise dominion over his life unless he first subjects himself to the dominion of God. Evaluate this statement and find evidence for your view from 1 Kings. Record your reflections in essay form.

6. Complete one warm-up essay every day.

FINAL PROJECT

Students should correct and rewrite all essays and place them in their Final Portfolio.

WARM-UP ESSAYS:

	DAY 1	DAY 2	DAY 3	DAY 4	DAY 5
Précis	Write a précis of your favorite song.	Write a précis of your favorite movie.	Write a précis of your favorite book.	Write a précis of a boring book.	Write a précis of a sermon you heard.

LESSON 9 TEST

ESSAY (100 POINTS)

In a one-page essay, compare and contrast the following two passages. Which one is a **précis**? Which is a **summary**? Why?

ESSAY A

Gene Forrester, the narrator of *A Separate Peace*, returns to Devon, his private high school in New Hampshire. As he walks around Devon School, the reader realizes that something terrible happened there. When Gene comes to rest at the foot of a huge tree overhanging a riverbank on the edge of campus and pauses to reflect, our story begins in a flashback to the summer between Gene's junior and senior years.

The reader quickly meets the main character of the story and its hero, Gene's best friend, Finny. Finny is a boy who stands out from the crowd. He's brave to the point of foolhardiness, outspoken, athletic, bright, funny—yet, Finny is also an enigma. He challenges the other boys to make a leap from the fateful tree on the riverbank into cold waters. This challenge, repeated throughout the book, ultimately proves to be Finny's destruction.

ESSAY B

The story is a story within a story, or a frame story. Gene is remembering a particular school year that occurred years before. However, the story is really about Gene, not the happenings at Devon School. Unlike his friends who seem to remain static characters, Gene grows and matures as a protagonist. The entire novel, in fact, is about Gene's maturation. He comes to a sort of peace within himself. He learns that peace is a state of mind unrelated to outside circumstances.

LESSON 9 TEST ANSWERS

ESSAY (100 POINTS)

In a one-page essay, compare and contrast the two following passages. Which one is a **précis**? Which is a **summary**? Why?

ANSWER: *Essay A is a summary; Essay B is a précis. Essay A is merely a recapitulation of the story. Essay B is both a recapitulation and some cursory analysis of the story.*

LESSON 10

Goals/Objectives: What is the purpose of this lesson?	Strategies to meet these goals: How will I obtain these goals/objectives?	Evaluation: How will I know when I have met these goals/objectives?
Concept: Character Profile Speech (cognitive goal)	The parent/educator will engage students in discussions about ways to write and present speeches. In front of an audience, students will present a Character Profile Speech.	Students will be able to write and to present an inspired speech. Suggested evaluation sheet includes: Oratory Evaluation I. Poise: Calm presentation? Appropriate word inflections? Familiarity with oratory/dramatic reading? Cue cards used appropriately? (20 points) II. Articulation: Distinct enunciation? Appropriate tone? Appropriate volume? (30 points) III. Organization: Introduction? Thesis stated? Points supported? Conclusion effective? Accomplish the stated purpose? (50 points)
Concept: improved writing skills (cognitive goal)	Students will write five warm-up essays/week.	With minimal errors students will write these essays in 15-20 minutes.
Concept: increased vocabulary (cognitive goal)	Students will collect at least five new vocabulary words and use these words in their warm-up essays and character profile essay.	Students will use five vocabulary words in conversation during the week, as well as use the words in their essays.

Goals/Objectives: What is the purpose of this lesson?	Strategies to meet these goals: How will I obtain these goals/objectives?	Evaluation: How will I know when I have met these goals/objectives?
Concept: reflective writing (affective/spiritual goal)	Using the Journal Guide Questions in the Appendices, students will record at least three entries this week. Suggested Scripture: 1 Kings 1-17.	Students will show evidence that they have reflected on this issue, including informed discussions and written responses.
Concept: increased knowledge of the assigned essay (cognitive goal)	Students will take Lesson 10 Test.	Students will score at least 80% on Lesson 10 Test.
Concept: character profile (cognitive goal)	Students will write a character profile of a close friend.	Students, with minimal errors, will clearly write character profile of a close friend.
Concept: working in a group setting (behavioral goal)	In a class, in a co-op experience, or during a family discussion, students will give a character profile of a close friend.	Students will exhibit practical listening skills and will manifest understanding of opposing worldviews.

SUGGESTED
Weekly *Implementation*

DAY 1	DAY 2	DAY 3	DAY 4	DAY 5
Write a Warm-up Essay.	Write a Warm-up Essay.	Write a Warm-up Essay.	Write a Warm-up Essay.	Write a Warm-up Essay.
Read 35-50 pages/day.	Read 35-50 pages/day.	Read 35-50 pages/day.	Read 35-50 pages/day.	Read 35-50 pages/day.
Find five new vocabulary words.	Find five new vocabulary words.	Find five new vocabulary words.	Find five new vocabulary words.	Find five new vocabulary words.
Reflect on the speech assignment for the week.	Compose a first draft of your speech.	Revise your speech and submit to your evaluator/ parent.	Prepare to present your speech tomorrow.	Present your speech to a live audience.
Write an outline and thesis for your character profile.	Work on the first draft for your character profile.	Revise and finish the first draft of your character profile.	Finish the final copy of your character profile.	Submit your assignments to your evaluator/ parent.
Make a journal entry.	Make a journal entry.	Make a journal entry.	Make a journal entry.	Submit a copy of your paper to a peer for evaluation.
				Make a journal entry.
				Take Lesson 10 Test

ENRICHMENT ACTIVITIES/PROJECTS

Students should contact someone who significantly helped their walk in the Lord.

SPEECH ASSIGNMENT: CHARACTER PROFILE

In front of an audience, present a character profile of a close friend.

ANSWER: *See the character profile description below.*

WRITING ASSIGNMENTS

1. Write a character profile of a close friend. Your essay should include an outline, rough draft, thesis statement, final copy, and five new (circled) vocabulary words. Pay particular attention to style (focus, content, organization). Give a copy to your peer/friend to complete a peer evaluation form (Appendix) and to your instructor for evaluation.

ANSWER: *The following is a character profile of a homeless man named Jimmy:*

Home is the Place where,
When you have to go there,
They have to take you in.
(Robert Frost in "Death of a Hired Hand"
http://www.internal.org/view_poem.phtml?poemI D=145)

"Oh no," I groaned to myself, "Jimmy!"

Jimmy, a street person, sat in a corner of my tired inner-city Pittsburgh church basement. Unshaven, polluting the room with his pungent body odor, he pulled his moth-eaten (but nonetheless impressive) Harris Tweed jacket around his shoulders.

With a sigh, I issued a polite hello.

Jimmy was the last person I wanted to meet this early December morning. I had come to my office to grab a few quiet moments, but I had been greeted by light leaking from beneath our poorly insulated basement door. Exorbitant light bills demanded that I investigate.

I found Jimmy, who had managed, somehow, to enter the church last night. He had stolen nothing, but this was due less to altruism on Jimmy's part than that there was absolutely nothing to steal in this tired inner-city church.

Jimmy was the kind of person who would disappoint you every time you trusted him.

"I need five bucks," he would plead. "Pay you back next week," he lied.

It was not the money or the lying that bothered me; it was his persistent, unmitigated gall.

While the rest of us lived with limits, Jimmy, by lying, stealing, and conning, managed to exceed the limits every time.

Like the time he lived in a hotel by telling the Red Cross his house had burned down. The truth was, for almost fifteen years now, he had never lived in a house, only in doorways, abandoned buildings, and shelters.

But Jimmy had enjoyed his hotel accommodations while they lasted. Jimmy always enjoyed the fruits of his sins! Maybe that irritated me a little, too.

Jimmy had never joined my church, but he had not missed a service in more than a year. Of course not! Church services were an entrepreneurial venture for Jimmy! He worked the north door during Sunday school, the basement door between services (to catch unrepentant smokers who were more than willing to do penance for their nasty sin), and brazenly worked the front door (sometimes standing a few yards from me!) after church services. When he was seriously conning, Jimmy could make $40 an hour! While preparing our budget, my former church officers jokingly thought of making Jimmy a separate budget line item.

Now this December morning Jimmy had decided to camp in our church basement.

Well, he wouldn't con me this morning. I was going to keep my five bucks.

Something was different though. He always smelled bad, but he really smelled bad this morning. His color was a jaded yellow. His eyes were lined with red, and he was breathing heavy, wheezing really and . . .

"Did you visit Dr. David?" I asked. His silence told me that he had.

"Oh no," I thought. "Jimmy's not here to sleep, eat, or con anyone. His colon cancer has finally caught up with him."

After being in urban ministry for ten years, I was no longer a sentimentalist. I had to learn, usually the hard way, to think quickly, to act decisively. The urban world was unforgiving. God forgive me, but, I had had enough of abused children and welfare moms and Jimmys. I wondered why he couldn't die in somebody else's church.

"Did you hear that the Pirates took the Expos last night?" Jimmy asked me. He knew I was caught. He had never read Matthew, but he still knew I had to help him. What else could I do? If I could not help a man die in dignity, what meaning did any of this ministry stuff have? I was tired and cynical, but I was still his pastor. And I loved him in my own way. I would help him, and it still bothered me that Jimmy knew it and expected it.

Coming home for Christmas. Jimmy had come home for Christmas—to die. And he knew that home is the place where you go when you have to go there, and a place where they have to take you in. I made him comfortable and phoned Dr. David.

Within a week, in our basement, at home, Jimmy the street person died. (James P. Stobaugh)

2. Read 35 to 50 pages each day and keep vocabulary cards.

3. Complete the speech assignment and have a teacher complete a speech evaluation form (Appendix).

4. Pay attention to stylistic tendencies. Make a special effort to write clear sentences. Avoid misplaced modifiers.

5. Review 1 Kings 1–17 and reflect upon what God has taught you thus far.

6. Complete one warm-up essay every day.

WARM-UP ESSAYS:

	DAY 1	DAY 2	DAY 3	DAY 4	DAY 5
Character Profiles	Write a character profile of yourself.	Write a character profile of your pastor.	Write a character profile of your pet.	Write a character profile of a sibling.	Write a character profile of your grandmother.

FINAL PROJECT

Students should correct and rewrite all essays and place them in their Final Portfolio.

LESSON 10 TEST

ESSAY (100 POINTS)

Write a one-page character profile of your favorite pet.

LESSON 10 TEST ANSWERS

ESSAY (100 POINTS)

Write a one-page character profile of your favorite pet.

ANSWER: *As I stepped into our yard I quietly moved toward my dad's kennel. Dad's prize-winning bird dogs, Sandy and Jim (my namesake), were delighted to see me.*

Jim was a purebred boxy male setter with caramel colored spots on a short white hair base. His most distinguishing feature was his voice that sounded more like a bloodhound than a prize-winning quail dog.

Sandy was an impressive black and white long hair setter who my father claimed was smarter than my dim-witted Uncle Homer. Sandy could locate a covey of quail faster than any dog I had ever known; Uncle Homer diurnally could barely locate his false teeth.

Sandy deeply loved me. She was older than I, and my father claimed that raising me had fulfilled her frustrated maternal instincts that had been severely curtailed when my father had Sandy spaded.

On this morning they wanted something I did not have: they supposed that I was the harbinger of a bird hunting expedition or at least a romp over to Mr. Stalling's pasture to harass his two yearlings. While my father loved unconditionally and unimaginatively never wavered on that score, not even jokingly, Helen loved unconditionally in a whimsical, mischievous way. While Jim and Sandy were undeniably my father's dogs, they, like the rest of us, recognized and accepted Helen's peremptory influence over everything. Unfortunately, they had embraced Helen's teasing love rather than my father's steady, consistent love. I sincerely apologized to Jim and Sandy, and I vigorously scratched their prickly ears. Sincere appeasement accomplished nothing. Sandy and Jim rudely snubbed the young offspring of their master by turning their backs and growling. (James Stobaugh)

LESSON 11

Writing Skill: General Analysis Essay (Writing)

Style (Writing and Speaking): Sentences—Writing Complete Sentences

Public Speaking Skill: Converting a General Analysis Essay into a Speech.

Looking Ahead: The General Synthesis Essay (Writing)

Goals/Objectives: What is the purpose of this lesson?	Strategies to meet these goals: How will I obtain these goals/objectives?	Evaluation: How will I know when I have met these goals/objectives?
Concept: writing a speech with the audience in mind (cognitive goal)	The parent/educator will engage students in discussions about ways to write and present speeches. In front of a friendly audience, students should present a 1-3 minute speech on the topic "Home-schooling in the Twenty-first Century." Then they should do the same in front of a hostile audience.	Students will be able to write and to present an inspired speech. Suggested evaluation sheet includes: Oratory Evaluation I. Poise: How does the student present himself/herself? Is the oratory/dramatic reading memorized? (25 points) II. Articulation: Does the student speak clearly, and slowly? (25 points) III. Presentation: What is the overall effect of the speech? Does it accomplish its purpose? (50 points)
Concept: improved writing skills (cognitive goal)	Students will write five warm-up essays/week.	With minimal errors students will write these essays in 15-20 minutes.
Concept: increased vocabulary (cognitive goal)	Students will collect at least five new vocabulary words and use these words in their warm-up essays and analysis essay.	Students will use five vocabulary words in conversation during the week, as well as use the words in their essays.

Goals/Objectives: What is the purpose of this lesson?	Strategies to meet these goals: How will I obtain these goals/objectives?	Evaluation: How will I know when I have met these goals/ objectives?
Concept: reflective writing (affective/spiritual goal)	Using the Journal Guide Questions in the Appendices, students will record at least three entries this week. Suggested Scripture: 1 Kings 16:30.	Students will show evidence that they have reflected on this issue, including informed discussions and written responses.
Concept: increased knowledge of the assigned essay (cognitive goal)	Students will take Lesson 11 Test.	Students will score at least 80% on Lesson 11 Test.
Concept: analysis essay (cognitive goal)	Students will write an analysis of their family by comparing each family member to an animal.	Students, with minimal errors, will clearly write an analysis of their family by comparing each family member to an animal.
Concept: working in a group setting (behavioral goal)	In a class, in a co-op experience, or during a family discussion, students should analyze the removal of prayer from public schools.	Students will exhibit practical listening skills and will manifest understanding of opposing world-views.

SUGGESTED
Weekly *Implementation*

DAY 1	DAY 2	DAY 3	DAY 4	DAY 5
Write a Warm-up Essay.	Write a Warm-up Essay.	Write a Warm-up Essay.	Write a Warm-up Essay.	Write a Warm-up Essay.
Read 35-50 pages/day.	Read 35-50 pages/day.	Read 35-50 pages/day.	Read 35-50 pages/day.	Read 35-50 pages/day.
Find five new vocabulary words.	Find five new vocabulary words.	Find five new vocabulary words.	Find five new vocabulary words.	Find five new vocabulary words.
Reflect on the speech assignment for the week.	Compose a first draft of your speech.	Revise your speech and submit to your evaluator/ parent.	Prepare to present your speech tomorrow.	Present your speech to a live audience.
Write an outline and thesis for your analysis essay.	Work on the first draft for your analysis essay.	Revise and finish the first draft of your analysis essay.	Finish the final copy of your analysis essay.	Submit your assignments to your evaluator/ parent.
Make a journal entry.	Make a journal entry.	Make a journal entry.	Make a journal entry.	Submit a copy of your paper to a peer for evaluation.
				Make a journal entry.
				Take Lesson 11 Test

ENRICHMENT ACTIVITIES/PROJECTS

Students should analyze the causes of the destruction of the World Trade Towers on September 11, 2001.

SPEECH ASSIGNMENT

Give a three-minute analysis speech where you compare each family member to an animal. In your speech, employ as many rhetorical questions as you can.

ANSWER: *Answers will vary. For example:*

What sort of creature is this mom of mine? In the morning Mom wakes up everyone, makes breakfast, sets the table, creates a list of chores, grades papers from yesterday's assignments, and manages to have a 30-minute devotion.

(The clear implication is that she is "as busy as a beaver.")

ASSIGNMENTS

1. Analyze your family by comparing each family member to an animal. Carefully defend your choice. This essay should include an outline, rough draft, thesis statement, final copy, and five new (circled) vocabulary words. The essay must pay particular attention to style (focus, content, organization). Give a copy to your peer/friend to complete a peer evaluation form (Appendix) and to your instructor for evaluation.

ANSWER: *Answers will vary.*

2. Read 35 to 50 pages each day and keep vocabulary cards.
3. Complete the speech assignment and have a teacher complete a speech evaluation form (Appendix).
4. Pay attention to your stylistic tendencies this week.

5. According to 1 Kings 16:30, "Ahab son of Omri did more evil in the eyes of the LORD than any of those before him." Why would the prophet say such an awful thing about King Ahab? Record your reflections in your prayer journal. This journal is meant to be private, but you are invited to share your reflections with others.

6. Complete one warm-up essay every day.

FINAL PROJECT

Students should correct and rewrite all essays and place them in their Final Portfolio.

WARM-UP ESSAYS:

	DAY 1	DAY 2	DAY 3	DAY 4	DAY 5
Analysis	Analyze why your room is so messy.	Analyze the way one should eat a piece of pie.	Analyze the causes of your father's baldness.	Analyze one of your pastor's sermons.	Analyze the way your mother handles stress.

LESSON 11 TEST

ESSAY (100 POINTS)

Write a one-page analysis of the best vacation your
family has experienced.

LESSON 11 TEST ANSWER

ESSAY (100 POINTS)

Write a one-page analysis of the best vacation your family has experienced.

ANSWER: *Answers will vary.*

LESSON 12

Writing Skill: General Synthesis Essay (Writing)

Style (Writing and Speaking): Sentences—Writing Clear Sentences

Public Speaking Skill: Converting a General Synthesis Essay to a Speech.

Looking Ahead: The General Evaluation Essay (Writing)

Goals/Objectives: What is the purpose of this lesson?	Strategies to meet these goals: How will I obtain these goals/objectives?	Evaluation: How will I know when I have met these goals/objectives?
Concept: convert a synthesis essay into a speech (cognitive goal)	The parent/educator will engage students in discussions about ways to write and present speeches.	Students will be able to write and to present an inspired speech. Suggested evaluation sheet includes: Oratory Evaluation I. Poise: How does the student present himself/herself? Is the oratory/dramatic reading memorized? (25 points) II. Articulation: Does the student speak clearly, and slowly? (25 points) III. Presentation: What is the overall effect of the speech? Does it accomplish its purpose? (50 points)
Concept: improved writing skills (cognitive goal)	Students will write five warm-up essays/week.	With minimal errors students will write these essays in 15-20 minutes.
Concept: increased vocabulary (cognitive goal)	Students will collect at least five new vocabulary words and use these words in their warm-up essays and synthesis essay.	Students will use five vocabulary words in conversation during the week, as well as use the words in their essays.

Goals/Objectives: What is the purpose of this lesson?	Strategies to meet these goals: How will I obtain these goals/objectives?	Evaluation: How will I know when I have met these goals/objectives?
Concept: reflective writing (affective/spiritual goal)	Using the Journal Guide Questions in the Appendices, students will record at least three entries this week. Suggested Scripture: 1 Kings 16:30.	Students will show evidence that they have reflected on this issue, including informed discussions and written responses.
Concept: increased knowledge of the assigned essay (cognitive goal)	Students will take Lesson 12 Test.	Students will score at least 80% on Lesson 12 Test.
Concept: synthesis essay (cognitive goal)	Students will write a synthesis essay on this topic: Last year a million plus Evangelical Christians graduated from high school. Many of them have gone to college and will become our next generation of leaders. Speculate about what effect this influx of students will have on American society and culture.	With minimal errors, students will clearly write a synthesis of the effect of Evangelicalism on American society.
Concept: working in a group setting (behavioral goal)	In a class, in a co-op experience, or during a family discussion, students should write a synthesis essay upon the effect of Saul's disobedience (1 Samuel) upon himself and the nation of Israel.	Students will exhibit practical listening skills and will manifest understanding of opposing worldviews.

SUGGESTED
Weekly *Implementation*

DAY 1	DAY 2	DAY 3	DAY 4	DAY 5
Write a Warm-up Essay.	Write a Warm-up Essay.	Write a Warm-up Essay.	Write a Warm-up Essay.	Write a Warm-up Essay.
Read 35-50 pages/day.	Read 35-50 pages/day.	Read 35-50 pages/day.	Read 35-50 pages/day.	Read 35-50 pages/day.
Find five new vocabulary words.	Find five new vocabulary words.	Find five new vocabulary words.	Find five new vocabulary words.	Find five new vocabulary words.
Reflect on the speech assignment for the week.	Compose a first draft of your speech.	Revise your speech and submit to your evaluator/ parent.	Prepare to present your speech tomorrow.	Present your speech to a live audience.
Write an outline and thesis for your synthesis essay.	Work on the first draft for your analysis essay.	Finish the first draft of your analysis essay.	Finish the final copy of your synthesis essay.	Submit your assignments to your evaluator/ parent.
Make a journal entry.	Make a journal entry.	Make a journal entry.	Make a journal entry.	Submit a copy of your paper to a peer for evaluation.
				Make a journal entry.
				Take Lesson 12 Test

ENRICHMENT ACTIVITIES/PROJECTS

Write a mission statement for yourself and for your family.

SPEECH ASSIGNMENT

While attending a local state university, you have written a very impressive paper entitled "A Case for the Mosaic Authorship of the Pentateuch." Your unbelieving professor is so impressed that he wants to speak to you privately. You recognize this invitation as an opportunity to share the Gospel with this professor. Write a three-minute synthesis speech organizing and presenting evidence for the Mosaic authorship of the Pentateuch.

ANSWER: (Sample) *Sir, I know it seems remarkable that Moses could write all the literature from Genesis to Deuteronomy. I know it is more remarkable that he could discuss things in which he had no firsthand participation—like Creation. I believe I have proven, nonetheless, that he did. What I did not put in my paper—because I am not sure it has any credibility in your eyes—is the main reason I believe Moses wrote the Pentateuch. What is that? Jesus Christ Himself believed that Moses wrote the Pentateuch (Matthew 8:3-5, 19:6-8). Jesus Christ and His Word are the supreme authority in my life. I wonder if you would be interested in hearing how He changed my life.*

WRITING ASSIGNMENTS

1. Last year a million plus Evangelical Christians graduated from high school. Many of them have gone

to college and will become our next generation of leaders. Speculate about what effect this influx of graduates will have on American society and culture. This essay should include an outline with thesis statement, rough draft, revised draft, final copy, and five new (circled) vocabulary words. Pay particular attention to style (focus, content, organization). Give a copy to a peer/friend to complete a peer evaluation form (Appendix) and to your instructor to evaluate.

ANSWER: *Maturation calls into sharp focus our views of reality, the meaning of life, and other existential concepts. In the book* Father Sergius *by Leo Tolstoy, the protagonist Augusto Perez shakes his fist at God and asks, "Am I a creature of fiction?" This question haunts modern society. In a way, too, it is the question many young people ask.*

In Western society in 2004, we ask that question at universities.

The first modern university was Halle University, founded in 1694. From the beginning, universities have wrestled with accepting truth as an absolute reality or seeing truth as an objective intellectual quest. The quest, unfortunately, has led us to many dead ends.

The modern university is a hostile environment for most Christians. It appears to be King Belshazzar's feast (Daniel 5), an undisciplined intellectual orgy of knowledge worship, instead of a time on Mount Horeb, a humble recognition of God's omnipotence. Moses, at the burning bush (Exodus 3), freely admits his human limits and extols God's holy name. Like Moses, present-day Christians must know who they are and who their God is.

Christian students are called to act as if they are on Mount Horeb even if they are in the middle of Belshazzar's feast. They are called to be salt and light in a hostile environment. The good news is that they appear to be ready. Imagine what effect one million elite college graduates *will have on American culture! In about four years, in my opinion, there will be a new group of playwrights, politicians, and business leaders. Many of these will be Evangelical Christians. This influx of Christian graduates will significantly change the cultural landscape of 21st century America.*

2. Read 200 to 250 pages this week and find vocabulary words.

3. Complete the speech assignment and have a teacher complete a speech evaluation (Appendix).

4. In 1 Kings 18:9, Obadiah, the faithful man of God, says to Elijah, "What have I done wrong,. . . that you are handing your servant over to Ahab to be put to death?" Meditate on this passage and others. Has God ever asked you to do something that has put you into a place of danger? This journal is meant to be private, but you are invited to share your reflections with others.

5. Pay particular attention to your writing style this week. Watch for shifts in agreement between nouns and verbs and between adjectives and their antecedents.

6. Write a warm-up essay every day. As you experience the daily writing, you should see improvement in your ability to express your thoughts on paper. This daily writing is preparation for composing effective essays.

FINAL PROJECT

Students should correct and rewrite all essays and place them in their Final Portfolio.

WARM-UP ESSAYS:

	DAY 1	DAY 2	DAY 3	DAY 4	DAY 5
Synthesis	Create a new game by combining baseball and hockey.	Create a solution to your brother's/sister's long times in the bathroom.	Create a solution to your mother's/father's insistence that students eat broccoli.	Create an alternative solution to the rule that students cannot watch TV on school nights.	Create a nonviolent video game that would sell.

LESSON 12 TEST

ESSAY (100 POINTS)

Write a one-page synthesis of the best vacation your family has experienced. In other words, speculate upon what would be a perfect vacation as you think about your best vacation.

LESSON 12 TEST ANSWER

ESSAY (100 POINTS)

Write a one-page synthesis of the best vacation your family has experienced. In other words, speculate upon what would be a perfect vacation as you think about your best vacation.

ANSWER: *Answers will vary.*

LESSON 13

Writing Skill: Literary Analysis Essay (Writing)

Style (Writing and Speaking): Sentences – Sentence Variety

Public Speaking Skill: Converting a Literary Analysis Essay into a Speech.

Looking Ahead: The General Evaluation Essay (Writing)

Goals/Objectives: What is the purpose of this lesson?	Strategies to meet these goals: How will I obtain these goals/objectives?	Evaluation: How will I know when I have met these goals/ objectives?
Concept: converting a literary analysis essay to a speech (cognitive goal)	The parent/educator will engage students in discussions about ways to write and present speeches. Students will present a literary analysis speech.	Students will be able to write and to present an inspired speech. Suggested evaluation sheet includes: Oratory Evaluation I. Poise: Calm presentation? Appropriate word inflections? Familiarity with oratory/dramatic reading? Cue cards used appropriately? (20 points) II. Articulation: Distinct enunciation? Appropriate tone? Appropriate volume? (30 points) III. Organization: Introduction? Thesis stated? Points supported? Conclusion effective? Accomplish the stated purpose? (50 points)
Concept: improved writing skills (cognitive goal)	Students will write five warm-up essays/week.	With minimal errors, students will write these essays in 15-20 minutes.
Concept: increased vocabulary (cognitive goal)	Students will collect at least five new vocabulary words and use these words in their warm-up essays and literary analysis.	Students will use five vocabulary words in conversation during the week, as well as use the words in their essays.

Goals/Objectives: What is the purpose of this lesson?	Strategies to meet these goals: How will I obtain these goals/objectives?	Evaluation: How will I know when I have met these goals/objectives?
Concept: reflective writing (affective/spiritual goal)	Using the Journal Guide Questions in the Appendices, students will record at least three entries this week. Suggested Scripture: 1 Kings 18	Students will show evidence that they have reflected on this issue, including informed discussions and written responses.
Concept: increased knowledge of the assigned essay (cognitive goal)	Students will take Lesson 13 Test.	Students will score at least 80% on Lesson 13 Test.
Concept: literary analysis (cognitive goal)	Students will write a literary analysis of their favorite novel.	With minimal errors, students will clearly write a literary analysis of a favorite novel.
Concept: working in a group setting (behavioral goal)	In a class, in a co-op experience, or during a family discussion, students will discuss their favorite prose work.	Students will exhibit practical listening skills and will manifest understanding of opposing worldviews.

SUGGESTED
Weekly *Implementation*

DAY 1	DAY 2	DAY 3	DAY 4	DAY 5
Write a Warm-up Essay. Read 35-50 pages/day. Find five new vocabulary words. Reflect on the speech assignment for the week. Write an outline with thesis for your literary analysis. Make a journal entry.	Write a Warm-up Essay. Read 35-50 pages/day. Find five new vocabulary words. Compose a first draft of your speech. Work on the first draft for your literary analysis. Make a journal entry.	Write a Warm-up Essay. Read 35-50 pages/day. Find five new vocabulary words. Revise your speech and submit to your evaluator/ parent. Finish the first draft and then the revised draft of your literary analysis. Make a journal entry.	Write a Warm-up Essay. Read 35-50 pages/day. Find five new vocabulary words. Prepare to present your speech tomorrow. Submit a copy of your paper to a peer for evaluation. Finish the final copy of your literary analysis. Make a journal entry.	Write a Warm-up Essay. Read 35-50 pages/day. Find five new vocabulary words. Present your speech to a live audience. Submit your assignments to your evaluator/ parent. Take Lesson 13 Test. Make a journal entry.

ENRICHMENT ACTIVITIES/PROJECTS

Students should do an oral analysis their favorite movie.

SPEECH ASSIGNMENT

Create a thinking game and concept map of your favorite literary piece. Use this outline to create a 1-3 minute speech to an audience.

   ANSWER: *The favorite book could concern the causes of the American Civil War.*

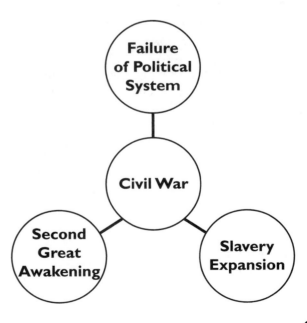

WRITING ASSIGNMENTS

1. Write a literary analysis of your favorite novel, short story, or poem. Include an outline with thesis statement, rough draft, revised draft, and final copy and five new (circled) vocabulary words. Pay particular attention to style (focus, content, organization). For evaluation, give a copy to a peer/friend who will complete a peer evaluation form (Appendix) and another copy to your parent/educator.

ANSWER: *The following is an example of literary analysis:*

The way in which the reader is drawn into Ethan Frome is truly effective. Narration creates a closer relationship between the reader and Frome. The reader is not just enlightened to the plot but also to the development of the protagonist. The reader is invited into Frome's thoughts and feelings. All this is accomplished through the narration.

Although the narrator is a neutral outsider, the reader is nonetheless drawn into Ethan's private thoughts. The reader experiences things he is seeing, feeling, desiring, and dreading. "All the long misery of his baffled past, of his youth of failure, hardship and vain effort, rose in his soul in bitterness and seemed to take shape before him in the woman (Zeena) who at every turn had barred his way." These insights into Ethan's heart are critical later in the novel when he and Mattie try to commit suicide. The reader watches Ethan move toward that fateful moment.

Through skillful narration, the reader feels the struggle, and the anguish at the prospect of Mattie leaving Ethan to this "bitter querulous woman" who is his wife. When Ethan considers divorce, the reader feels an understanding not resentment, having already seen into his mind both options for his future.

Narration in Ethan Frome draws the reader into the heart and soul of poor Ethan Frome. Readers want to see Ethan and young Mattie runaway to the west and leave Zeena in her own misery. They want to see the Ethan of long ago cheerful and well. When all hope is gone, when Ethan and Mattie climb on the sled, readers vicariously join them.

(Jessica Stobaugh)

2. Read 150 to 200 pages this week and find vocabulary words.

3. Complete the speech assignment and have a teacher complete a speech evaluation form (Appendix).

4. In 1 Kings 18, Elijah faces the priests of Baal. Answer the question "What is the cause and effect of apostasy?" Meditate on this passage and others. Have you had a Mt. Carmel experience?

5. Pay particular attention to your writing style this week.

6. Write a warm-up essay every day. Over time and as you experience daily writing, you should see improvement in your ability to express your thoughts on paper. This daily writing is preparation for composing effective essays.

FINAL PROJECT

Students should correct and rewrite all essays and place them in their Final Portfolio.

WARM-UP ESSAYS:

	DAY 1	DAY 2	DAY 3	DAY 4	DAY 5
Literary Analysis	Write a literary analysis of a recent sermon.	Write a literary analysis of a favorite poem.	Write a literary analysis of a favorite short story.	Write a literary analysis of a favorite movie.	Write a literary analysis of a favorite nonfiction story.

LESSON 13 TEST

ESSAY (100 POINTS)

Using appropriate "language of analysis," write a one-page literary analysis of the following short story by Edgar Allan Poe:

"The Cask of Amontillado"

(www.classicreader.com/read.php/sid.6/bookid.454/

The thousand injuries of Fortunato I had borne as I best could; but when he ventured upon insult, I vowed revenge. You, who so well know the nature of my soul, will not suppose, however, that I gave utterance to a threat. At length I would be avenged; this was a point definitively settled—but the very definitiveness with which it was resolved, precluded the idea of risk. I must not only punish, but punish with impunity. A wrong is unredressed when retribution overtakes its redresser. It is equally unredressed when the avenger fails to make himself felt as such to him who has done the wrong.

It must be understood, that neither by word nor deed had I given Fortunato cause to doubt my good will. I continued, as was my wont, to smile in his face, and he did not perceive that my smile now was at the thought of his immolation.

He had a weak point—this Fortunato—although in other regards he was a man to be respected and even feared. He prided himself on his connoisseurship in wine. Few Italians have the true virtuoso spirit. For the most part their enthusiasm is adopted to suit the time and opportunity—to practise imposture upon the British and Austrian millionaires. In painting and gemmary, Fortunato, like his countrymen , was a quack—but in the matter of old wines he was sincere. In this respect I did not differ from him materially: I was skilful in the Italian vintages myself, and bought largely whenever I could.

It was about dusk, one evening during the supreme madness of the carnival season, that I encountered my friend. He accosted me with excessive warmth, for he had been drinking much. The man wore motley. He had on a tight-fitting parti-striped dress, and his head was surmounted by the conical cap and bells. I was so pleased to see him, that I thought I should never have done wringing his hand.

I said to him—"My dear Fortunato, you are luckily met. How remarkably well you are looking to-day! But I have received a pipe of what passes for Amontillado, and I have my doubts."

"How?" said he. "Amontillado? A pipe? Impossible! And in the middle of the carnival!"

"I have my doubts," I replied; "and I was silly enough to pay the full Amontillado price without consulting you in the matter. You were not to be found, and I was fearful of losing a bargain."

"Amontillado!"

"I have my doubts."

"Amontillado!"

"And I must satisfy them."

"Amontillado!"

"As you are engaged, I am on my way to Luchesi. If any one has a critical turn, it is he. He will tell me—"

"Luchesi cannot tell Amontillado from Sherry."

"And yet some fools will have it that his taste is a match for your own."

"Come, let us go."

"Whither?"

"To your vaults."

"My friend, no; I will not impose upon your good nature. I perceive you have an engagement. Luchesi—"

"I have no engagement;—come."

"My friend, no. It is not the engagement, but the severe cold with which I perceive you are afflicted. The vaults are insufferably damp. They are encrusted with nitre."

"Let us go, nevertheless. The cold is merely nothing. Amontillado! You have been imposed upon. And as for Luchesi, he cannot distinguish Sherry from Amontillado."

Thus speaking, Fortunato possessed himself of my arm. Putting on a mask of black silk, and drawing a roquelaire closely about my person, I suffered him to hurry me to my palazzo. There were no attendants at home; they had absconded to make merry in honor of the time. I had told them that I should not return until the morning, and had given them explicit orders not to stir from the house. These orders were sufficient, I well knew, to insure their immediate disappearance, one and all, as soon as my back was turned.

I took from their sconces two flambeaux, and giving one to Fortunato, bowed him through several suites of rooms to the archway that led into the vaults. I passed down a long and winding staircase, requesting him to be cautious as he followed. We came at length to the foot of the descent, and stood together on the damp ground of the catacombs of the Montresors. The gait of my friend was unsteady, and the bells upon his cap jingled as he strode.

"The pipe," said he.

"It is farther on," said I; "but observe the white web-work which gleams from these cavern walls."

He turned towards me, and looked into my eyes with two filmy orbs that distilled the rheum of intoxication .

"Nitre?" he asked, at length.

"Nitre," I replied. "How long have you had that cough?"

"Ugh! ugh! ugh!—ugh! ugh! ugh!—ugh! ugh! ugh!—ugh! ugh! ugh!—ugh! ugh!"

My poor friend found it impossible to reply for many minutes.

"It is nothing," he said, at last.

"Come," I said, with decision, "we will go back; your health is precious. You are rich, respected, admired, beloved; you are happy, as once I was. You are a man to be missed. For me it is no matter. We will go back; you will be ill, and I cannot be responsible. Besides, there is Luchesi—"

"Enough," he said; "the cough is a mere nothing; it will not kill me. I shall not die of a cough."

"True—true," I replied; "and, indeed, I had no intention of alarming you unnecessarily—but you should use all proper caution. A draught of this Medoc will defend us from the damps." Here I knocked off the neck of a bottle which I drew from a long row of its fellows that lay upon the mould.

"Drink," I said, presenting him the wine. He raised it to his lips with a leer. He paused and nodded to me familiarly, while his bells jingled.

"I drink," he said, "to the buried that repose around us."

"And I to your long life."

He again took my arm, and we proceeded.

"These vaults," he said, "are extensive."

"The Montresors," I replied, "were a great and numerous family."

"I forget your arms."

"A huge human foot d'or, in a field azure; the foot crushes a serpent rampant whose fangs are imbedded in the heel."

"And the motto?"

"Nemo me impune lacessit ."

"Good!" he said.

The wine sparkled in his eyes and the bells jingled. My own fancy grew warm with the Medoc. We had passed through walls of piled bones, with casks and puncheons intermingling, into the inmost recesses of the catacombs. I paused again, and this time I made bold to seize Fortunato by an arm above the elbow.

"The nitre!" I said : "see, it increases. It hangs like moss upon the vaults. We are below the river's bed. The drops of moisture trickle among the bones. Come, we will go back ere it is too late. Your cough—"

"It is nothing," he said; "let us go on. But first, another draught of the Medoc."

I broke and reached him a flaçcon of De Grââve. He emptied it at a breath. His eyes flashed with a fierce light. He laughed and threw the bottle upwards with a gesticulation I did not understand.

I looked at him in surprise. He repeated the movement—a grotesque one.

"You do not comprehend?" he said.

"Not I," I replied.

"Then you are not of the brotherhood."

"How?"

"You are not of the masons."

"Yes, yes," I said, "yes, yes."

"You? Impossible! A mason?"

"A mason," I replied.

"A sign," he said.

"It is this," I answered, producing a trowel from beneath the folds of my roquelaire.

"You jest," he exclaimed, recoiling a few paces. "But let us proceed to the Amontillado."

"Be it so," I said, replacing the tool beneath the cloak, and again offering him my arm. He leaned upon it heavily. We continued our route in search of the Amontillado. We passed through a range of low arches, descended, passed on, and descending again, arrived at a deep crypt, in which the foulness of the air caused our flambeaux rather to glow than flame.

At the most remote end of the crypt there appeared another less spacious. Its walls had been lined with human remains, piled to the vault overhead, in the fashion of the great catacombs of Paris. Three sides of this interior crypt were still ornamented in this manner. From the fourth the bones had been thrown down, and lay promiscuously upon the earth, forming at one point a mound of some size. Within the wall thus exposed by the displacing of the bones, we perceived a still interior recess, in depth about four feet, in width three, in height six or seven. It seemed to have been constructed for no especial use in itself, but formed merely the interval between two of the colossal supports of the roof of the catacombs, and was backed by one of their circumscribing walls of solid granite.

It was in vain that Fortunato, uplifting his dull torch, endeavored to pry into the depths of the recess. Its termination the feeble light did not enable us to see.

"Proceed," I said; "herein is the Amontillado. As for Luchesi—"

"He is an ignoramus," interrupted my friend, as he stepped unsteadily forward, while I followed immediately at his heels. In an instant he had reached the extremity of the niche, and finding his progress arrested by the rock, stood stupidly bewildered. A moment more and I had fettered him to the granite. In its surface were two iron staples, distant from each other about two feet, horizontally. From one of these depended a short chain, from the other a padlock. Throwing the links about his waist, it was but the work of a few seconds to secure it. He was too much astounded to resist. Withdrawing the key I stepped back from the recess.

"Pass your hand," I said, "over the wall; you cannot help feeling the nitre. Indeed it is very damp. Once more let me implore you to return. No? Then I must positively leave you. But I must first render you all the little attentions in my power."

"The Amontillado!" ejaculated my friend, not yet recovered from his astonishment.

"True," I replied; "the Amontillado."

As I said these words I busied myself among the pile of bones of which I have before spoken. Throwing them aside, I soon uncovered a quantity of building stone and mortar. With these materials and with the aid of my trowel, I began vigorously to wall up the entrance of the niche.

I had scarcely laid the first tier of my masonry when I discovered that the intoxication of Fortunato had in a great measure worn off. The earliest indication I had of this was a low moaning cry from the depth of the recess. It was not the cry of a drunken man. There was then a long and obstinate silence. I laid the second tier, and the third, and the fourth; and then I heard the furious vibrations of the chain. The noise lasted for several minutes, during which, that I might hearken to it with the more satisfaction, I ceased my labors and sat down upon the bones. When at last the clanking subsided, I resumed the trowel, and finished without interruption the fifth, the sixth, and the seventh tier. The wall was now nearly upon a level with my breast. I again paused, and holding the flambeaux over the mason-work, threw a few feeble rays upon the figure within.

A succession of loud and shrill screams, bursting suddenly from the throat of the chained form, seemed to thrust me violently back. For a brief moment I hesitated—I trembled.

Unsheathing my rapier, I began to grope with it about the recess: but the thought of an instant reassured me. I placed my hand upon the solid fabric of the catacombs, and felt satisfied. I reapproached the wall. I replied to the yells of him who clamored. I re-echoed—I aided—I surpassed them in volume and in strength. I did this, and the clamorer grew still.

It was now midnight, and my task was drawing to a close. I had completed the eighth, the ninth, and the tenth tier. I had finished a portion of the last and the eleventh; there remained but a single stone to be fitted and plastered in. I struggled with its weight; I placed it partially in its destined position. But now there came from out the niche a low laugh that erected the hairs upon my head. It was succeeded by a sad voice, which I had difficulty in recognising as that of the noble Fortunato. The voice said -

"Ha! ha! ha!—he! he!—a very good joke indeed—an excellent jest. We will have many a rich laugh about it at the palazzo—he! he! he!—over our wine—he! he! he!"

"The Amontillado!" I said.

"He! he! he!—he! he! he!—yes, the Amontillado. But is it not getting late? Will not they be awaiting us at the palazzo, the Lady Fortunato and the rest? Let us be gone."

"Yes," I said, "let us be gone."

" For the love of God, Montressor! "

"Yes," I said, "for the love of God!"

But to these words I hearkened in vain for a reply. I grew impatient. I called aloud -

"Fortunato!"

No answer. I called again -

"Fortunato!"

No answer still. I thrust a torch through the remaining aperture and let it fall within. There came forth in return only a jingling of the bells. My heart grew sick—on account of the dampness of the catacombs. I hastened to make an end of my labor. I forced the last stone into its position; I plastered it up. Against the new masonry I re-erected the old rampart of bones. For the half of a century no mortal has disturbed them. *In pace requiescat*!

LESSON 13 TEST ANSWER

ESSAY (100 POINTS)

Using appropriate "language of analysis," write a one-page literary analysis of the following short story by Edgar Allan Poe:

ANSWER: Students should use the language presented in the introduction of this lesson. *The characters are well developed in a short amount of time. The setting is well described. The plot concerns an internal conflict and external conflict, and it is well presented. The tone (i.e., suspense) is developed brilliantly through the narration. Overall, it is a well-written short story—all the elements of a short story are present.*

LESSON 14

Writing Skill: Evaluation Essay (Writing)

Style (Writing and Speaking): Words—Using the Dictionary vs. the Thesaurus

Public Speaking Skill: Converting the Evaluation Essay to a Speech.

Looking Ahead: The Cause/Effect Essay

Goals/Objectives: What is the purpose of this lesson?	Strategies to meet these goals: How will I obtain these goals/objectives?	Evaluation: How will I know when I have met these goals/objectives?
Concept: Evaluation speech (cognitive goal)	The parent/educator will engage students in discussions about ways to write and present speeches. Students will present an evaluation speech.	Students will be able to write and to present an inspired speech. Suggested evaluation sheet includes: Oratory Evaluation I. Poise: Calm presentation? Appropriate word inflections? Familiarity with oratory/dramatic reading? Cue cards used appropriately? (20 points) II. Articulation: Distinct enunciation? Appropriate tone? Appropriate volume? (30 points) III. Organization: Introduction? Thesis stated? Points supported? Conclusion effective? Accomplish the stated purpose? (50 points)
Concept: improved writing skills (cognitive goal)	Students will write five warm-up essays/week.	With minimal errors, students will write these essays in 15-20 minutes.
Concept: increased vocabulary (cognitive goal)	Students will collect at least five new vocabulary words and use these words in their warm-up essays and evaluation essay.	Students will use five vocabulary words in conversation during the week, as well as use the words in their essays.

Goals/Objectives: What is the purpose of this lesson?	Strategies to meet these goals: How will I obtain these goals/objectives?	Evaluation: How will I know when I have met these goals/ objectives?
Concept: reflective writing (affective/spiritual goal)	Using the Journal Guide Questions in the Appendices, students will record at least three entries this week. Suggested Scripture: 1 Kings 16–19.	Students will show evidence that they have reflected on this issue, including informed discussions and written responses.
Concept: increased knowledge of the assigned essay (cognitive goal)	Students will take Lesson 14 Test.	Students will score at least 80% on Lesson 14 Test.
Concept: evaluation (cognitive goal)	Students will write a short essay on this topic, "What obstacles are in the way of racial reconciliation in contemporary America?"	Students, with minimal errors, will clearly evaluate the obstacles to racial reconciliation.
Concept: working in a group setting (behavioral goal)	In a class, in a co-op experience, or during a family discussion, students will discuss what will bring racial reconciliation to America.	Students will exhibit practical listening skills and will manifest understanding of opposing worldviews.

SUGGESTED
Weekly *Implementation*

DAY 1	DAY 2	DAY 3	DAY 4	DAY 5
Write a Warm-up Essay.	Write a Warm-up Essay.	Write a Warm-up Essay.	Write a Warm-up Essay.	Write a Warm-up Essay.
Read 35-50 pages/day.	Read 35-50 pages/day.	Read 35-50 pages/day.	Read 35-50 pages/day.	Read 35-50 pages/day.
Find five new vocabulary words.	Find five new vocabulary words.	Find five new vocabulary words.	Find five new vocabulary words.	Find five new vocabulary words.
Reflect on the speech assignment for the week.	Compose a first draft of your speech.	Revise your speech and submit to your evaluator/ parent.	Prepare to present your speech tomorrow.	Present your speech to a live audience.
Write an outline with thesis for your evaluation essay.	Work on the first draft for your evaluation essay.	Finish the first draft and then the revised draft of your evaluation essay.	Submit a copy of your paper to a peer for evaluation.	Submit your assignments to your evaluator/ parent.
Make a journal entry.	Make a journal entry.	Make a journal entry.	Finish the final copy of your evaluation essay.	Take Lesson 14 Test.
			Make a journal entry.	Make a journal entry.

ENRICHMENT ACTIVITIES/PROJECTS

Students should orally evaluate the effectiveness of their performance in this course.

SPEECH ASSIGNMENT

In a three-minute speech, evaluate the significance to world history of an important individual.

ANSWER: *See essay below.*

WRITING ASSIGNMENTS

1. Evaluate the significance to world history of an important individual. Include an outline with thesis statement, rough draft, revised draft, and final copy and five new (circled) vocabulary words. Pay particular attention to style (focus, content, organization). For evaluation, give a copy to a peer/friend who will complete a peer evaluation form (Appendix) and another copy to your parent/educator.

ANSWER: *The following is an essay on Abraham Lincoln by author James Russell Lowell (October 6, 1884): (www.barleby.com/28/16.html)*

A war—which, whether we consider the expanse of the territory at stake, the hosts brought into the field, or the reach of the principles involved, may fairly be reckoned the most momentous of modern times—was to be waged by a people divided at home, unnerved by fifty years of peace, under a chief magistrate without experience and without reputation, whose every measure was sure to be cunningly hampered by a jealous and unscrupulous minority, and who, while dealing with unheard-of complications at home, must soothe a hostile neutrality abroad, waiting only a pretext to become war. All this was to be done without warning and without preparation, while at the same time a social revolution was to be accomplished in the political condition of millions of people, by softening the prejudices, allaying the fears, and gradually obtaining the cooperation, of their unwilling liberators. Surely, if ever there were an occasion when the heightened imagination of the historian might see Destiny visibly intervening in human affairs, here was a knot worthy of her shears. Never, perhaps, was any system of government tried by so continuous and searching a strain as ours during the last three years; never has any shown itself stronger; and never could that strength be so directly traced to the virtue and intelligence of the people,—to that general enlightenment and prompt efficiency of public opinion possible only under the influence of a political framework like our

own. We find it hard to understand how even a foreigner should be blind to the grandeur of the combat of ideas that has been going on here,—to the heroic energy, persistency, and self-reliance of a nation proving that it knows how much dearer greatness is than mere power; and we own that it is impossible for us to conceive the mental and moral condition of the American who does not feel his spirit braced and heightened by being even a spectator of such qualities and achievements. That a steady purpose and a definite aim have been given to the jarring forces which, at the beginning of the war, spent themselves in the discussion of schemes which could only become operative, if at all, after the war was over; that a popular excitement has been slowly intensified into an earnest national will; that a somewhat impracticable moral sentiment has been made the unconscious instrument of a practical moral end; that the treason of covert enemies, the jealousy of rivals, the unwise zeal of friends, have been made not only useless for mischief, but even useful for good; that the conscientious sensitiveness of England to the horrors of civil conflict has been prevented from complicating a domestic with a foreign war; all these results, any one of which might suffice to prove greatness in a ruler, have been mainly due to the good sense, the good humor, the sagacity, the large-mindedness, and the unselfish honesty of the unknown man whom a blind fortune, as it seemed, had lifted from the crowd to the most dangerous and difficult eminence of modern times. It is by presence of mind in untried emergencies that the native metal of a man is tested; it is by the sagacity to see, and the fearless honesty to admit, whatever of truth there may be in an adverse opinion, in order more convincingly to expose the fallacy that lurks behind it, that a reasoner at length gains for his mere statement of a fact the force of argument; it is by a wise forecast which allows hostile combinations to go so far as by the inevitable reaction to become elements of his own power; that a politician proves his genius for statecraft; and especially it is by so gently guiding public sentiment that he seems to follow it, by so yielding doubtful points that he can be firm without seeming obstinate in essential ones, and thus gain the advantages of compromise without the weakness of concession; by so instinctively comprehending the temper and prejudices of a people as to make them gradually conscious of the superior wisdom of his freedom from temper and prejudice,—it is by qualities such as these that a magistrate shows himself worthy to be chief in a commonwealth of freemen. And it is for qualities such as these that we firmly believe history will rank Mr. Lincoln among the most prudent of statesmen and the most successful of rulers. If we wish to appreciate him, we have only to conceive the inevitable chaos in which we should now be weltering, had a weak man or an unwise one been chosen in his stead.

For additional value in this exercise, identify the differences between the writing standards of this piece of writ-

ing and that of today. Comment on paragraphing, sentence structure, word choice, grammar, and punctuation.

2. Read 150 to 200 pages this week and find vocabulary words.

3. Complete the speech assignment and have a teacher complete a speech evaluation form (Appendix).

4. Pay particular attention to your writing style this week.

5. Read 1 Kings 16–19. The student should reflect upon who is worse: the passive and ineffective Ahab, or the officious and shrewd Jezebel.

6. Write a warm-up essay every day. As you experience the daily writing, you should see improvement in your ability to express your thoughts on paper. This daily writing is preparation for composing effective essays.

FINAL PROJECT

Students should correct and rewrite all essays and place them in their Final Portfolio.

WARM-UP ESSAYS:

	DAY 1	DAY 2	DAY 3	DAY 4	DAY 5
Evaluation	Evaluate your favorite television show.	Evaluate your favorite sport.	Evaluate your favorite Bible verse.	Evaluate your favorite meal.	Evaluate your favorite movie star.

LESSON 14 TEST

ESSAY (100 POINTS)

Using reference books, write an analysis essay of the
causes of America's involvement in World War II.
Then, write an essay speculating about what would
have happened if America had not entered the war
(synthesis essay). Finally, evaluate whether or not
America was justified in entering the war on the side of
the Allies. Make each essay from 75-150 words.

LESSON 14 TEST ANSWER

ESSAY (100 POINTS)

Using reference books, write an analysis essay of the causes of America's involvement in World War II. Then, write an essay speculating about what would have happened if America had not entered the war (synthesis essay). Finally, evaluate whether or not America was justified in entering the war on the side of the Allies. Make each essay from 75-150 words.

ANSWER:

Sample Analysis Essay: *World War II may have begun in Europe, but 1939 Depression-era America was not yet ready to fight. Preoccupied with domestic problems, Americans had no intention of entering another European War as we had done in 1917. Let the Europeans fight their own war! These Americans were called "Isolationists," and without a doubt they were the majority of Americans. Most scholars believe that both Russia and England would have lost World War II without American support.*

The outbreak of World War II in Europe proved to be an important turning point in the development of American foreign policy. This shift echoed the American of 1889 who now wished to be left alone and out of European politics. Most American sympathies, however, lay with the underdogs—Great Britain and France—and it was difficult to remain neutral, especially after France fell in 1940 and Great Britain was about to fall.

The situation in Asia was no better. In the early 1930s Japan began her conquest of China and vigorously continued her efforts in 1937 with her attack on Nanking, "the rape of Nanking." President Roosevelt responded slowly to these threats. His domestic problems were all he could bear and, besides, from the beginning, Roosevelt saw Hitler as a greater threat. Roosevelt supported non-violent means to control Japanese aggression. By 1941, America had imposed an embargo on certain goods—notably scrap iron. These measures persuaded Japan to take a great gamble.

Japan could either retreat from her world conquest and lose face, or she could make a bold gamble and attack the U.S. She chose the latter course of action.

On December 7, 1941, America was attached at Pearl Harbor by the Empire of Japan. The next day, December 8, 1941, the same day that the U.S. declared war on Japan, Germany declared war on America. Now, the whole world was at war.

The Japanese attack on American soil at Pearl Harbor motivated America in a way no one expected. America brought her entire industrial might to bear on the Axis (Japan-Italy-German) powers. It took four years to do so, but by August, 1945, World War II had ended.

LESSON 15

Writing Skill: Cause/Effect Essay

Style (Writing and Speaking): Words—Connotation vs. Denotation

Public Speaking Skill: Converting the Cause/Effect Essay to a Speech.

Looking Ahead: The Comparison/Contrast Essay

Goals/Objectives: What is the purpose of this lesson?	Strategies to meet these goals: How will I obtain these goals/objectives?	Evaluation: How will I know when I have met these goals/objectives?
Concept: Cause/Effect Speech (cognitive goal)	The parent/educator will engage students in discussions about ways to write and to present a cause/effect speech. Students will present a cause/effect speech.	Students will be able to write and to present an inspired speech. Suggested evaluation sheet includes: Oratory Evaluation I. Poise: Calm presentation? Appropriate word inflections? Familiarity with oratory/dramatic reading? Cue cards used appropriately? (20 points) II. Articulation: Distinct enunciation? Appropriate tone? Appropriate volume? (30 points) III. Organization: Introduction? Thesis stated? Points supported? Conclusion effective? Accomplish the stated purpose? (50 points)
Concept: improved writing skills (cognitive goal)	Students will write five warm-up essays/week.	With minimal errors, students will write these essays in 15-20 minutes.
Concept: increased vocabulary (cognitive goal)	Students will collect at least five new vocabulary words and use these words in their warm-up essays and cause/effect essay.	Students will use five vocabulary words in conversation during the week, as well as use the words in their essays.

Goals/Objectives: What is the purpose of this lesson?	Strategies to meet these goals: How will I obtain these goals/objectives?	Evaluation: How will I know when I have met these goals/objectives?
Concept: reflective writing (affective/spiritual goal)	Using the Journal Guide Questions in the Appendices, students will record at least three entries this week. Suggested Scripture: 1 Kings 19.	Students will show evidence that they have reflected on this issue including informed discussions and written responses.
Concept: increased knowledge of the assigned essay (cognitive goal)	Take Lesson 15 Test.	Students will score at least 80% on Lesson 15 Test.
Concept: cause/effect essay (cognitive goal)	Students will write an essay on the causes and results of bad choices.	Students, with minimal errors, will clearly write a cause/effect essay about bad choices.
Concept: working in a group setting (behavioral goal)	In a class, in a co-op experience, or during a family discussion, students will confess their bad choices and work their parents on solutions.	Students will exhibit practical listening skills and will manifest understanding of opposing worldviews.

SUGGESTED
Weekly *Implementation*

DAY 1	DAY 2	DAY 3	DAY 4	DAY 5
Write a Warm-up Essay.	Write a Warm-up Essay.	Write a Warm-up Essay.	Write a Warm-up Essay.	Write a Warm-up Essay.
Read 35-50 pages/day.	Read 35-50 pages/day.	Read 35-50 pages/day.	Read 35-50 pages/day.	Read 35-50 pages/day.
Find five new vocabulary words.	Find five new vocabulary words.	Find five new vocabulary words.	Find five new vocabulary words.	Find five new vocabulary words.
Reflect on the speech assignment for the week.	Compose a first draft of your speech.	Revise your speech and submit to your evaluator/ parent.	Prepare to present your speech tomor-row.	Present your speech to a live audience.
Write an outline with thesis for your cause/effect essay.	Work on the rough draft for your cause/effect essay.	Finish the first draft and then the revised draft of your cause/effect essay.	Submit a copy of your paper to a peer for evaluation.	Submit your assign-ments to your eval-uator/ parent.
Make a journal entry.	Make a journal entry.	Make a journal entry.	Finish the final copy of your cause/effect essay.	Take Lesson 15 Test.
			Make a journal entry.	Make a journal entry.

ENRICHMENT ACTIVITIES/PROJECTS

Students should discuss the cause and effect of high inflation in America.

SPEECH ASSIGNMENT

Convert a cause/effect essay into a speech.

ANSWER: *The following is an essay/speech by Charles Darwin defining and explaining the result of Natural Selection:* "Again, it may be asked, how is it that varieties, which I have called incipient species, become ultimately converted into good and distinct species, which in most cases obviously differ from each other far more than do the varieties of the same species? How do those groups of species, which constitute what are called distinct genera and which differ from each other more than do the species of the same genus, arise? All these results, as we shall more fully see in the next chapter, follow from the struggle for life. Owing to this struggle, variations, however slight and from whatever cause proceeding, if they be in any degree profitable to the individuals of a species, in their infinitely complex relations to other organic beings and to their physical conditions of life, will tend to the preservation of such individuals, and will gener-ally be inherited by the offspring. The offspring, also, will thus have a better chance of surviving, for, of the many individuals of any species which are periodically born, but a small number can survive. I have called this principle, by which each slight varia-tion, if useful, is preserved, by the term natural selection, in order to mark its relation to man's power of selection. But the expres-sion often used by Mr. Herbert Spencer, of the Survival of the Fittest, is more accurate, and is sometimes equally convenient. We have seen that man by selection can certainly produce great *results, and can adapt organic beings to his own uses, through the accumulation of slight but useful variations, given to him by the hand of Nature. But Natural Selection, we shall hereafter see, is a power incessantly ready for action, and is as immeasurably superior to man's feeble efforts, as the works of Nature are to those of Art."*

(*Origin of the Species*, Charles Darwin, www.classicreader.com/booktoc.php/sid.2/bookid.107/)

Darwin is arguing all differences in species arise from struggles in life, or natural selection. This causes, as it were, an evolution of species from simplicity to complexity, from futility to utilitarianism.

WRITING ASSIGNMENTS

1. Evaluate the last time you made some bad choices. What were the causes of these bad choices? What was the outcome? This essay should include an outline with thesis statement, rough draft, revised draft, and final copy and five new (circled) vocabulary words. The essay must pay particular attention to style (focus, content, organization). For evaluation, give a copy to a peer/friend who will complete a peer evaluation form (Appendix) and another copy to your parent/educator.

ANSWER: *Answers will vary. The following is a cause/effect reflection by Booker T. Washington upon when he became interested in education:*

One day, while at work in the coal-mine, I happened to overhear two miners talking about a great school for coloured people somewhere in Virginia. This was the first time that I had ever heard anything about any kind of school or college that was more pretentious than the little coloured school in our town.

In the darkness of the mine I noiselessly crept as close as I could to the two men who were talking. I heard one tell the other that not only was the school established for the members of any
race, but the opportunities that it provided by which poor but worthy students could work out all or a part of the cost of a board, and at the same time be taught some trade or industry.

As they went on describing the school, it seemed to me that it must be the greatest place on earth, and not even Heaven presented more attractions for me at that time than did the Hampton Normal and Agricultural Institute in Virginia, about which these men were talking. I resolved at once to go to that school, although I had no idea where it was, or how many miles away, or how I was going to reach it; I remembered only that I was on fire constantly with one ambition, and that was to go to Hampton. This thought was with me day and night."
(www.classicreader.com, Chapter III, *Up from Slavery: an Autobiography,* Booker T. Washington).

2. Read 200-250 pages this week and find vocabulary words.

3. Complete the speech assignment and have a teacher complete a speech evaluation form (Appendix).

4. Pay particular attention to your writing style this week. Focus on usage rules.

5. Read 1 Kings 19. Have you ever felt hopeless like Elijah (19:4–5)? How does God react to Elijah? How does Elijah react to God? Record your reflections in your prayer journal. This journal is meant to be private, but you are invited to share your reflections with others.

6. Write a warm-up essay every day. As you experience the daily writing, you should see improvement in your ability to express your thoughts on paper. This daily writing is preparation for composing effective essays.

FINAL PROJECT

Students should correct and rewrite all essays and place them in their Final Portfolio.

WARM-UP ESSAYS:

	DAY 1	DAY 2	DAY 3	DAY 4	DAY 5
Cause/Effect	What causes inflation?	What is the cause of crime?	What were the causes of the Gulf War?	What causes snow?	What causes our country to abort millions of children?

LESSON 15 TEST

ESSAY (100 POINTS)

In a one-page essay, discuss the reason gasoline prices
are so high in the United States.

LESSON 15 TEST ANSWER

ESSAY (100 POINTS)

In a one-page essay, discuss the reason gasoline prices are so high in the United States.

ANSWER: *Answers will vary. Students could mention the problem of supply and demand, the conflict in the Middle East, or even greediness among gasoline producers. Check for cause/effect thinking in the essay.*

LESSON 16

Writing Skill: Comparison/Contrast Essay

Style (Writing and Speaking): Words—Standard and Sub-standard English

Public Speaking Skill: Converting the Comparison/Contrast Essay to a Speech.

Looking Ahead: The Problem/Solution Essay

Goals/Objectives: What is the purpose of this lesson?	Strategies to meet these goals: How will I obtain these goals/objectives?	Evaluation: How will I know when I have met these goals/objectives?
Concept: Comparison/Contrast Speech (cognitive goal)	The parent/educator will engage students in discussions about ways-write and present speeches. Students will present a comparison/contrast speech.	Students will be able to write and to present an inspired speech. Suggested evaluation sheet includes: Oratory Evaluation I. Poise: Calm presentation? Appropriate word inflections? Familiarity with oratory/dramatic reading? Cue cards used appropriately? (20 points) II. Articulation: Distinct enunciation? Appropriate tone? Appropriate volume? (30 points) III. Organization: Introduction? Thesis stated? Points supported? Conclusion effective? Accomplish the stated purpose? (50 points)
Concept: improved writing skills (cognitive goal)	Students will write five warm-up essays/week.	With minimal errors, students will write these essays in 15-20 minutes.
Concept: increased vocabulary (cognitive goal)	Students will collect at least five new vocabulary words and use these words in their warm-up essays and comparison/contrast essay.	Students will use five vocabulary words in conversation during the week, as well as use the words in their essays.

Goals/Objectives: What is the purpose of this lesson?	Strategies to meet these goals: How will I obtain these goals/objectives?	Evaluation: How will I know when I have met these goals/objectives?
Concept: reflective writing (affective/spiritual goal)	Using the Journal Guide Questions in the Appendices, students will record at least three entries this week. Suggested Scripture: 1 Kings 19	Students will show evidence that they have reflected on this issue, including informed discussions and written responses.
Concept: increased knowledge of the assigned essay (cognitive goal)	Students will take Lesson 16 Test.	Students will score at least 80% on Lesson 16 Test.
Concept: comparison/contrast essay (cognitive goal)	Students will write a comparison/contrast of two close friends.	Students, with minimal errors, will clearly write a comparison/contrast of two close friends.
Concept: working in a group setting (behavioral goal)	In a class, in a co-op experience, or during a family discussion, students will discuss what a good friend is.	Students will exhibit practical listening skills and will manifest understanding of opposing worldviews.

SUGGESTED
Weekly *Implementation*

DAY 1	DAY 2	DAY 3	DAY 4	DAY 5
Write a Warm-up Essay.	Write a Warm-up Essay.	Write a Warm-up Essay.	Write a Warm-up Essay.	Write a Warm-up Essay.
Read 35-50 pages/day.	Read 35-50 pages/day.	Read 35-50 pages/day.	Read 35-50 pages/day.	Read 35-50 pages/day.
Find five new vocabulary words.	Find five new vocabulary words.	Find five new vocabulary words.	Find five new vocabulary words.	Find five new vocabulary words.
Reflect on the speech assignment for the week.	Compose a first draft of your speech.	Revise your speech and submit to your evaluator/ parent.	Prepare to present your speech tomorrow.	Present your speech to a live audience.
Write an outline with thesis for your compare/contrast essay.	Work on the first draft for your compare/contrast essay.	Finish the first draft and then the revised draft of your compare/contrast essay.	Submit a copy of your paper to a peer for evaluation.	Submit your assignments to your evaluator/ parent.
Make a journal entry.	Make a journal entry.	Make a journal entry.	Finish the final copy of your compare/contrast essay.	Take Lesson 16 Test.
			Make a journal entry.	Make a journal entry.

ENRICHMENT ACTIVITIES/PROJECTS

Students should orally compare and contrast their football team with the world champion, all American football team, Pittsburgh Steelers.

Students should orally compare and contrast their culinary skills with Betty Crocker or Martha Stewart.

Students should orally compare and contrast their future parenting goals with those of their grandparents.

SPEECH ASSIGNMENT

In a 2-3 minute speech, compare and contrast two personal friends.

ANSWER: *Answers will vary.*

WRITING ASSIGNMENTS

1. Compare and contrast two personal friends. Your essay should include an outline with thesis statement, rough draft, revised draft, and final copy and five new (circled) vocabulary words. Pay particular attention to style (focus, content, organization). For evaluation, give a copy to a peer/friend who will complete a peer evaluation form (Appendix) and another copy to your parent/educator.

ANSWER: (In the following sample identify the differences in English standards between that era and the current era.)

These are the most memorable circumstances recorded in history of Demosthenes and Cicero which have come to our knowledge. But omitting an exact comparison of their respective faculties in speaking, yet thus much seems fit to be said; that Demosthenes, to make himself a master in rhetoric, applied all the faculties he had, natural or acquired, wholly that way; that he far surpassed in force and strength of eloquence all his contemporaries in political and judicial speaking, in grandeur and majesty all the panegyrical orators, and in accuracy and science all the logicians and rhetoricians of his day; that Cicero was highly educated, and by his diligent study became a most accomplished general scholar in all these branches, having left behind him numerous philosophical treatises of his own on Academic principles; as, indeed, even in his written speeches, both political and judicial, we see him continually trying to show his learning by the way. And one may discover the different temper of each of them in their speeches. For Demosthenes' oratory was without all embellishment and jesting, wholly composed for real effect and seriousness; not smelling of the lamp, as Pytheas scoffingly said, but of the temperance, thoughtfulness, austerity, and grave earnestness of his temper. Whereas Cicero's love of mockery often ran him into scurrility; and in his love of laughing away serious arguments in judicial cases by jests and facetious remarks, with a view to the advantage of his clients, he paid too little regard to what was decent; saying, for example, in his defence of Cælius, that he had done no absurd thing in such plenty and affluence to indulge himself in pleasures, it being a kind of madness not to enjoy the things we possess, especially since the most eminent philosophers have asserted pleasure to be the chiefest good. So also we are told, that when Cicero, being consul, undertook the defence of Murena against Cato's prosecution, by way of bantering Cato, he made a long series of jokes upon the absurd paradoxes, as they are called, of the Stoic sect; so that a loud laughter passing from the crowd to the judges, Cato, with a quiet smile, said to those that sat next to him, "My friends, what an amusing consul we have." And, indeed, Cicero was by natural temper very much disposed to mirth and pleasantry, and always appeared with a smiling and serene countenance. But Demosthenes had constant care and thoughtfulness in his look, and a serious anxiety, which he seldom, if ever, laid aside; and, therefore, was accounted by his enemies, as he himself confessed, morose and ill-mannered. Also, it is very evident, out of their several writings, that Demosthenes never touched upon his own praises but decently and without offence when there was need of it, and for some weightier end; but, upon other occasions modestly and sparingly.

But Cicero's immeasurable boasting of himself in his orations argues him guilty of an uncontrollable appetite for distinction, his cry being evermore that arms should give place to the gown, and the soldier's laurel to the tongue. And at last we find him extolling not only his deeds and actions, but his orations also, as well those that were only spoken, as those that

were published; as if he were engaged in a boyish trial of skill, who should speak best, with the rhetoricians, Isocrates and Anaximenes, not as one who could claim the task to guide and instruct the Roman nation. It is necessary, indeed, for a political leader to be an able speaker; but it is an ignoble thing for any man to admire and relish the glory of his own eloquence. And, in this matter, Demosthenes had a more than ordinary gravity and magnificence of mind, accounting his talent in speaking nothing more than a mere accomplishment and matter of practice, the success of which must depend greatly on the good-will and candor of his hearers, and regarding those who pride themselves on such accounts to be men of a low and petty disposition. The power of persuading and governing the people did, indeed, equally belong to both, so that those who had armies and camps at command stood in need of their assistance; as Chares, Diopithes, and Leosthenes of Demosthenes, Pompey and young Cæsar of Cicero's, as the latter himself admits in his Memoirs addressed to Agrippa and Mæcenas. But what are thought and commonly said most to demonstrate and try the tempers of men, namely, authority, and place, by moving every passion, and discovering every frailty, these are things which Demosthenes never received; nor was he ever in a position to give such proof of himself, having never obtained any eminent office, nor led any of those armies into the field against Philip which he raised by his eloquence. Cicero, on the other hand, was sent quæstor into Sicily, and proconsul into Cilicia and Cappadocia, at a time when avarice was at the height, and the commanders and governors who were employed abroad, as though they thought it a mean thing to steal, set themselves to seize by open force; so that it seemed no heinous matter to take bribes, but he that did it most moderately was in good esteem. And yet he, at this time, gave the most abundant proofs alike of his contempt of riches and of his humanity and good-nature. And at Rome, when he was created consul in name, but indeed received sovereign and dictatorial authority against Catiline and his conspirators, he attested the truth of Plato's prediction, that then the miseries of states would be at an end, when by a happy fortune supreme power, wisdom, and justice should be united in one. It is said, to the reproach of Demosthenes, that his eloquence was mercenary; that he privately made orations for Phormion and Apollodorus, though adversaries in the same cause; that he was charged with moneys received from the king of Persia, and condemned for bribes from Harpalus. And should we grant that all those (and they are not few) who have made these statements against him have spoken what is untrue, yet that Demosthenes was not the character to look without desire on the presents offered him out of respect and gratitude by royal persons, and that one who lent money on maritime usury was likely to be thus indifferent, is what we cannot assert. But that Cicero refused, from the Sicilians when he was quæstor, from the king of Cappadocia when he was proconsul, and from his *friends at Rome when he was in exile, many presents, though urged to receive them, has been said already. Moreover, Demosthenes' banishment was infamous, upon conviction for bribery; Cicero's very honorable, for ridding his country of a set of villains. Therefore, when Demosthenes fled his country, no man regarded it; for Cicero's sake the senate changed their habit, and put on mourning, and would not be persuaded to make any act before Cicero's return was decreed. Cicero, however, passed his exile idly in Macedonia. But the very exile of Demosthenes made up a great part of the services he did for his country; for he went through the cities of Greece, and everywhere, as we have said, joined in the conflict on behalf of the Grecians, driving out the Macedonian ambassadors, and approving himself a much better citizen than Themistocles and Alcibiades did in the like fortune.*

And, after his return, he again devoted himself to the same public service, and continued firm to his opposition to Antipater and the Macedonians. Whereas Lælius reproached Cicero in the senate for sitting silent when Cæsar, a beardless youth, asked leave to come forward, contrary to the law, as a candidate for the consulship; and Brutus, in his epistles, charges him with nursing and rearing a greater and more heavy tyranny than that they had removed. Finally, Cicero's death excites our pity; for an old man to be miserably carried up and down by his servants, flying and hiding himself from that death which was, in the course of nature, so near at hand; and yet at last to be murdered. Demosthenes, though he seemed at first a little to supplicate, yet, by his preparing and keeping the poison by him,

demands our admiration; and still more admirable was his using it. When the temple of the god no longer afforded him a sanctuary, he took refuge, as it were, at a mightier altar, freeing himself from arms and soldiers, and laughing to scorn the cruelty of Antipater.

("Comparison of Demosthenes and Cicero," in *Lives*, Plutarch, www.bartleby.com/12/7.html).

2. Read 200-250 pages/week and find vocabulary words.

3. Complete the speech assignment and have a teacher complete a speech evaluation form (Appendix).

4. Pay particular attention to your writing style this week.

5. Read 1 Kings 19:10–18. Consider where Elijah finds God. Has God appeared to you in unusual places and in unusual circumstances? Answer these questions and others in your prayer journal.

6. Write a warm-up essay every day. As you experience the daily writing, you should see improvement in your ability to express your thoughts on paper. This daily writing is preparation for composing effective essays.

FINAL PROJECT

Students should correct and rewrite all essays and place them in their Final Portfolio.

WARM-UP ESSAYS:

	DAY 1	DAY 2	DAY 3	DAY 4	DAY 5
Compare/Contrast	Compare your brother with Matt Damon.	Contrast your dad to Harrison Ford.	Compare your favorite car with the car your family owns.	Contrast a movie to the book you read by the same name.	Contrast your youth director to your pastor.

LESSON 16 TEST

ESSAY (100 POINTS)

Compare and contrast the way your parents (or two other people) drive.

LESSON 16 TEST ANSWERS

ESSAY (100 POINTS)

Compare and contrast the way your parents (or two other people) drive.

ANSWER: *Answers will vary.*

LESSON 17

Writing Skill: Problem/Solution Essay

Style: (Writing and Speaking): Words—Idioms

Public Speaking Skill: Converting the Problem/Solution Essay to a Speech.

Looking Ahead: The Definition Essay

Goals/Objectives: What is the purpose of this lesson?	Strategies to meet these goals: How will I obtain these goals/objectives?	Evaluation: How will I know when I have met these goals/objectives?
Concept: introduction to a speech (cognitive goal)	The parent/educator will engage students in discussions about ways to write and present speeches. Students will discuss what a good introduction is.	Students will write an appropriate, accurate introduction of a speech of their choice.
Concept: improved writing skills (cognitive goal)	Students will write five warm-up essays/week.	With minimal errors, students will write these essays in 15-20 minutes.
Concept: increased vocabulary (cognitive goal)	Students will collect at least five new vocabulary words and use these words in their warm-up essays and problem/solution essay.	Students will use five vocabulary words in conversation during the week, as well as use the words in their essays.
Concept: reflective writing (affective/spiritual goal)	Using the Journal Guide Questions in the Appendices, students will record at least three entries this week. Suggested Scripture: 1 Kings 19.	Students will show evidence that they have reflected on this issue, including informed discussions and written responses.
Concept: increased knowledge of the assigned essay (cognitive goal)	Students will take Lesson 17 Test.	Students will score at least 80% on Lesson 17 Test.

Goals/Objectives: What is the purpose of this lesson?	Strategies to meet these goals: How will I obtain these goals/objectives?	Evaluation: How will I know when I have met these goals/objectives?
Concept: problem/solution essay (cognitive goal)	Students will write an essay on the following topic: As this century begins, Christians are becoming a declining minority in American culture and society. In a one-page essay, answer this question, "Is this a problem? Why? What are some solutions?"	With minimal errors students will clearly write a problem and solution essay.
Concept: working in a group setting (behavioral goal)	In a class, in a co-op experience, or during a family discussion, students will discuss how Christians can be more effective witnesses for our Lord in this hostile, post-Christian world.	Students will exhibit practical listening skills and will manifest understanding of opposing worldviews.

SUGGESTED
Weekly *Implementation*

DAY 1	DAY 2	DAY 3	DAY 4	DAY 5
Write a Warm-up Essay.	Write a Warm-up Essay.	Write a Warm-up Essay.	Write a Warm-up Essay.	Write a Warm-up Essay.
Read 35-50 pages/day.	Read 35-50 pages/day.	Read 35-50 pages/day.	Read 35-50 pages/day.	Read 35-50 pages/day.
Find five new vocabulary words.	Find five new vocabulary words.	Find five new vocabulary words.	Find five new vocabulary words.	Find five new vocabulary words.
Reflect on the speech assignment for the week.	Compose a first draft of your speech.	Revise your speech and submit to your evaluator/ parent.	Prepare to present your speech tomorrow.	Present your speech to a live audience.
Write an outline with thesis for your problem/ solution essay.	Work on the first draft for your problem/ solution essay.	Finish the first draft and then the revised draft of your problem/ solution essay.	Submit a copy of your paper to a peer for evaluation.	Submit your assignments to your evaluator/ parent.
Make a journal entry.	Make a journal entry.	Make a journal entry.	Finish the final copy of your problem/ solution essay.	Make a journal entry.
			Make a journal entry.	Take Lesson 17 Test.

ENRICHMENT ACTIVITIES/PROJECTS

Students and their families should identify a major problem in their family and offer solutions.

SPEECH ASSIGNMENT

Present a 2-3 minute speech on the topic: As this century begins, Christians are becoming a declining minority in American culture and society. In a one-page essay, answer the questions, "Is this a problem? Why? What are some solutions?"

ANSWER: *See # 1 under "Writing Assignments."*

WRITING ASSIGNMENTS

1. As this century begins, Christians are becoming a declining minority in American culture and society. In a one-page essay, answer this question, "Is this a problem? Why? What are some solutions?" This essay should include an outline with thesis statement, rough draft, revised draft, and final copy and five new (circled) vocabulary words. The essay must pay particular attention to style (focus, content, organization). For evaluation, give a copy to a peer/friend who will complete a peer evaluation form (Appendix) and another copy to your parent/educator.

ANSWER: *By side-stepping the Enlightenment, Christian home schooling has opened up a whole new arena for* *debate. While conceding that faith is not a makeshift bridge to overcome some Kierkegaardian gap between beliefs and evidence, home schooling posits that it still is important that we look beyond our experience for reality. Human needs and aspirations are greater than the world can satisfy, so it is reasonable to look elsewhere for that satisfaction. Worth is the highest and best reality (a decidedly anti-Enlightenment notion) and its genesis and maintenance come exclusively from relationship with God alone. Home schooling families, with their sacrificial love of one another and their extravagant gift of time to one another, offer a radical path into this new way of looking at reality.*

Christian home schooling, then, moves backward in time, far back in time, when intellectualism was not separate from religion. It blows to bits the claims of the Enlightenment. Home schooling has brought stability back into the lives of countless millions of America when the majority of Americans are living in a context of clashing reactions where the very ground of meaning, the foundations and structures of thought, language, and social discourse are up for grabs, where the very concepts of personhood, spirituality, truth, integrity, and objectivity are all being demolished, breaking up, giving way. Home schoolers do it the old-fashioned way: Parents educate their children at home and in the process lay down their lives for all our futures.

Home schooling. Millions strong. Unpretentious to a fault, this new cultural revolution invites Americans back to traditional truths that have been with us always and to others that need to be rediscovered. Home schooling invites Americans to a comfortable marriage of intellectualism and transcendentalism that fares our culture and our nation well in the years ahead. In that sense, then, perhaps home schooling families are the new patriots, the hope for our weary nation and our dysfunctional culture. We shall see. . .

(James P. Stobaugh)

2. Read 200-250 pages/week and create vocabulary cards of unfamiliar words found in your reading.

3. Complete the speech assignment and have a teacher complete a speech evaluation form (Appendix).

4. Pay particular attention to writing style this week.

5. First Kings 19:19–21 is a description of the call of Elisha. Elijah rebukes Elisha for returning to say good-bye to his parents. Why? Have you ever experienced such a call? Answer these questions and others in your prayer journal.

6. Write a warm-up essay every day. As you experience the daily writing, you should see improvement in your ability to express your thoughts on paper. This daily writing is preparation for composing effective essays.

FINAL PROJECT

Students should correct and rewrite all essays and place them in their Final Portfolio.

WARM-UP ESSAYS:

	DAY 1	DAY 2	DAY 3	DAY 4	DAY 5
Problem/ Solution	The solution to the problem of children watching too much TV violence.	The solution to the problem of teenage pregnancy.	The solution to the problem of 80 percent of urban children having no father.	The solution to the problem of Judeo-Christian morality disappearing from our culture.	The solution to the problem of ozone disappearing from the atmosphere.

LESSON 17 TEST

ESSAY (100 POINTS)

Pretend that your brother/sister is borrowing your toothbrush. In a one-page essay, discuss the problem and the solution to this problem.

LESSON 17 TEST ANSWER

ESSAY (100 POINTS)

Pretend that your brother/sister is borrowing your toothbrush. In a one-page essay, discuss the problem and the solution to this problem.

ANSWER: *Students should establish that borrowing a toothbrush is a problem. Why is it a problem? Is the sibling brushing teeth with the toothbrush or cleaning the tub grout or ...? Next, offer a solution. Perhaps the toothbrush owner will dip the toothbrush in red pepper ....*

LESSON 18

Goals/Objectives: What is the purpose of this lesson?	Strategies to meet these goals: How will I obtain these goals/objectives?	Evaluation: How will I know when I have met these goals/objectives?
Concept: converting a definition essay to a definition speech (cognitive goal)	The parent/educator will engage students in discussions about ways to write and present speeches. In front of an audience, students will present a definition speech defining sound.	Students will be able to write and to present an inspired speech. Suggested evaluation sheet includes: Oratory Evaluation I. Poise: How does the student present himself/herself? Is the oratory/dramatic reading memorized? (25 points) II. Articulation: Does the student speak clearly, and slowly? (25 points) III. Presentation: What is the overall effect of the speech? Does it accomplish its purpose? (50 points)
Concept: improved writing skills (cognitive goal)	Students will write five warm-up essays/week.	With minimal errors students will write these essays in 15-20 minutes.
Concept: increased vocabulary (cognitive goal)	Students will collect at least five new vocabulary words and use these words in their warm-up essays and definition essay.	Students will use five vocabulary words in conversation during the week, as well as use the words in their essays.

Goals/Objectives: What is the purpose of this lesson?	Strategies to meet these goals: How will I obtain these goals/objectives?	Evaluation: How will I know when I have met these goals/objectives?
Concept: reflective writing (affective/spiritual goal)	Using the Journal Guide Questions in the Appendices, students will record at least three entries this week. Suggested Scripture: 1 Kings 20	Students will show evidence that they have reflected on this issue including informed discussions and written responses.
Concept: increased knowledge of the assigned essay (cognitive goal)	Students will take Lesson 18 Test.	Students will score at least 80% on Lesson 18 Test.
Concept: definition essay (cognitive goal)	Students will write an essay defining sound.	Students, with minimal errors, will clearly write a definition essay.
Concept: working in a group setting (behavioral goal)	In a class, in a co-op experience, or during a family discussion, students will courtship vs. dating.	Students will exhibit practical listening skills and will manifest understanding of opposing worldviews.

SUGGESTED
Weekly *Implementation*

DAY 1	DAY 2	DAY 3	DAY 4	DAY 5
Write a Warm-up Essay.	Write a Warm-up Essay.	Write a Warm-up Essay.	Write a Warm-up Essay.	Write a Warm-up Essay.
Read 35-50 pages/day.	Read 35-50 pages/day.	Read 35-50 pages/day.	Read 35-50 pages/day.	Read 35-50 pages/day.
Find five new vocabulary words.	Find five new vocabulary words.	Find five new vocabulary words.	Find five new vocabulary words.	Find five new vocabulary words.
Reflect on the speech assignment for the week.	Compose a first draft of your speech.	Revise your speech and submit to your evaluator/ parent.	Prepare to present your speech tomorrow.	Present your speech to a live audience.
Write an outline with thesis for your definition essay.	Work on the first draft for your definition essay.	Finish the first draft and then the revised draft of your definition essay.	Submit a copy of your paper to a peer for evaluation.	Submit your assignments to your evaluator/ parent.
Make a journal entry.	Make a journal entry.	Make a journal entry.	Finish the final copy of your definition essay.	Make a journal entry.
			Make a journal entry.	Take Lesson 18 Test.

ENRICHMENT ACTIVITIES/PROJECTS

Students should discuss their answers to their warm-up essays with their instructors.

SPEECH ASSIGNMENT

You should present a two or three-minute speech defining sound.

ANSWER: *Answers will be opinions.*

WRITING ASSIGNMENTS

1. In a one-page essay, define *sound*. Does a tree falling in the forest make sound if no human hears it? This essay should include an outline, rough draft, thesis

statement, final copy, and five new (circled) vocabulary words. The essay must pay particular attention to style (focus, content, organization). Give a copy to a peer/friend to complete a peer evaluation (Appendix) and to instructor for evaluation.

ANSWER: *Answers will vary. The following is a definition essay by John Stuart Mills entitled* On Liberty. *(www.bartleby.com/25/2). Notice the differences between English standards from Mills's era and the present era. Also notice how Mills defines liberty by discussing what it is not:*

The subject of this Essay is not the so-called Liberty of the Will, so unfortunately opposed to the misnamed doctrine of Philosophical Necessity; but Civil, or Social Liberty: the nature and limits of the power which can be legitimately exercised by society over the individual. A question seldom stated, and hardly ever discussed, in general terms, but which profoundly influences the practical controversies of the age by its latent presence, and is likely soon to make itself recognized as the vital question of the future. It is so far from being new, that, in a certain sense, it has divided mankind, almost from the remotest ages, but in the stage of progress into which the more civilized portions of the species have now entered, it presents itself under new conditions, and requires a different and more fundamental treatment. 1 The struggle between Liberty and Authority is the most conspicuous feature in the portions of history with which we are earliest familiar, particularly in that of Greece, Rome, and England. But in old times this contest was between subjects, or some classes of subjects, and the government. By liberty, was meant protection against the tyranny of the political rulers. The rulers were conceived (except in some of the popular governments of Greece) as in a necessarily antagonistic position to the people whom they ruled. They consisted of a governing One, or a governing tribe or caste, who derived their authority from inheritance or conquest; who, at all events, did not hold it at the pleasure of the governed, and whose supremacy men did not venture, perhaps did not desire to contest, whatever precautions might be taken against its oppressive exercise. Their power was regarded as necessary, but also as highly dangerous; as a weapon which they would attempt to use against their subjects, no less than against external enemies. To prevent the weaker members of the community from being preyed upon by innumerable vultures, it was needful that there should be an animal of prey stronger than the rest, commissioned to keep them down. But as the king of the vultures would be no less bent upon preying upon the flock than any of the minor harpies, it was indispensable to be in a perpetual attitude of defence against his beak and claws. The aim, therefore, of patriots, was to set limits to the power which the ruler should be suffered to exercise over the community; and this limitation was what they meant by liberty. It was attempted in two ways. First, by obtaining a recognition of certain immunities, called political liberties or rights, which it was to be regarded as a breach of duty in the ruler to infringe, and which, if he did infringe, specific resistance, or general rebellion, was held to be justifiable. A second, and generally a later expedient, was the establishment of constitutional checks; by which the consent of the community, or of a body of some sort supposed to represent its interests, was made a necessary condition to some of the more important acts of the governing power. To the first of these modes of limitation, the ruling power, in most European countries, was compelled, more or less, to submit. It was not so with the second; and to attain this, or when already in some degree possessed, to attain it more completely, became everywhere the principal object of the lovers of liberty. And so long as mankind were content to combat one enemy by another, and to be ruled by a master, on condition of being guaranteed more or less efficaciously against his tyranny, they did not carry their

aspirations beyond this point. 2 A time, however, came in the progress of human affairs, when men ceased to think it a necessity of nature that their governors should be an independent power, opposed in interest to themselves. It appeared to them much better that the various magistrates of the State should be their tenants or delegates, revocable at their pleasure. In that way alone, it seemed, could they have complete security that the powers of government would never be abused to their disadvantage. By degrees, this new demand for elective and temporary rulers became the prominent object of the exertions of the popular party, wherever any such party existed; and superseded, to a considerable extent, the previous efforts to limit the power of rulers. As the struggle proceeded for making the ruling power emanate from the periodical choice of the ruled, some persons began to think that too much importance had been attached to the limitation of the power itself. That (it might seem) was a resource against rulers whose interests were habitually opposed to those of the people. What was now wanted was, that the rulers should be identified with the people; that their interest and will should be the interest and will of the nation. The nation did not need to be protected against its own will. There was no fear of its tyrannizing over itself. Let the rulers be effectually responsible to it, promptly removable by it, and it could afford to trust them with power of which it could itself dictate the use to be made. Their power was but the nation's own power, concentrated, and in a form convenient for exercise. This mode of thought, or rather perhaps of feeling, was common among the last generation of European liberalism, in the Continental section of which, it still apparently predominates. Those who admit any limit to what a government may do, except in the case of such governments as they think ought not to exist, stand out as brilliant exceptions among the political thinkers of the Continent. A similar tone of sentiment might by this time have been prevalent in our own country, if the circumstances which for a time encouraged it had continued unaltered.

2. Read 200-250 pages/week and make vocabulary cards.

3. Complete the speech assignment and have a teacher complete a speech evaluation (Appendix).

4. Pay particular attention to your writing style this week.

5. Meditate on 1 Kings 20. Reflect on this passage, and others, in your prayer journal.

6. Write a warm-up essay every day.

FINAL PROJECT

Students should correct and rewrite all essays and place them in their Final Portfolio.

WARM-UP ESSAYS:

	DAY 1	DAY 2	DAY 3	DAY 4	DAY 5
Definition	Define *immortality*.	Define *salvation*.	Define *sanctification*.	Define *grace*.	Define *judgment*

LESSON 18 TEST

ESSAY (100 POINTS)

Connotation is the implied meaning of a word or expression. *Denotation* is the literary definition, or meaning, of a word or expression. For instance, what a word or expression says and what it means can be two different things. A mom can say with a smile, "Go to bed," and the connotation is benign. On the other hand, she can say "Go to bed" with a frown, and the connotation is entirely different. On the other hand, the denotation of the expression never changes.

Write an essay discussing first the denotation and then the connotation of one of the words/phrases below or choose your own topic:

1. Racism
2. Prayer in schools
3. The Supreme Court
4. The FBI
5. Evangelicalism

LESSON 18 TEST ANSWER

ESSAY (100 POINTS)

Write an essay discussing first the denotation and then the connotation of one of the words/phrases below or choose your own topic:

1. Racism
2. Prayer in schools
3. The Supreme Court
4. The FBI
5. Evangelicalism

ANSWER SAMPLE: *Perhaps no word is more misunderstood or abused in American society than the word "Racism." In contemporary America there is no shortage of discussion of racial anger among the black community. Many Americans readily concede its existence and pray for its departure. Racial anger has arisen through the way we have handled race. What are the ways that America has decided to deal with race over the last three hundred years? Why have they not worked? Some scholars argue that racism is an insignificant category—in the long run worth ignoring. They argue that the only legitimate categories are "Christian" or "non-Christian." To judge or to evaluate the efficacy of human relationships according to any other category—like race or class—is wrong. The scholar Dinesh D'Souza advances this position. He persuasively argues that America's obsession with race is a distinctly Western phenomenon and should be given up. Evoking the Exodus narratives, D'Souza argues that America's three-hundred-year struggle with racism is over, and it is time to leave the wilderness and to enter the promised land.*

On the other side of the argument is the view that argues that race is the most important category for human identity. One major supporter of this view is Sang Hyun Lee, Professor of Systematic Theology and Director of the Asian American Program at Princeton Theological Seminary. He calls this racial/cultural separatism "marginality." Men like John Dawson are correct when they call the church to repent. That is the unavoidable starting point for all meaningful reconciliation. John Dawson correctly calls the whole Church to prayer and then to honest, heartfelt repentance. Dawson calls the Church to approach racism with fear and trembling and with a lot of prayer. Dawson calls the believer to engage in strategic level spiritual warfare. He reminds us that racism is a national sin, and a repentant church should lead our country to repentant prayer. This is infinitely more difficult for churches to do and therefore more valuable for America than all the reparations we would ever pay. Many groups are doing just that. The National Black Evangelical Association and the National Association of Evangelicals recently issued a joint statement of repentance: "Racism is a fundamental sin of the United States, fueled by economic greed and the foundations, institutions and cultural mores of this country. It has prevented formation of a true cultural democracy. Racism has enslaved, impoverished, and oppressed people of color in the United States." Likewise, the Southern Baptist Convention has extended a plea to the African American community, asking its forgiveness for the Convention's 100 or more years of racial insensitivity and spiritual irresponsibility. (James P. Stobaugh)

LESSON 19

Writing Skill: Explanatory Essay

Grammar Review (Writing and Speaking): Words—Precise Language

Public Speaking Skill: Converting the Explanitory Essay to a Speech

Looking Ahead: Fact, Inference, and Opinion

Goals/Objectives: What is the purpose of this lesson?	Strategies to meet these goals: How will I obtain these goals/objectives?	Evaluation: How will I know when I have met these goals/objectives?
Concept: explanatory speech (cognitive goal)	The parent/educator will engage students in discussions about ways-write and present speeches. Students will convert an explanatory essay into an explanatory speech.	Students will be able to write and to present an inspired speech. Suggested evaluation sheet includes: Oratory Evaluation I. Poise: How does the student present himself/herself? Is the oratory/dramatic reading memorized? (25 points) II. Articulation: Does the student speak clearly, and slowly? (25 points) III. Presentation: What is the overall effect of the speech? Does it accomplish its purpose? (50 points)
Concept: improved writing skills (cognitive goal)	Students will write five warm-up essays/week.	With minimal errors students will write these essays in 15-20 minutes.
Concept: increased vocabulary (cognitive goal)	Students will collect at least five new vocabulary words and use these words in their warm-up essays and explanatory essay.	Students will use five vocabulary words in conversation during the week, as well as use the words in their essays.

Goals/Objectives: What is the purpose of this lesson?	Strategies to meet these goals: How will I obtain these goals/objectives?	Evaluation: How will I know when I have met these goals/objectives?
Concept: reflective writing (affective/spiritual goal)	Using the Journal Guide Questions in the Appendices, students will record at least three entries this week. Suggested Scripture: 1 Kings 20:35-41.	Students will show evidence that they have reflected on this issue including informed discussions and written responses.
Concept: increased knowledge of the assigned essay (cognitive goal)	Students will take Lesson 19 Test.	Students will score at least 80% on Lesson 19 Test.
Concept: explanatory essay (cognitive goal)	Students will write an explanatory essay on the causes of World War I.	Students, with minimal errors, will clearly write an explanatory essay of the causes of World War I.
Concept: working in a group setting (behavioral goal)	In a class, in a co-op experience, or during a family discussion, students will discuss the best thing that has happened to them.	Students will exhibit practical listening skills and will manifest understanding of opposing worldviews.

SUGGESTED
Weekly *Implementation*

DAY 1	DAY 2	DAY 3	DAY 4	DAY 5
Write a Warm-up Essay.	Write a Warm-up Essay.	Write a Warm-up Essay.	Write a Warm-up Essay.	Write a Warm-up Essay.
Read 35-50 pages/day.	Read 35-50 pages/day.	Read 35-50 pages/day.	Read 35-50 pages/day.	Read 35-50 pages/day.
Find five new vocabulary words.	Find five new vocabulary words.	Find five new vocabulary words.	Find five new vocabulary words.	Find five new vocabulary words.
Reflect on the speech assignment for the week.	Compose a first draft of your speech.	Revise your speech and submit to your evaluator/ parent.	Prepare to present your speech tomorrow.	Present your speech to a live audience.
Write an outline with thesis for your explanatory essay.	Work on the first draft for your explanatory essay.	Finish the first draft and then the revised draft of your explanatory essay.	Submit a copy of your paper to a peer for evaluation.	Submit your assignments to your evaluator/ parent.
Make a journal entry.	Make a journal entry.	Make a journal entry.	Finish the final copy of your explanatory essay.	Make a journal entry.
			Make a journal entry.	Take Lesson 19 Test.

ENRICHMENT ACTIVITIES/PROJECTS

Students should explain how to solve a quadratic equation to a younger sibling.

SPEECH ASSIGNMENT

Present a 3-5 minute speech explaining the causes of World War I.

ANSWER: *See essay below.*

WRITING ASSIGNMENTS

1. In a one-page essay, explain what caused World War I. Include an outline, rough draft, thesis statement, final copy, and five new (circled) vocabulary words.

Your essay must pay particular attention to style (focus, content, organization). Give a copy to a peer/friend to complete a peer evaluation (Appendix) and to your instructor to evaluate.

ANSWER: SAMPLE ESSAY

Last summer, while my wife and her mother vigorously reconnoitered and then exploited local shopping opportunities in a Scottish highland community, my father-in-law and I walked around the same quaint village. In the center of this small community—no more than 1200 people—there was the obligatory war monument. We see the same sort of thing in America, so I was not at first particularly impressed. For instance, in my home-town there is a memorial to American war dead in the center of our town square. In fact, there is a list of American World War veterans on the wall at our local post office too. While waiting for stamps, I read through the names almost every day. The ones who died have a small, impressive golden star next to their names. Only 2 names have stars.

However, on the monument in the central square of this beautiful Scottish village, there were 128 names. These were names of the dead, not the participants. A community that was then about 850 people had 128 dead casualties in World War I. The implication is that double that number was permanently maimed. Indeed, on one summer day in 1916, at the Somme, some towns lost their entire local soccer team and most of the volunteer fire company. Suppose there were about 425 men who lived in this community in 1914. In 1918 over 250 of them had been killed or wounded. Can you imagine the impact that World War I had on this small, unpretentious Scottish community? It lost almost half its male population. As I traveled across Scotland this story was repeated time and time again. This carnage is unique to European communities; there is nothing to compare in American history.

For the last time, during World War I, the British army recruited its regiments by county and town, but the trend was exaggerated in the Kitchener armies recruited for World War I. The British army made a promise very early on, when they weren't sure how many volunteers they were going to get, that if a volunteer joined up in a group, the group would be kept together. And, the phrase was: "Join up with your pals or your chums, your friends." This certainly maintained morale an increased recruitment numbers. That is, it improved morale until they were all killed together on some nameless battlefield in France.

Of the 65 million men who participated in the war, more than 10 million were killed and more than 20 million wounded. The term "World War I" did not come into general use until after World War II. Before that, the war was known as the "Great War." World War I was the first total war. No war had been quite like it. All the participating countries mobilized all their resources to achieve victory on the battlefield. The home front, then, became as important as the battlefield. In fact, in some places in France, the home front was only a few miles behind the war front.

What caused this conflagration to spread all over the world?

By 1900, the world was changing with increased speed and pronounced intensity that before then seemed to be fanciful. Space, time, and physical dimensions had been transformed in a way that a century before, literally, no one could have imagined. Telephone defied time and space to take the human voice instantly across time and space. Cities were lit by electricity all the time. Literally, there was less darkness by 1900 than any previous century. It did not take eighty days to travel around the world; eighty hours was a possibility. Indeed there were limitless possibilities—mankind could even travel under the ocean.

People were moving from the farm to the city. Advances in medicine, surplus crops assured that there was a substantial population explosion.

Suddenly, by 1914, countries had a surplus number of young men to throw into the war engine. The expansion of education, the expansion of entertainments, the emergence of the film industry, newsreels—all brought to masses of people visions of worlds they had never thought available. All this progress conspired to give people realistic reasons to hope that things would be better than they were today.

It could also mean intense frustration for those poor people who did not participate in this progress. Inequality and injustice among classes had always existed. However, with the advent of a national media, people now knew about it. And this suddenly mattered a whole lot. People wanted more things and more control over their lives.

The industrial revolution had increased productivity and made possible a flourishing military. Europe knew the industrial basis of military power. In order to provide for the steel and the machinery necessary to stand up to the powers of the day, countries knew that they had to grow economically if they were to have military power. And the converse was also true. If they wished to have military power, they needed to build a strong, thriving industrial infrastructure. Nations—no matter how large—that did not have a strong industrial base lost wars. This was why Russia with its massive army and large land mass lost to lowly Japan in 1905. The same was true 30 years earlier when industrial Germany defeated agrarian France in the Franco-Prussian War of 1870. This was a fundamental anxiety that plagued all European nations and contributed in no small way to the War when it finally came less than two decades into the new century. The instability of European life is that Germany grew too rapidly for the political structures which were old, and nobody knew how to change them, short of war.

Once a nation felt it was threatened, it had to move quickly to meet the challenge. In the European industrial states, the nation that mobilized first usually won the resulting war. Thus, small conflict could easily become big world wars.

That is exactly what happened in a backwater part of the Balkans.

In the summer of 1914, a Serbian nationalist—a citizen of the aging Austria-Hungarian Empire—assassinated the Archduke Francis Ferdinand, the heir to the throne of Austria-Hungary. Germany, perhaps foolishly, issued a blank check to Austria-Hungary and said it would support her no matter what. Russia, whose ally was Serbia, said the same thing. Then, everyone rushed to declare war on each other so that they could mobilize first. Quickly a local, insignificant conflict became a world war. (James Stobaugh)

2. Read 200-250 pages/week and find vocabulary words.

3. Complete the speech assignment and have a teacher complete a speech evaluation (Appendix).

4. Pay particular attention to writing style this week.

5. Meditate on 1 Kings 20:35-41. Reflect on this passage, and others, in your prayer journal.

6. Write a warm-up essay every day.

FINAL PROJECT

Students should correct and rewrite all essays and place them in their Final Portfolio.

WARM-UP ESSAYS:

	DAY 1	DAY 2	DAY 3	DAY 4	DAY 5
Explanatory	Explain how to bake a chocolate cake.	Explain how to go to your best friend's house.	Explain how to ice-skate.	Explain whether pizza should be eaten from the pointed end or the outside edge.	Explain why Brussels sprouts are wonderful to eat.

LESSON 19 TEST

ESSAY (100 POINTS)

In a one-page essay, explain how to build an Egyptian pyramid.

LESSON 19 TEST ANSWER

ESSAY (100 POINTS)

In a one-page essay, explain how to build an Egyptian pyramid.

ANSWER: Sample Essay

The first pyramids were built around 2650 BC.

The 4th Dynasty that began in 2550-2490 BC was a time of great peace. The kings were able to put their energies in art. King Khufu's Great Pyramid of Giza was built. People prayed to the sun god Re. The first religious words were written on the walls of the royal tombs.

During the 5th Dynasty (2465-2323 BC), for the first time high officials came from people outside of the royal family. The pyramids begin to be smaller and less solid. The ancient Egyptians built more than 90 royal pyramids, from about 2650 BC until about 1550 BC. During that time, the pyramid form evolved from a series of stepped terraces that resembled the stories of a battleship to the better known, sloped pyramidal shape we see today. Pyramids, of course, were simply large tombs which stored the remains of important people—generally speaking, the larger the pyramid, the more important the person. Egyptian religious leaders argued that this was the best way to send off deceased people to their afterlife. Inside the tombs/pyramids were stored important items needed on the journey to the afterlife.

Building a pyramid was a great engineering feat. It required a lot of planning to build such a large and complicated structure. Normally a tertiary director coordinated the whole project. He would gather a team of engineers and thousands of workers/slaves to help him. No one knows how many workers it took to build a pyramid but presumably it took a lot.

The first task for the engineers was to cut the stone from a quarry. Large sandstone blocks would be used for the interior stones with limestone on the exterior. At the same time, usually before the project was started, sandstone and limestone were quarried from a close source. Limestone was especially suited for the task. Limestone in its natural state was pliable and soft but hardened on exposure to air. After estimating how much stone was needed, builders quarried the sandstone and the limestone before the project was started. The limestone was then set out in the desert to cure and harden through exposure to the air.

As soon as a block was cut, it was pushed out to the work site using large, smooth beams rolling on rocks. Often the biggest problem for the workers was not starting the process—it was stopping the process! Going downhill, the block could easily accelerate out of control and needed to be controlled by ropes held around stout anchor poles bedded in the ground. The stones could also be pulled up a gentle rise by a team of oxen. Workers built up from each new base, much like skyscrapers are built today. (James Stobaugh)

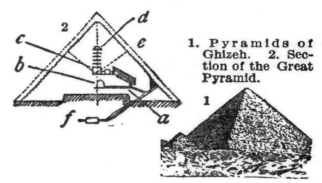

1. Pyramids of Ghizeh. 2. Section of the Great Pyramid.

a, passageways; *b,* queen's chamber; *c,* king's chamber; *d,* five small chambers to relieve pressure; *e,* one of two ventilators; *f,* a subterranean room.

LESSON 20

Writing Skill: Fact, Inference, and Opinion

Grammar Review (Writing and Speaking): Usage – Pronoun and Subject/Verb Agreement

Public Speaking Skill: Converting the Fact, Inference, and Opinion Essay to a Speech.

Looking Ahead: The Historical Profile

Goals/Objectives: What is the purpose of this lesson?	Strategies to meet these goals: How will I obtain these goals/objectives?	Evaluation: How will I know when I have met these goals/objectives?
Concept: factual, inference, and opinion speech (cognitive goal)	The parent/educator will engage students in discussions about ways to write and present speeches. In front of an audience, students will present a fact, inference, and opinion essay.	Students will be able to write and to present an inspired speech. Suggested evaluation sheet includes: Oratory Evaluation I. Poise: How does the student present himself/herself? Is the oratory/dramatic reading memorized? (25 points) II. Articulation: Does the student speak clearly, and slowly? (25 points) III. Presentation: What is the overall effect of the speech? Does it accomplish its purpose? (50 points)
Concept: improved writing skills (cognitive goal)	Students will write five warm-up essays/week.	With minimal errors students will write these essays in 15-20 minutes.
Concept: increased vocabulary (cognitive goal)	Students will collect at least five new vocabulary words and use these words in their warm-up essays and factual, inference, and opinion essay.	Students will use five vocabulary words in conversation during the week, as well as use the words in their essays.

Goals/Objectives: What is the purpose of this lesson?	Strategies to meet these goals: How will I obtain these goals/objectives?	Evaluation: How will I know when I have met these goals/objectives?
Concept: reflective writing (affective/spiritual goal)	Using the Journal Guide Questions in the Appendices, students will record at least three entries this week. Suggested Scripture: 1 Kings 21.	Students will show evidence that they have reflected on this issue including informed discussions and written responses.
Concept: increased knowledge of the assigned essay (cognitive goal)	Students will take Lesson 20 Test.	Students will score at least 80% on Lesson 20 Test.
Concept: factual, inference, and opinion essay (cognitive goal)	Students will write a factual, inference, and opinion essay on the Lord's Supper.	Students, with minimal errors, will clearly write a factual, inference, and opinion essay.
Concept: working in a group setting (behavioral goal)	In a class, in a co-op experience, or during a family discussion, students will discuss religious fundamentalism.	Students will exhibit practical listening skills and will manifest understanding of opposing worldviews.

SUGGESTED
Weekly *Implementation*

DAY 1	DAY 2	DAY 3	DAY 4	DAY 5
Write a Warm-up Essay.	Write a Warm-up Essay.	Write a Warm-up Essay.	Write a Warm-up Essay.	Write a Warm-up Essay.
Read 35-50 pages/day.	Read 35-50 pages/day.	Read 35-50 pages/day.	Read 35-50 pages/day.	Read 35-50 pages/day.
Find five new vocabulary words.	Find five new vocabulary words.	Find five new vocabulary words.	Find five new vocabulary words.	Find five new vocabulary words.
Reflect on the speech assignment for the week.	Compose a first draft of your speech.	Revise your speech and submit to your evaluator/ parent.	Prepare to present your speech tomorrow.	Present your speech to a live audience.
Write an outline with thesis for your fact, inference, and opinion essay.	Work on the first draft for your fact, inference, and opinion essay.	Finish the first draft and then the revised draft of your fact, inference, and opinion essay.	Submit a copy of your paper to a peer for evaluation.	Submit your assignments to your evaluator/ parent.
Make a journal entry.	Make a journal entry.	Make a journal entry.	Finish the final copy of your fact, inference, and opinion essay.	Make a journal entry.
			Make a journal entry.	Take Lesson 20 Test.

ENRICHMENT ACTIVITIES/PROJECTS

Students will read a newspaper and give examples of fact, inference, and opinion.

SPEECH ASSIGNMENT

Present a 3-5 minute speech on some aspect of the Christian life.

ANSWER: *Answers will vary. The following essay discusses the Christian life and argues against "fence crawling":*

The Christian life, if it is anything, is losing and finding, attachment and detachment: losing what we once thought was important; gaining what we discover is really important;

detachment from our world; attachment to Christ. This rhythm, this motion cannot be broken—even when we sin. We try—like Adam and Eve—to hide, but God comes and looks and finds us. After Adam and Eve ate the forbidden fruit, they were painfully aware of their naked sinfulness. God came to the garden to find them. Their/our sin will not thwart us. We are, as it were, lost sheep. But He still seeks us. He loves us so—the lost sheep.

In fact, some of us need to be "found" more than we care to mention. Some of us are losing and detaching more than finding and attaching. Some of us are "fence crawlers." We are not satisfied with our journey of faith—we want more right now! We are always sure that the grass on the other side of the fence is greener than our present fare. We are sure that we can do things better than God—He is so slow! So we are restless. In sheepish terms, we carefully work our way along every fence or hedge, hoping to find a hole where we can push our way out. It may be a broken board, a loosened rail, a gap in a stone fence, or even a gate someone carelessly left open. We find it. We may find a pastor, an elder, or a brother or sister who irritates us, and we take that opportunity to slip out of the safety of the flock. Since we hate to go alone, we take along some company.

Fence crawlers are dangerous. They create problems for everyone. Because the good shepherd is obligated to find his lost sheep, the flock stops moving and waits for that wayward sheep. Everyone loses.

Inevitably, the fence crawler finds his adventure, but he usually finds a lion or two, too. The Good Shepherd rescues him, but sometimes not before the poor sheep is mauled or injured or even killed.

Fence crawlers always become casualties. They hate lostness; that is why they try to take other sheep with them. They become lost sheep. They are disoriented and miserable. They make all the other sheep miserable. (James Stobaugh)

Writing Assignments

1. In a one-page essay, write an essay on the Lord's Supper. In your essay examine other opinions but state what you see as the facts. This essay should include an outline, rough draft, thesis statement, final copy, and five new (circled) vocabulary words. The essay must pay particular attention to style (focus, content, organization). Give a copy to a peer/friend to complete a peer evaluation form (Appendix) and to your instructor to evaluate.

ANSWER: *Answers will vary but the following is an essay on The Lord's Supper:*

Our perceptions and our understandings of reality are often incomplete or inaccurate.

I remember just such a case in my own life. While I was a student at Harvard Divinity School, I visited a girl friend from Lake Village, Arkansas. She was spending the summer at Hampton Beach, New Hampshire, with other Baptist youth, sharing her faith with vacationers.

Now I know that some of you probably think that Hampton Beach is beautiful, but I have to tell you, in 1976 at least, it was a loathsome commercialized stretch of pop machines and greasy hotdog stands.

Nonetheless, I enjoyed spending the afternoon with my Arkansas girl friend, whose father's one million dollars and 1500 acres of rice somewhat mitigated her marginal good looks and bland personality, and we returned to her headquarters to end our date the way we always ended our dates . . . we prayed!

"Oh Lord," she began as I poured sand out of my tennis shoes, "Thank you that some day I will marry a minister."

Well, I do not know whether or not this young lady married a clergyman, but I knew that I had no intentions of marrying her—1500 acres notwithstanding—so I figured I better end that prayer and our relationship as soon as possible. I was delighted to end my first day in New Hampshire and to return to Harvard Yard.

This friend of mine was operating from the wrong set of assumptions. All her sincerity, innocence, and good intentions—and they were legion—while they were commendable did not help her get a husband.

Likewise, we are wrong if we see the Lord's Supper exclusively as a somber and unhappy occasion. True, He was leaving the disciples after the Last Supper. However, at the same time, He was leaving so that the Holy Spirit could come, which He did at Pentecost.

I have reason to argue that as the disciples waited in the Upper Room, they probably enjoyed the Last Supper. In fact, in the early Church, which at this time was hardly more than a sect of Judaism, the Lord's Supper was observed every time the Body of Christ gathered. It was not until the 4th Century before the Church owned property, but from the beginning they observed the Lord's Supper.

At first their entire service was a Eucharistic meal or Agape meal. As they enjoyed a meal together in the home of one of their members, the early church shared the gifts of the Holy Spirit. Men and women alike were leaders and celebrants of the communion. It is my belief that the first pastors arose from the deacons, and they did not participate in ecclesiological duties. Pastors and other leaders were identified by the fruits of their personal lives and the evidence of the Holy Spirit being alive and well in their lives.

As time progressed, the Eucharist was separated from other liturgical events and was only observed on special occasions.

Giving thanks, and remembrance, were two central motifs of the Passover and later Eucharistic celebrations. Remembering: good and bad times but always sacred times because God gave them to us to learn something.

No doubt the disciples were remembering better times. Peter and James remembering their calling by Jesus: fishing for fish was a lot easier than fishing for men. They remembered other meals—feeding the 5000 and the wedding at Cana. All of these types of memories can give us joy and hope. We are reminded that God is consistently good to us even if we do not enjoy His chastisement.

They remembered His words, "This is my body . . . this is my blood." As I once heard a preacher say, "At times Christendom has stretched and pulled Jesus' life and message almost beyond recognition, but these words we have never forgotten." (James Stobaugh)

2. Read 200-250 pages/week and make vocabulary cards.

3. Complete the speech assignment and have a teacher complete a speech evaluation (Appendix).

4. Pay particular attention to your writing style this week.

5. Read 1 Kings 21. In your prayer journal, tell this story from the perspectives of Naboth, Ahab, Elijah, and Jezebel.

6. Write a warm-up essay every day.

FINAL PROJECT

Students should correct and rewrite all essays and place them in their Final Portfolio.

WARM-UP ESSAYS:

	DAY 1	DAY 2	DAY 3	DAY 4	DAY 5
Facts/ Inferences/ Opinion	You think your sister has been using your toothbrush to remove dirt from her shoes. Write a factual paper arguing your point.	You think your sister has been using your toothbrush to remove dirt from her shoes. Write an inference paper arguing your point.	You think your sister has been using your toothbrush to remove dirt from her shoes. Write an opinion paper arguing your point.	Using facts argue that you should be allowed to go on a mission trip to Mongolia.	Using opinions argue that you should be allowed to go on a mission trip to Mongolia.

LESSON 20 TEST

FACT, INFERENCE OR OPINION (40 POINTS)

A. Tell whether the following statements are facts, inferences, or opinions:

German people are naturally neater than other kinds of people.

Abortion is murder.

Creation science is a religious myth.

Human beings evolved from a lower primate.

Harvard University was founded in 1636.

Harvard University is the best college in the country.

Based on statistical evidence, going to Harvard Business School will guarantee a high salary.

President Bush prefers gray suits to black ones.

O.J. Simpson was acquitted of all charges.

O.J. Simpson was really guilty.

O.J. Simpson kept a low profile for a while because he was tired of all the publicity.

Jesus Christ is the Son of God.

ESSAY (60 POINTS)

B. Write a factual essay on euthanasia. Next, write an inference essay concerning the outcomes of euthanasia. Finally, write an essay stating an opinion about euthanasia. Or do the same assignment with any topic that interests you.

LESSON 20 TEST ANSWER

FACT, INFERENCE OR OPINION
(40 POINTS)

A. Tell whether the following statements are facts, inferences, or opinions:

ANSWER:

German people are naturally neater than other kinds of people. *Opinion*

Abortion is murder. *Fact*

Creation science is a religious myth. *Opinion*

Human beings evolved from a lower primate. *Opinion*

Harvard University was founded in 1636. *Fact*

Harvard University is the best college in the country. *Opinion*

Based on statistical evidence, going to Harvard Business School will guarantee a high salary. *Inference*

President Bush prefers gray suits to black ones. *Inference or Opinion*

O.J. Simpson was acquitted of all charges. *Fact*

O.J. Simpson was really guilty. *Opinion*

O.J. Simpson kept a low profile for a while because he was tired of all the publicity. *Inference*

Jesus Christ is the Son of God. *Fact*

ESSAY (60 POINTS)

B. Write a factual essay on euthanasia. Next, write an inference essay concerning the outcomes of euthanasia. Finally, write an essay stating an opinion about euthanasia. Or do the same assignment with any topic that interests you.

ANSWER: *Answers will vary.*

LESSON 21

Goals/Objectives: What is the purpose of this lesson?	Strategies to meet these goals: How will I obtain these goals/objectives?	Evaluation: How will I know when I have met these goals/objectives?
Concept: historical profile speech (cognitive goal)	The parent/educator will engage students in discussions about ways to write and present speeches. In front of an audience, students will present an historical profile.	Students will be able to write and to present an inspired speech. Suggested evaluation sheet includes: Oratory Evaluation I. Poise: How does the student present himself/herself? Is the oratory/dramatic reading memorized? (25 points) II. Articulation: Does the student speak clearly, and slowly? (25 points) III. Presentation: What is the overall effect of the speech? Does it accomplish its purpose? (50 points)
Concept: improved writing skills (cognitive goal)	Students will write five warm-up essays/week.	With minimal errors students will write these essays in 15-20 minutes.
Concept: increased vocabulary (cognitive goal)	Students will collect at least five new vocabulary words and use these words in their warm-up essays and historical profile essay.	Students will use five vocabulary words in conversation during the week, as well as use the words in their essays.

Goals/Objectives: What is the purpose of this lesson?	Strategies to meet these goals: How will I obtain these goals/objectives?	Evaluation: How will I know when I have met these goals/objectives?
Concept: reflective writing. (affective/spiritual goal)	Using the Journal Guide Questions in the Appendices, students will record at least three entries this week. Suggested Scripture: 1 Kings (entire book).	Students will show evidence that they have reflected on this issue including informed discussions and written responses.
Concept: increased knowledge of the assigned essay (cognitive goal)	Students will take Lesson 21 Test.	Students will score at least 80% on Lesson 21 Test.
Concept: historical profile (cognitive goal)	Students will write a historical profile of William Wilberforce.	Students, with minimal errors, will clearly write a historical profile of William Wilberforce.
Concept: working in a group setting (behavioral goal)	In a class, in a co-op experience, or during a family discussion, students will give a historical profile of a close friend.	Students will exhibit practical listening skills and will manifest understanding of opposing worldviews.

SUGGESTED
Weekly Implementation

DAY 1	DAY 2	DAY 3	DAY 4	DAY 5
Write a Warm-up Essay.	Write a Warm-up Essay.	Write a Warm-up Essay.	Write a Warm-up Essay.	Write a Warm-up Essay.
Read 35-50 pages/day.	Read 35-50 pages/day.	Read 35-50 pages/day.	Read 35-50 pages/day.	Read 35-50 pages/day.
Find five new vocabulary words.	Find five new vocabulary words.	Find five new vocabulary words.	Find five new vocabulary words.	Find five new vocabulary words.
Reflect on the speech assignment for the week.	Compose a first draft of your speech.	Revise your speech and submit to your evaluator/ parent.	Prepare to present your speech tomorrow.	Present your speech to a live audience.
Write an outline and thesis for your historical profile.	Work on the first draft for your historical profile.	Finish the first draft of your historical profile.	Finish the final copy of your historical profile.	Submit your assignments to your evaluator/ parent.
Make a journal entry.	Make a journal entry.	Make a journal entry.	Make a journal entry.	Submit a copy of your paper to a peer for evaluation.
				Make a journal entry.
				Take Lesson 21 Test

ENRICHMENT ACTIVITIES/PROJECTS

Students should give oral historical profiles of their grandparents.

SPEECH ASSIGNMENT

Present a 1-3 minute historical profile of William Wilberforce.

ANSWER: *See the essay below.*

WRITING ASSIGNMENTS

1. Write a historical profile of William Wilberforce. This essay should include an outline, rough draft, thesis statement, final copy, and five new (circled) vocabulary words. Pay particular attention to style (focus, content, organization). Give a copy to your peer/friend to complete a peer evaluation (Appendix) and to your instructor to evaluate.

ANSWER: *William Wilberforce (1759-1833) was one of the greatest men of all world history. He is an inspiration to us all of what I call the "long obedience." He dedicated his life to righteous causes and stuck with them until they were won. Wilberforce embraced Christ as Savior in 1784 and along with other Evangelical believers later devoted himself to social reform activities. The fight to abolish the slave trade soon attracted Wilberforce, and he became the abolitionist movement's chief spokesman in the House of Commons. In 1807 Wilberforce secured enactment of legislation prohibiting the trade. He joined the struggle for the complete abolition of slavery, and the bill abolishing slavery became law one month after his death.*

2. Read 150-250 pages/week and keep vocabulary cards.

3. Complete the speech assignment and have a teacher complete a speech evaluation (Appendix).

4. Pay attention to stylistic tendencies this week. Practice combining sentences to make your paper more interesting.

5. In the book of 1 Kings there is a despicable character named Jezebel. Meditate upon why she is so despicable and record reflections in your prayer journal.

6. Complete one warm-up essay every day.

FINAL PROJECT

Students should correct and rewrite all essays and place them in their Final Portfolio.

LESSON 21 TEST

ESSAY (100 POINTS)

Write a historical profile of Winnie the Pooh.

WARM-UP ESSAYS:

	DAY 1	DAY 2	DAY 3	DAY 4	DAY 5
Historical Profile	Write a historical profile of your next door neighbor.	Write a historical profile your pastor.	Write a historical profile of your teacher.	Write a historical profile of the president.	Write a historical profile of the apostle Paul.

LESSON 21 TEST

ESSAY (100 POINTS)

Write a historical profile of Winnie the Pooh.

LESSON 21 TEST ANSWER

ESSAY (100 POINTS)

Write a historical profile of Winnie the Pooh.

ANSWER: *Winnie the Pooh was created by A. A. Milne (1882-1956). He wrote these stories for his son, Christopher Robin.*

LESSON 22

FINAL PORTFOLIO DUE

Students will give to their teacher their corrected essays, speech evaluations, peer evaluations, and other material in an attractive organized and labeled folder.

Students should include fifteen to twenty literary reviews.

Student will submit at least three warm-up essays for each week (a total of sixty-three) and show evidence of others.

Students will include evidence that they have produced at least three weekly journal entries (a total of sixty-three). A sample cover sheet for your Final Portfolio is shown below.

Skills for Rhetoric Folder

Name
Month day, year

LESSONS 23 TO 34

RESEARCH PAPER OVERVIEW

Writing the Research Paper: Each lesson will emphasize a separate aspect of the research paper.

Writing Style: Different writing styles will continue to be emphasized.

Journal Writing: Students should continue to journal.

Writing Assignments: Over the next twelve lessons, students will write a research paper. At the same time, they should continue to read classics and complete literary reviews (located in the Appendix). The best writers inevitably read vast amounts of good books in their career. The student should also continue to write warm-up essays.

LESSON 23

Writing Skill: Research Paper: Designing a Working Plan by Choosing a Topic; Initial Research; and Organization

Style (Writing and Speaking): Usage—*Fewer* vs. *Less*, *Good* vs. *Well*, and Double Negatives

Public Speaking Skill: Effective Listening

Looking Ahead: The Research Paper: Thesis Statement

Goals/Objectives: What is the purpose of this lesson?	Strategies to meet these goals: How will I obtain these goals/objectives?	Evaluation: How will I know when I have met these goals/objectives?
Concept: Effective Listening (cognitive goal)	The parent/educator will engage students in discussions about effective listening. Students will recall a speech or sermon they heard this week.	Students will be able to write and to recall a speech they heard.
Concept: improved writing skills. (cognitive goal)	Students will write five warm-up essays/week.	With minimal errors students will write these essays in 15-20 minutes.
Concept: increased vocabulary. (cognitive goal)	Students will collect at least five new vocabulary words and use these words in their warm-up essays.	Students will use five vocabulary words in conversation during the week, as well as use the words in their essays.
Concept: reflective writing. (affective/spiritual goal)	Using the Journal Guide Questions in the Appendices, students will record at least three entries this week. Suggested Scripture:1 Kings 21:29.	Students will show evidence that they have reflected on this issue including informed discussions and written responses.
Concept: increased knowledge of the assigned essay. (cognitive goal)	Students will take Lesson 23 Test.	Students will score at least 80% on Lesson 23 Test.
Concept: narrowing research paper topics. (cognitive goal)	Students will complete a Thinking Game in order to narrow their topics.	Students, with minimal errors, will narrow their topic.

SUGGESTED
Weekly *Implementation*

DAY 1	DAY 2	DAY 3	DAY 4	DAY 5
Write a Warm-up Essay.	Write a Warm-up Essay.	Write a Warm-up Essay.	Write a Warm-up Essay.	Write a Warm-up Essay.
Read 35-50 pages/day.	Read 35-50 pages/day.	Read 35-50 pages/day.	Read 35-50 pages/day.	Read 35-50 pages/day.
Find five new vocabulary words.	Find five new vocabulary words.	Find five new vocabulary words.	Find five new vocabulary words.	Find five new vocabulary words.
Reflect on the speech assignment for the week.	Compose a first draft of your speech.	Revise your speech and submit to your evaluator/ parent.	Prepare to present your speech tomorrow.	Present your speech to a live audience.
Write an outline with thesis for your historical profile.	Work on the first draft for your historical profile.	Finish the first draft and then the revised draft of your historical profile.	Submit a copy of your paper to a peer for evaluation.	Submit your assignments to your evaluator/ parent.
Make a journal entry.	Make a journal entry.	Make a journal entry.	Finish the final copy of your historical profile.	Submit a copy of your paper to a peer for evaluation.
			Make a journal entry.	Take Lesson 23 Test.
				Make a journal entry.

ENRICHMENT ACTIVITIES/PROJECTS

Students will analyze 2-3 newspaper articles and determine if the articles are appropriately written. In other words, are the articles sufficiently broad in scope to generate interest but still focused enough to make a point?

SPEECH ASSIGNMENT

Listen carefully to a speech or sermon and relate the main points to your teacher/parent/ guardian.

   ANSWER: *Answers will vary.*

WRITING ASSIGNMENTS

   1. You will be assigned a research topic this week.

After being assigned a paper topic, narrow that topic by using the Thinking Game (Appendix).

   ANSWER: *The Thinking Game*

State problem/issue
   Five Sentences: *The South saw the end of slavery expansion as being tantamount to the very end of slavery and therefore the end of their way of life. Likewise, the North saw slavery expansion as a threat to the free labor/free soil concept that people should be rewarded for hard work. Also, the growth of more efficient transportation, massive immigration, and abolitionism exacerbated an already fragile situation. The Cane Ridge Revival and Second Great Awakening promised Americans new freedoms that they did not yet have. Finally, the political system did not seem to be able to solve the problem.*
   Two Sentences: *Slavery expansion, reform movements,*

and fears of immigration caused great disunity in the United States. The political system could not solve these problems.

One Sentence: *Because of many different reasons, by 1860 the United States was irreparably divided, and the political system could not bring the nation together.*

Name three or more subtopics of problem.

The uneasiness and fear generated by problems in the middle period of American history.

The problem of slavery.

The problem of immigration.

Name three or more subtopics of the subtopics.

Uneasiness and fear

Abolitionism

Transportation explosion

Slavery

Free Labor

Immoral

Immigration

Assimilation

Free Soil/Free Labor

Roman Catholicism

What information must be known to solve the problem or to answer the question?

Evidence must be gathered to support the above problems.

State the answer to the question/problem

Five sentences: *The American Civil War was caused by many things. For one thing, the fear of slavery expansion in the North and the fear of its cessation in the South caused great anxiety in all of the United States. Next, immigration and fear of immigration exacerbated the already disturbed American society. Add this to the Second Great Awakening and Reform movements whose impact promised Americans unprecedented freedom, and the nation was ripe for war. It came when the American political system could no longer solve its problems, as it had so adroitly done in the first part of the 19th century.*

Two Sentences: *America was in a great upheaval caused by massive immigration, the Second Great Awakening, radical reform movements, and violent debate around slavery expansion. Ultimately, though, the Civil War was caused by the inability of the political system to solve these problems.*

One Sentence: *America at the middle of the 19th century was in an uproar, and the inability of the political system to calm that uproar caused the Civil War.*

Stated in terms of outcomes, what evidences will I see to confirm that I have made the right decision?

Once the military conflict solved the problems that the political system could not solve, the nation was reunited.

Once the problem/question is answered/solved, what one or two new problems/answers will arise?

Why did it take so long for the nation to be reunited after the Civil War ended? The Reconstruction era was particularly violent.

2. Read 150 to 200 pages this week and create vocabulary cards.

3. Complete the speech assignment and have a teacher complete a speech evaluation. (Appendix).

4. While preparing the warm-up essays, pay particular attention to your writing style this week.

5. Meditate on 1 Kings 21:29 and imagine how Elijah felt when his archenemy King Ahab was shown mercy by God. Meditate on this passage and others. Has God ever disappointed you?

6. Write a warm-up essay every day.

RESEARCH PAPER BENCHMARK

In the next 11 lessons you will write a research paper. If you complete the assignments for each lesson, by Lesson 34 you will have a complete research paper. Do not skip any step! During this lesson you will obtain/choose and narrow your research paper topic.

WARM-UP ESSAYS:

	DAY 1	DAY 2	DAY 3	DAY 4	DAY 5
Narrow a topic in the first paragraph of a research paper.	Topic: Adolescent pimples.	Topic: Drinking milk with pizza.	Topic: Pesky little brothers/ sisters.	Topic: Should curfew be negotiated?	Topic: Is there a pot of gold at the end of a rainbow?

LESSON 23 TEST

THINKING GAME (100 POINTS)

Complete the Thinking Game structure on the research paper topic "The Collapse of the American Family."

LESSON 23 TEST ANSWER

THINKING GAME (100 POINTS)

Complete the following Thinking Game on the research paper topic "The Collapse of the American Family."

ANSWER: *The Thinking Game*

Five sentences: The social welfare system is a runaway juggernaut. We have spent over $5 trillion since 1965, and we are worse off. If all this money had given us happy, healthy families, it would have been worth it. However, the opposite is true. It has consigned untold millions of children to lives of bitterness and failure. In 1960 five of every 100 American births were illegitimate. By 1991 that figure was thirty of every 100, and the upward trend shows no sign of slowing. Government welfare programs dealing with the problem have also increased. However, the cost of illegitimacy is not measured only in dollars.

Two sentences: A country that raises its young men without fathers is inviting chaos. It will surely reap a whirlwind.

One sentence: The American family is under tremendous stress and is in danger of collapsing as a viable institution.

Name three or more subtopics of problem.
 I. Collapse of Morality
 II. Welfare State
 III. Tangential problems

Name three or more subtopics of the subtopics.

I. Collapse of Morality
Post-modernism

II. Welfare State
A. Positive-Liberal State
B. John Perkins

III. Tangential problems
A. Racism
B. Crime
C. No fathers

What information must be known to solve the problem or to answer the question?

How big is the problem? What are its causes?
State the answer to the question/problem

Five sentences: In a word the cause of the problem is the absence of viable fathers. Most historians—and social scientists—agree that a stable, two parent American family is the key to a revitalization of American society. Whether it is 1850 Cincinnati described by the historian Mary Ryan or 1995 Los Angeles, a two parent family brings significant bonuses to American society. Its absence creates all sorts of problems. Fathers are becoming an extinct species.

Two sentences: American society must make it possible for fathers to live and prosper in American families again. There must be a reexamination of the welfare state mentality.

One sentence: American society must make it possible for fathers to live and prosper in American families again.

Stated in terms of outcomes, what evidences will I see confirming that I have made the right decision?

When there are more two parent families in America.

Once the problem/question is answered/solved, what one or two new problems/answers will arise?

How do families survive in adverse economic times?

LESSON 24

Goals/Objectives: What is the purpose of this lesson?	Strategies to meet these goals: How will I obtain these goals/objectives?	Evaluation: How will I know when I have met these goals/objectives?
Concept: Oratory. (cognitive goal)	The parent/educator will engage students in discussions about ways to write and present speeches. In front of an audience, being aware of their presentation, students will present an oratory.	Students will be able to write and to present an inspired speech. Suggested evaluation sheet includes: Oratory Evaluation I. Poise: How does the student present himself/herself? Is the oratory/dramatic reading memorized? (25 points) II. Articulation: Does the student speak clearly, and slowly? (25 points) III. Presentation: What is the overall effect of the speech? Does it accomplish its purpose? (50 points)
Concept: improved writing skills. (cognitive goal)	Students will write five warm-up essays/week.	With minimal errors students will write these essays in 15-20 minutes.
Concept: increased vocabulary. (cognitive goal)	Students will collect at least five new vocabulary words and use these words in their warm-up essays.	Students will use five vocabulary words in conversation during the week, as well as use the words in their essays.

Goals/Objectives: What is the purpose of this lesson?	Strategies to meet these goals: How will I obtain these goals/objectives?	Evaluation: How will I know when I have met these goals/objectives?
Concept: reflective writing. (affective/spiritual goal)	Using the Journal Guide Questions in the Appendices, students will record at least three entries this week. Suggested Scripture: 1 Kings 22.	Students will show evidence that they have reflected on this issue including informed discussions and written responses.
Concept: increased knowledge of the assigned essay. (cognitive goal)	Students will take Lesson 24 Test.	Students will score at least 80% on Lesson 24 Test.
Concept: thesis statement. (cognitive goal)	Students will write a thesis statement for their research paper.	Students, with minimal errors, will clearly articulate a thesis statement for their research paper.

SUGGESTED
Weekly *Implementation*

DAY 1	DAY 2	DAY 3	DAY 4	DAY 5
Write a Warm-up Essay.	Write a Warm-up Essay.	Write a Warm-up Essay.	Write a Warm-up Essay.	Write a Warm-up Essay.
Read 35-50 pages/day.	Read 35-50 pages/day.	Read 35-50 pages/day.	Read 35-50 pages/day.	Read 35-50 pages/day.
Find five new vocabulary words.	Find five new vocabulary words.	Find five new vocabulary words.	Find five new vocabulary words.	Find five new vocabulary words.
Reflect on the speech assignment for the week.	Compose a first draft of your speech.	Revise your speech and submit to your evaluator/ parent.	Prepare to present your speech tomorrow.	Present your speech to a live audience.
Review information on how to write a thesis statement.	Make a journal entry.	Write several thesis statements for your research paper. Narrow your choices.	Submit a copy of your thesis statement to a peer for evaluation.	Submit your assignments to your evaluator/ parent.
Make a journal entry.		Make a journal entry.	Make your final choice for your thesis statement.	Take Lesson 24 Test.
			Make a journal entry.	Make a journal entry.

ENRICHMENT ACTIVITIES/PROJECTS

Students should read 1-3 newspaper articles and orally state the thesis statement of each article.

SPEECH ASSIGNMENT: PRESENTING AN ORATORY

Write and then present a three-minute oratory on a subject of your choice.

The Roman statesman Cicero, in "To Cerealis," discusses how you should create your oratory (www.bartleby.com/9/4/1024.html):

1. The entrance, or the introduction
2. The narration, or the background details
3. The proposition, or the thesis
4. The division, or a brief list of your points
5. The confirmation, or the evidence for these points
6. The confutation, or anticipation of the rebuttal
7. The conclusion

ANSWER: *Answers will vary. A great example of a near- perfect oratory is President Franklin Roosevelt's First Inaugural Address on March 4, 1933:*

I am certain that my fellow Americans expect that on my induction into the Presidency I will address them with a candor and a decision which the present situation of our Nation impels. This is preeminently the time to speak the truth, the whole truth, frankly and boldly. Nor need we shrink from honestly facing conditions in our country today. This great Nation will endure as it has endured, will revive and will prosper. So, first of all, let me assert my firm belief that the only thing we have to fear is fear itself—nameless, unreasoning, unjustified terror which paralyzes needed efforts to convert retreat into advance. In every dark hour of our national life a leadership of frankness and vigor has met with that understanding and support of the people themselves which is essential to victory. I am convinced that you will again give that support to leadership in these critical days.

In such a spirit on my part and on yours we face our common difficulties. They concern, thank God, only material things. Values have shrunken to fantastic levels; taxes have risen; our ability to pay has fallen; government of all kinds is faced by serious curtailment of income; the means of exchange are frozen in the currents of trade; the withered leaves of industrial enterprise lie on every side; farmers find no markets for their produce; the savings of many years in thousands of families are gone.

More important, a host of unemployed citizens face the grim problem of existence, and an equally great number toil with little return. Only a foolish optimist can deny the dark realities of the moment.

Yet our distress comes from no failure of substance. We are stricken by no plague of locusts. Compared with the perils which our forefathers conquered because they believed and were not afraid, we have still much to be thankful for. Nature still offers her bounty and human efforts have multiplied it. Plenty is at our doorstep, but a generous use of it languishes in the very sight of the supply. Primarily this is because the rulers of the exchange of mankind's goods have failed, through their own stubbornness and their own incompetence, have admitted their failure, and abdicated. Practices of the unscrupulous money changers stand indicted in the court of public opinion, rejected by the hearts and minds of men.

True they have tried, but their efforts have been cast in the pattern of an outworn tradition. Faced by failure of credit they have proposed only the lending of more money. Stripped of the lure of profit by which to induce our people to follow their false leadership, they have resorted to exhortations, pleading tearfully for restored confidence. They know only the rules of a generation of self-seekers. They have no vision, and when there is no vision the people perish.

The money changers have fled from their high seats in the temple of our civilization. We may now restore that temple to the ancient truths. The measure of the restoration lies in the extent to which we apply social values more noble than mere monetary profit.

Happiness lies not in the mere possession of money; it lies in the joy of achievement, in the thrill of creative effort. The joy and moral stimulation of work no longer must be forgotten in the mad chase of evanescent profits. These dark days will be worth all they cost us if they teach us that our true destiny is not to be ministered unto but to minister to ourselves and to our fellow men.

Recognition of the falsity of material wealth as the standard of success goes hand in hand with the abandonment of the false belief that public office and high political position are to be valued only by the standards of pride of place and personal profit; and there must be an end to a conduct in banking and in business which too often has given to a sacred trust the likeness of callous and selfish wrongdoing. Small wonder that confidence languishes, for it thrives only on honesty, on honor, on the sacredness of obligations, on faithful protection, on unselfish performance; without them it cannot live.

Restoration calls, however, not for changes in ethics alone. This Nation asks for action, and action now.

Our greatest primary task is to put people to work. This is no unsolvable problem if we face it wisely and courageously. It can be accomplished in part by direct recruiting by the Government itself, treating the task as we would treat the emer-

gency of a war, but at the same time, through this employment, accomplishing greatly needed projects to stimulate and reorganize the use of our natural resources.

Hand in hand with this we must frankly recognize the overbalance of population in our industrial centers and, by engaging on a national scale in a redistribution, endeavor to provide a better use of the land for those best fitted for the land. The task can be helped by definite efforts to raise the values of agricultural products and with this the power to purchase the output of our cities. It can be helped by preventing realistically the tragedy of the growing loss through foreclosure of our small homes and our farms. It can be helped by insistence that the Federal, State, and local governments act forthwith on the demand that their cost be drastically reduced. It can be helped by the unifying of relief activities which today are often scattered, uneconomical, and unequal. It can be helped by national planning for and supervision of all forms of transportation and of communications and other utilities which have a definitely public character. There are many ways in which it can be helped, but it can never be helped merely by talking about it. We must act and act quickly.

Finally, in our progress toward a resumption of work we require two safeguards against a return of the evils of the old order; there must be a strict supervision of all banking and credits and investments; there must be an end to speculation with other people's money, and there must be provision for an adequate but sound currency.

There are the lines of attack. I shall presently urge upon a new Congress in special session detailed measures for their fulfillment, and I shall seek the immediate assistance of the several States.

Through this program of action we address ourselves to putting our own national house in order and making income balance outgo. Our international trade relations, though vastly important, are in point of time and necessity secondary to the establishment of a sound national economy. I favor as a practical policy the putting of first things first. I shall spare no effort to restore world trade by international economic readjustment, but the emergency at home cannot wait on that accomplishment.

The basic thought that guides these specific means of national recovery is not narrowly nationalistic. It is the insistence, as a first consideration, upon the interdependence of the various elements in all parts of the United States—a recognition of the old and permanently important manifestation of the American spirit of the pioneer. It is the way to recovery. It is the immediate way. It is the strongest assurance that the recovery will endure.

In the field of world policy I would dedicate this Nation to the policy of the good neighbor—the neighbor who resolutely respects himself and, because he does so, respects the rights of others—the neighbor who respects his obligations and respects the sanctity of his agreements in and with a world of neighbors.

If I read the temper of our people correctly, we now realize as we have never realized before our interdependence on each other; that we can not merely take but we must give as well; that if we are to go forward, we must move as a trained and loyal army willing to sacrifice for the good of a common discipline, because without such discipline no progress is made, no leadership becomes effective. We are, I know, ready and willing to submit our lives and property to such discipline, because it makes possible a leadership which aims at a larger good. This I propose to offer, pledging that the larger purposes will bind upon us all as a sacred obligation with a unity of duty hitherto evoked only in time of armed strife.

With this pledge taken, I assume unhesitatingly the leadership of this great army of our people dedicated to a disciplined attack upon our common problems.

Action in this image and to this end is feasible under the form of government which we have inherited from our ancestors. Our Constitution is so simple and practical that it is possible always to meet extraordinary needs by changes in emphasis and arrangement without loss of essential form. That is why our constitutional system has proved itself the most superbly enduring political mechanism the modern world has produced. It has met every stress of vast expansion of territory, of foreign wars, of bitter internal strife, of world relations.

It is to be hoped that the normal balance of executive and legislative authority may be wholly adequate to meet the unprecedented task before us. But it may be that an unprecedented demand and need for undelayed action may call for temporary departure from that normal balance of public procedure.

I am prepared under my constitutional duty to recommend the measures that a stricken nation in the midst of a stricken world may require. These measures, or such other measures as the Congress may build out of its experience and wisdom, I shall seek, within my constitutional authority, to bring to speedy adoption.

But in the event that the Congress shall fail to take one of these two courses, and in the event that the national emergency is still critical, I shall not evade the clear course of duty that will then confront me. I shall ask the Congress for the one remaining instrument to meet the crisis—broad Executive power to wage a war against the emergency, as great as the power that would be given to me if we were in fact invaded by a foreign foe.

For the trust reposed in me I will return the courage and the devotion that befit the time. I can do no less.

We face the arduous days that lie before us in the warm courage of the national unity; with the clear consciousness of seeking old and precious moral values; with the clean satisfaction that comes from the stern performance of duty by old and young alike. We aim at the assurance of a rounded and permanent national life.

We do not distrust the future of essential democracy. The people of the United States have not failed. In their need they have registered a mandate that they want direct, vigorous action. They have asked for discipline and direction under leadership. They have made me the present instrument of their wishes. In the spirit of the gift I take it.

In this dedication of a Nation we humbly ask the blessing of God. May He protect each and every one of us. May He guide me in the days to come. (Franklin Roosevelt, http:// odur.let.rug.nl/~usa/P/fr32/speeches/fdr1.htm)

WRITING ASSIGNMENTS

1. After being assigned a paper topic by your educator/teacher, write a thesis statement. Discuss with a parent/teacher what the thesis of this essay is.

ANSWER: *Answers will vary.*

2. Read 150 to 200 pages this week and create vocabulary cards.

3. Complete the speech assignment and have a teacher complete a speech evaluation (Appendix).

4. While preparing the warm-ups, pay particular attention to your writing style this week.

5. Meditate on 1 Kings 22 and reflect on the story of Micaiah.

6. Write a warm-up essay every day.

RESEARCH PAPER BENCHMARK

Last lesson student determined and narrowed his topic. During this lesson student will write his research paper thesis statement.

WARM-UP ESSAYS:

	DAY 1	DAY 2	DAY 3	DAY 4	DAY 5
Write a thesis statement for the following research paper topics.	Topic: Soccer is a game for the intelligent.	Topic: Home-schoolers should have a snow day.	Topic: The theory of relativity is relative.	Topic: Why home-schooled girls score as well as home-schooled boys on the SAT I.	Topic: Why bad things happen to good people.

LESSON 24 TEST

WRITING A THESIS STATEMENT (100 POINTS)

Write a thesis statement for the following essay by Mark Twain, from his book entitled *Christian Science* (1907) http://www.geocities.com/:

This last summer, when I was on my way back to Vienna from the Appetite-Cure in the mountains, I fell over a cliff in the twilight, and broke some arms and legs and one thing or another, and by good luck was found by some peasants who had lost an ass, and they carried me to the nearest habitation, which was one of those large, low, thatch-roofed farm-houses, with apartments in the garret for the family, and a cunning little porch under the deep gable decorated with boxes of bright colored flowers and cats; on the ground floor a large and light sitting-room, separated from the milch-cattle apartment by a partition; and in the front yard rose stately and fine the wealth and pride of the house, the manure-pile. That sentence is Germanic, and shows that I am acquiring that sort of mastery of the art and spirit of the language which enables a man to travel all day in one sentence without changing cars.

There was a village a mile away, and a horse doctor lived there, but there was no surgeon. It seemed a bad outlook; mine was distinctly a surgery case. Then it was remembered that a lady from Boston was summering in that village, and she was a Christian Science doctor and could cure anything. So she was sent for. It was night by this time, and she could not conveniently come, but sent word that it was no matter, there was no hurry, she would give me "absent treatment" now, and come in the morning; meantime she begged me to make myself tranquil and comfortable and remember that there was nothing the matter with me. I thought there must be some mistake.

"Did you tell her I walked off a cliff seventy-five feet high?"

"Yes."

"And struck a boulder at the bottom and bounced?"

"Yes."

"And struck another one and bounced again?"

"Yes."

"And struck another one and bounced yet again?"

"Yes."

"And broke the boulders?"

"Yes."

"That accounts for it; she is thinking of the boulders. Why didn't you tell her I got hurt, too?"

"I did. I told her what you told me to tell her: that you were now but an incoherent series of compound fractures extending from your scalp-lock to your heels, and that the comminuted projections caused you to look like a hat-rack."

"And it was after this that she wished me to remember that there was nothing the matter with me?"

"Those were her words."

"I do not understand it. I believe she has not diagnosed the case with sufficient care. Did she look like a person who was theorizing, or did she look like one who has fallen off precipices herself and brings to the aid of abstract science the confirmations of personal experience?"

"Bitte?"

It was too large a contract for the Stubenmädchen's vocabulary; she couldn't call the hand. I allowed the subject to rest there, and asked for something to eat and smoke, and something hot to drink, and a basket to pile my legs in; but I could not have any of these things.

"Why?"

"She said you would need nothing at all."

"But I am hungry and thirsty, and in desperate pain."

"She said you would have these delusions, but must pay no attention to them. She wants you to particularly remember that there are no such things as hunger and thirst and pain."

"She does, does she?"

"It is what she said."

"Does she seem to be in full and functionable possession of her intellectual plant, such as it is?"

"Bitte?"

"Do they let her run at large, or do they tie her up?"

"Tie her up?"

"There, good-night, run along, you are a good girl, but your mental Geschirr is not arranged for light and airy conversation. Leave me to my delusions."

LESSON 24 TEST ANSWERS

WRITING A THESIS STATEMENT (100 POINTS)

Write a thesis statement for the following essay by Mark Twain, from his book entitled *Christian Science* (1907).

ANSWER: *Twain is poking fun at Christian Science proponents by exaggerating their distinctives.*

LESSON 25

Goals/Objectives: What is the purpose of this lesson?	Strategies to meet these goals: How will I obtain these goals/objectives?	Evaluation: How will I know when I have met these goals/objectives?
Concept: dramatic reading. (cognitive goal)	The parent/educator will engage students in discussions about ways to present a dramatic reading. In front of an audience, students will present a dramatic reading.	Students will be able to write and to present an inspired speech. Suggested evaluation sheet includes: Oratory Evaluation I. Poise: How does the student present himself/herself? Is the oratory/dramatic reading memorized? (25 points) II. Articulation: Does the student speak clearly, and slowly? (25 points) III. Presentation: What is the overall effect of the speech? Does it accomplish its purpose? (50 points)
Concept: improved writing skills. (cognitive goal)	Students will write five warm-up essays/week.	With minimal errors students will write these essays in 15-20 minutes.
Concept: increased vocabulary. (cognitive goal)	Students will collect at least five new vocabulary words and use these words in their warm-up essays.	Students will use five vocabulary words in conversation during the week, as well as use the words in their essays.

Goals/Objectives: What is the purpose of this lesson?	Strategies to meet these goals: How will I obtain these goals/objectives?	Evaluation: How will I know when I have met these goals/ objectives?
Concept: reflective writing. (affective/spiritual goal)	Using the Journal Guide Questions in the Appendices, students will record at least three entries this week. Suggested Scripture: 1 Kings 22.	Students will show evidence that they have reflected on this issue including informed discussions and written responses.
Concept: increased knowledge of the assigned essay. (cognitive goal)	Students will take Lesson 25 Test.	Students will score at least 80% on Lesson 25 Test.
Concept: preliminary essay. (cognitive goal)	Students will create a preliminary bibliography.	Students, with minimal errors, will create a preliminary bibliography.

SUGGESTED
Weekly *Implementation*

DAY 1	DAY 2	DAY 3	DAY 4	DAY 5
Write a Warm-up Essay.	Write a Warm-up Essay.	Write a Warm-up Essay.	Write a Warm-up Essay.	Write a Warm-up Essay.
Read 35-50 pages/day.	Read 35-50 pages/day.	Read 35-50 pages/day.	Read 35-50 pages/day.	Read 35-50 pages/day.
Find five new vocabulary words.	Find five new vocabulary words.	Find five new vocabulary words.	Find five new vocabulary words.	Find five new vocabulary words.
Reflect on the speech assignment for the week.	Practice your dramatic reading. Start to memorize the passage.	Practice your dramatic reading. Memorize the passage.	Prepare to present your dramatic reading tomorrow.	Present your dramatic reading to a live audience.
Write a preliminary bibliography for your research paper.	Write a preliminary bibliography for your research paper.	Write a preliminary bibliography for your research paper.	Write a preliminary bibliography for your research paper.	Submit your assignments to your evaluator/ parent.
Make a journal entry.	Make a journal entry.	Make a journal entry.	Make a journal entry.	Take Lesson 25 Test
				Make a journal entry.

ENRICHMENT ACTIVITIES/PROJECTS

Students should read 2 famous oratories.

SPEECH ASSIGNMENT

Read the following biblical passages to an audience:

DANIEL 5:1–30

King Belshazzar held a great feast for 1,000 of his nobles and drank wine in their presence. Under the influence of the wine, Belshazzar gave orders to bring in the gold and silver vessels that his predecessor Nebuchadnezzar had taken from the temple in Jerusalem, so that the king and his nobles, wives, and concubines could drink from them. So they brought in the gold vessels that had been taken from the temple, the house of God in Jerusalem, and the king and his nobles, wives, and concubines drank from them. They drank the wine and praised their gods made of gold and silver, bronze, iron, wood, and stone.

At that moment the fingers of a man's hand appeared and began writing on the plaster of the king's palace wall next to the lampstand. As the king watched the hand that was writing, his face turned pale, and his thoughts so terrified him that his hip joints shook and his knees knocked together.

The king called out to bring in the mediums, Chaldeans, and astrologers. He said to these wise men of Babylon, "Whoever reads this inscription and gives me its interpretation will be clothed in purple, have a gold chain around his neck, and have the third highest position in the kingdom."

So all the king's wise men came in, but none could read the inscription or make known its interpretation to him. Then King Belshazzar became even more terrified, his face turned pale, and his nobles were bewildered.

Because of the outcry of the king and his nobles, the queen came to the banquet hall. "May the king live forever," she said. "Don't let your thoughts terrify you or your face be pale. There is a man in your kingdom who has the spirit of the holy gods in him. In the days of your predecessor he was found to have insight, intelligence, and wisdom like the wisdom of the gods. Your predecessor, King Nebuchadnezzar, appointed him chief of the diviners, mediums, Chaldeans, and astrologers. Your own predecessor, the king, [did this]* because Daniel, the one the king named Belteshazzar, was found to have an extraordinary spirit, knowledge and perception, and the ability to interpret dreams, explain riddles, and solve problems. Therefore, summon Daniel, and he will give the interpretation."

Then Daniel was brought before the king. The king said to him, "Are you Daniel, one of the Judean exiles that my predecessor the king brought from Judah? I've heard that you have the spirit of the gods in you, and that you have insight, intelligence, and extraordinary wisdom. Now the wise men and mediums were brought before me to read this inscription and make its interpretation known to me, but they could not give its interpretation. However, I have heard about you that you can give interpretations and solve problems. Therefore, if you can read this inscription and give me its interpretation, you will be clothed in purple, have a gold chain around your neck, and have the third highest position in the kingdom."

Then Daniel answered the king, "You may keep your gifts, and give your rewards to someone else; however, I will read the inscription for the king and make the interpretation known to him.

Your Majesty, the Most High God gave sovereignty, greatness, glory, and majesty to your predecessor Nebuchadnezzar. Because of the greatness He gave him, all peoples, nations, and languages were terrified and fearful of him. He killed anyone he wanted and kept alive anyone he wanted; he exalted anyone he wanted and humbled anyone he wanted. But when his heart was exalted and his spirit became arrogant, he was deposed from his royal throne and his glory was taken from him. He was driven away from people, his mind was like an animal's, he lived with the wild donkeys, he was fed grass like cattle, and his body was drenched with dew from the sky until he acknowledged that the Most High God is ruler over the kingdom of men and sets anyone He wants over it.

"But you his successor, Belshazzar, have not humbled your heart, even though you knew all this. Instead, you have exalted yourself against the Lord of heaven. The vessels from His house, were brought to you, and as you and your nobles, wives, and concubines drank wine from them, you praised the gods made of silver and gold, bronze, iron, wood, and stone, which do not see or hear or understand. But you have not glorified the God who holds your life-breath in His hand and who controls the whole course of your life. Therefore, He sent the hand, and this writing was inscribed.

"This is the writing that was inscribed:

MENE, MENE, TEKEL, PARSIN

This is the interpretation of the message:

Mene: God has numbered [the days of] your king-dom and brought it to an end.

Tekel: You have been weighed in the balance and found deficient.

Peres: Your kingdom has been divided and given to the Medes and Persians."

Then Belshazzar gave an order, and they clothed Daniel in purple, a gold chain around his neck, and issued a proclamation concerning him that he should be the third ruler in the kingdom.

That very night Belshazzar the king of the Chaldeans was killed, and Darius the Mede received the kingdom at the age of 62. (Holman CSB)

ISAIAH 6:1–8

In the year that King Uzziah died, I saw the Lord seated on a high and lofty throne, and His robe filled the temple. Seraphim were standing above Him; each one had six wings: with two he covered his face, with two he covered his feet, and with two he flew. And one called to another:

"Holy, holy, holy is the Lord of Hosts;
His glory fills the whole earth."

The foundations of the doorways shook at the sound of their voices, and the temple was filled with smoke.

Then I said: "Woe is me, for I am ruined, because I am a man of unclean lips and live among a people of unclean lips, [and] because my eyes have seen the King, the Lord of Hosts." Then one of the seraphim flew to me, and in his hand was a glowing coal that he had taken from the altar with tongs. He touched my mouth [with it] and said: "Now that this has touched your lips, your wickedness is removed, and your sin is atoned for."

Then I heard the voice of the Lord saying: "Who should I send? Who will go for Us?"

I said: "Here I am. Send me." (Holman CSB)

WRITING ASSIGNMENTS

1. Prepare a preliminary bibliography of at least ten sources of information. At least one of these sources must be a primary source and at least one must be a journal article. While you may use encyclopedias and indexes in preparing this bibliography, they will not count as sources. Each bibliographic entry should be typed and contain all the necessary bibliographic information: author's name, title, translator's name, editor's name, place of publication, publisher's name, date of publication, and page numbers. At this point, format is not important. Create bibliography cards on note cards, or you may use files created on your computer's word-processing software.

ANSWER SAMPLE:

PRELIMINARY BIBLIOGRAPHY

Ahlstrom, Sydney E. *A Religious History of the American People.* New Haven, Conn: Yale University Press, 1972.

Barnes, Eric Wollencott. *The War between the States.* New York: Whittlesey House, 1959.

Clark, James Lemuel. *Civil War Recollections.* Austin, Tex.: Republic of Texas Press, 1997.

Cooke, Allistair. *America.* New York: Alfred A. Knopf, 1974.

Crum, John W. *AP* [advanced placement] *American History.* New York: Prentice Hall, 1994.

Degler, Carl N. *Neither Black nor White.* Madison, Wis.: University of Wisconsin Press, 1971.

Essick, Abraham. *The Diary of Reverend Abraham Essick, 1849–1880.* Charlottesville, Va: University of Virginia Online Collection.

Fletcher, William A. *Rebel Private, Front and Rear.* New York: Dutton, 1995.

Grob, Gerald N., and George Athan Billias. *Interpretations of American History, Vol. I: To 1877.* New York: Macmillan, 1982.

Halstead, Murat. "Douglas Deadlock and Disunion." *American Heritage,* vol. 11, no. 4 (June 1960). New York: American Heritage Publishing Co.

Hunter, Taliaferro Robert Mercer. *Southern Historical Society Papers.* Vol. I, no. 1, Jan. 1876.

Israel, Fred L. *The Presidents, Vol. 3.* Danbury, Conn: Grolier Educational, 1997.

Jordan, Robert Paul. *The Civil War.* Washington, D. C.: National Geographic World, 1969.

Lincoln, Abraham. Lincoln Online. Http://www.abrahamlincoln.com.

McCullough, David. "The Unexpected Mrs. Stowe." *American Heritage,* vol. 24, no. 5 (Oct. 1973): 5–9, 76–80. Also in *A Sense of History.* Washington, D.C.: American Heritage Foundation, 1995.

Mohr, James C., editor. *The Cormany Diaries.* Pittsburgh, Pa: University of Pittsburgh Press, 1982.

Nash, Gary B., et al., editor. *The American People: Creating a Nation and a Society.* New York: Harper Collins, 1990.

Oakes, James. *The Ruling Race: A History of American Slaveholders.* New York: Vintage Books, 1983.

The New Book of Knowledge, Vol.3: U.S.A. Danbury, Conn: Grolier, 1989.

Pierson, George Wilson. *Tocqueville in America.* New York: Doubleday, 1959.

Republican National Platform (1860). Louisiana State University Special Civil War Collection. Baton Rouge, La.

Remini, Robert V. *Andrew Jackson.* New York: Twayne Publishers, 1966.

Rozwenc, Edward C. *Slavery as a Cause of the Civil War.* New York: D. C. Heath and Co., 1949.

Stobaugh, James P. "Racial Anger as an Obstacle to Racial Reconciliation." D.Min. dissertation, Gordon-Conwell Theological Seminary, South Hamilton, Mass.

Van Doren, Charles, and Robert McHenry. *Webster's Guide to American History.* Springfield, Mass: G. & C. Merriam Co., 1971.

Wagman, John, ed. *Civil War Front Pages.* New York: Fairfax Press, 1989.

Wheeler, Richard. *A Rising Thunder: From Lincoln's Election to the Battle of Bull Run: An Eyewitness History.* New York: Harper Perennial, 1994.

Weisberger, Bernard A. "A Nation of Immigrants." *American Heritage,* vol. 45 (Feb./Mar. 1994), 75–91. Also in *A Sense of History.* Washington, D.C.: American Heritage Foundation, 1995.

They Gathered at the River. Boston: Little, Brown, & Co., 1958.

Williams, T. Harry. *The History of American Wars.* New York: Alfred A. Knopf, 1981.

Note: Students should be aware that the above examples represent only one method of how a bibliography can be presented.

2. Read 150 to 200 pages this week and create vocabulary cards.

3. Complete the speech assignment and have a teacher complete a speech evaluation (Appendix).

4. While preparing the warm-ups, pay particular attention to your writing style this week.

5. Meditate on 1 Kings 22. Students should reflect on righteous Jehoshaphat's decision to ally himself with evil Ahab.

6. Write a warm-up essay every day.

RESEARCH PAPER BENCHMARK

So far student has determined and narrowed his topic and written his thesis statement. During this lesson student will write his research paper preliminary bibliography.

WARM-UP ESSAYS:

	DAY 1	DAY 2	DAY 3	DAY 4	DAY 5
Write an essay on what happens to you at the library	You knock over the potted plant next to the reference librarian.	You stand in line to check out library books, then happen to notice than a crucial resource is being checked out by another classmate.	You notice that an important (priceless) video, borrowed from the rare archives section, has been chewed up by your dog. What do you tell the librarian?	Your cheese sandwich is mistakenly caught in the microfiche machine.	Delayed by traffic, you arrive at 5:01, but the library closed at 5:00. Try to persuade a librarian, locking the door, to let you grab one book.

WRITING YOUR PAPER ON THE COMPUTER

Virtually all college papers will be written on computers. Two basic computer word-processing programs are used: Microsoft Word and WordPerfect. You should be comfortable working with both.

Create a folder (not a file) with the title of your paper. Include a thesis statement in the title or on top of the outline.

Create a preliminary bibliography.

Organize your paper into several relevant topics. Make computer files on each topic in your folder. These topics will become outline headings.

Create an outline based on file headings.

Take notes on relevant topics from the preliminary bibliography. Type these notes in sentence form in the files you have created. If they are written well, you will be ready to import the material into your document at a later time. Be sure to record page numbers and references for future footnoting (or endnoting). When you finish, most of the paper should already have been written.

When you are ready, write your rough draft. "Writing the rough draft" basically should mean importing information from your files.

Write a final copy and rewrite as often as necessary.

LESSON 25 TEST

PRELIMINARY BIBLIOGRAPHIES (100 POINTS)

Read the following preliminary bibliographies and decide what the topic of the research paper will be.

BIBLIOGRAPHY A

Annas, George J., and Michael A. Grodin, eds. *The Nazi Doctors and the Nuremberg Code: Human Rights in Human Experimentation*. New York: Oxford University Press, 1992.

Astor, Gerald. *The "Last" Nazi: The Life and Times of Dr. Joseph Mengele*. New York: D. I. Fine, 1985.

Die Auschwitz-Hefte: Texte der polnischen Zeitschrift "Przegląd lekarski" über historische, psychische und medizinische Aspekte des Lebens und Sterbens in Auschwitz. Hamburger Institut für Sozialforschung. Weinheim: Beltz, 1987.

Bernadac, Christian. *Les Médecins maudits: les expériences médicales humaines dans les camps de concentration*. Paris: France-Empire, 1977.

Breggin, Peter R. *Toxic Psychiatry*. New York: St. Martin's Press, 1991.

Caplan, Arthur, ed. *When Medicine Went Mad: Bioethics and the Holocaust*. Totowa, N.J.: Humana Press, 1992.

BIBLIOGRAPHY B

Abrahams, Roger D., ed. *Afro-American Folktales*. New York: Pantheon Books, 1985.

Adair, James A. "Racial Intermarriage and Christianity." Th.M. thesis, Pittsburgh-Xenia Theological Seminary, Pittsburgh, Pa.

Anderson, David C. *Children of Special Value*. New York: St. Martin's Press, 1971.

Andrews, Lori. *Black Power, White Blood: The Life and Times of Johnny Spain*. New York: Pantheon Books, 1996.

Asante, Molefi K., and Mark T. Mattson. *Historical and Cultural Atlas of African Americans*. New York: MacMillan, 1992.

Barbour, Floyd B., ed. *The Black Power Revolt*. Boston, Mass: Extending Horizons Books, 1968.

Barclay, William. *The Letter to the Romans*. Philadelphia: Westminster, 1975.

Barnes, Andrew E., and Peter N. Stearns, eds. *Social History and Issues in Human Consciousness: Some Interdisciplinary Connections*. New York: New York University Press, 1989.

Barone, Michael. "Slouching Toward Dystopia." *U.S. News and World Report*. Dec. 20, 1995.

Barth, Markus. *Justification*. Grand Rapids, Mich.: Eerdmans, 1971.

Barth, Karl. *The Epistle to the Romans*. New York: Oxford University Press.

Batey, Richard A. *Jesus and the Forgotten City: New Light on Sepphoris and the Urban World of Jesus*. Grand Rapids, Mich: Baker Books, 1994.

Beane, Becky. "Crossing the Color Line." *Jubilee* (The Magazine of Prison Fellowship Ministries), Spring 1996.

Beasley, Leon M. "A Beginning Attempt to Eradicate Racist Attitudes." *Social Casework*, Jan. 1972.

Becker, John T., and Stanli K. Becker. *All Blood Is Red — All Shadows Are Dark!* Cleveland, Ohio: Seven Shadows Press, 1984.

Beker, J. Christiaan. *Suffering and Hope: The Biblical Vision and the Human Predicament*. 2d ed. Grand Rapids: Eerdmans, 1994.

Note: Students should be aware that the above examples represent only one method of how a bibliography can be presented.

LESSON 25 TEST ANSWER

PRELIMINARY BIBLIOGRAPHIES (100 POINTS)

Read the following preliminary bibliographies and decide what the topic of the research paper will be.

ANSWER:
Bibliography A: Nazi medical experiments.
Bibliography B: Racial relations in the United States.

LESSON 26

Writing Skill: Research Paper: Taking Notes (A)

Style (Writing and Speaking): Usage – *There, And/Nor/Or, There/Their/They're*

Public Speaking Task: Poetry Reading

Looking Ahead: The Research Paper: Taking Notes (B)

Goals/Objectives: What is the purpose of this lesson?	Strategies to meet these goals: How will I obtain these goals/objectives?	Evaluation: How will I know when I have met these goals/objectives?
Concept: poetry reading. (cognitive goal)	The parent/educator will engage students in discussions about ways to write and present speeches. In front of an audience, students will present a poetry reading.	Students will be able to write and to present an inspired speech. Suggested evaluation sheet includes: Oratory Evaluation I. Poise: How does the student present himself/herself? Is the oratory/dramatic reading memorized? (25 points) II. Articulation: Does the student speak clearly, and slowly? (25 points) III. Presentation: What is the overall effect of the speech? Does it accomplish its purpose? (50 points)
Concept: improved writing skills. (cognitive goal)	Students will write five warm-up essays/week.	With minimal errors students will write these essays in 15-20 minutes.
Concept: increased vocabulary. (cognitive goal)	Students will collect at least five new vocabulary words and use these words in their warm-up essays.	Students will use five vocabulary words in conversation during the week, as well as use the words in their essays.
Concept: reflective writing. (affective/spiritual goal)	Using the Journal Guide Questions in the Appendices, students will record at least three entries this week. Suggested Scripture: 1 Kings 22.	Students will show evidence that they have reflected on this issue including informed discussions and written responses.

Goals/Objectives: What is the purpose of this lesson?	Strategies to meet these goals: How will I obtain these goals/objectives?	Evaluation: How will I know when I have met these goals/ objectives?
Concept: increased knowledge of the assigned essay. (cognitive goal)	Students will take Lesson 26 Test.	Students will score at least 80% on Lesson 26 Test.
Concept: note-taking. (cognitive goal)	Students will take notes on their research topic.	Students will collect at least 20-25 note/entries this week.

SUGGESTED
Weekly *Implementation*

DAY 1	DAY 2	DAY 3	DAY 4	DAY 5
Write a Warm-up Essay.	Write a Warm-up Essay.	Write a Warm-up Essay.	Write a Warm-up Essay.	Write a Warm-up Essay.
Read 35-50 pages/day.	Read 35-50 pages/day.	Read 35-50 pages/day.	Read 35-50 pages/day.	Read 35-50 pages/day.
Find five new vocabulary words.	Find five new vocabulary words.	Find five new vocabulary words.	Find five new vocabulary words.	Find five new vocabulary words.
Reflect on the speech assignment for the week.	Practice reading your poetry selection.	Memorize your poetry selection.	Prepare to present your poetry reading tomorrow.	Present your poetry reading to a live audience.
Take notes on your topic.	Take notes on your topic.	Take notes on your topic.	Take notes on your topic.	Submit your assignments to your evaluator/ parent
Make a journal entry.	Make a journal entry.	Make a journal entry.	Make a journal entry.	Make a journal entry.
				Take Lesson 26 Test

ENRICHMENT ACTIVITIES/PROJECTS
Students should ask their pastor to let them read Scripture during morning worship.

SPEECH ASSIGNMENT
In front of an audience, read the following ending of "The Rime of the Ancient Mariner" by the British poet Samuel Taylor Coleridge:

This Hermit good lives in that wood
Which slopes down to the sea.
How loudly his sweet voice he rears!
He loves to talk with marineres
That come from a far countree.

He kneels at morn and noon and eve—
He hath a cushion plump:
It is the moss that wholly hides
The rotted old oak-stump.

The skiff-boat neared: I heard them talk,
"Why this is strange, I trow!
Where are those lights so many and fair,
That signal made but now?"

"Strange, by my faith!" the Hermit said—
"And they answered not our cheer!
The planks looked warped! and see those sails,
How thin they are and sere!
I never saw aught like to them,
Unless perchance it were

"Brown skeletons of leaves that lag
My forest-brook along;
When the ivy-tod is heavy with snow,
And the owlet whoops to the wolf below,
That eats the she-wolf's young."

"Dear Lord! it hath a fiendish look—
(The Pilot made reply)
I am a-feared"—"Push on, push on!"
Said the Hermit cheerily.

The boat came closer to the ship,
But I nor spake nor stirred;
The boat came close beneath the ship,
And straight a sound was heard.

Under the water it rumbled on,
Still louder and more dread:
It reached the ship, it split the bay;
The ship went down like lead.

Stunned by that loud and dreadful sound,
Which sky and ocean smote,
Like one that hath been seven days drowned
My body lay afloat;
But swift as dreams, myself I found
Within the Pilot's boat.

Upon the whirl, where sank the ship,
The boat spun round and round;
And all was still, save that the hill
Was telling of the sound.

I moved my lips—the Pilot shrieked
And fell down in a fit;
The holy Hermit raised his eyes,
And prayed where he did sit.

I took the oars: the Pilot's boy,
Who now doth crazy go,
Laughed loud and long, and all the while
His eyes went to and fro.
"Ha! ha!" quoth he, "full plain I see,
The Devil knows how to row."

And now, all in my own countree,
I stood on the firm land!
The Hermit stepped forth from the boat,
And scarcely he could stand.

"O shrieve me, shrieve me, holy man!"
The Hermit crossed his brow.
"Say quick," quoth he, "I bid thee say—
What manner of man art thou?"

Forthwith this frame of mine was wrenched
With a woeful agony,
Which forced me to begin my tale;
And then it left me free.

Since then, at an uncertain hour,
That agony returns;
And till my ghastly tale is told,
This heart within me burns.

I pass, like night, from land to land;
I have strange power of speech;
That moment that his face I see,
I know the man that must hear me:
To him my tale I teach.

What loud uproar bursts from that door!
The wedding-guests are there:
But in the garden-bower the bride
And bride-maids singing are:
And hark the little vesper bell,
Which biddeth me to prayer!

O Wedding-Guest! this soul hath been
Alone on a wide wide sea:
So lonely 'twas, that God himself
Scarce seemed there to be.

O sweeter than the marriage-feast,
'Tis sweeter far to me,
To walk together to the kirk
With a goodly company!—

To walk together to the kirk,
And all together pray,
While each to his great Father bends,
Old men, and babes, and loving friends,
And youths and maidens gay!

Farewell, farewell! but this I tell
To thee, thou Wedding-Guest!
He prayeth well, who loveth well
Both man and bird and beast.

He prayeth best, who loveth best
All things both great and small;
For the dear God who loveth us
He made and loveth all.

The Mariner, whose eye is bright,
Whose beard with age is hoar,
Is gone: and now the Wedding-Guest
Turned from the bridegroom's door.

He went like one that hath been stunned,
And is of sense forlorn:
A sadder and a wiser man,
He rose the morrow morn.
(http://www.classicreader.com/read.php/sid.1/bookid.1
    293/sec.s/)

WRITING ASSIGNMENTS

1. For the next two lessons you will be taking notes on your topic. You will create 3-by-5 note cards, or you may create files on your computer's word-processing software.

ANSWER: *Answers will vary. Here is one note entry on a computer file:*

II. Body
   B. A flood of immigrants entered the United States from 1800 to 1860: population doubled every 20 years.
       1. Immigrants from Northern Europe.
       2. Immigrants from Ireland.
       3. Very few immigrants into the South: Stagnant economy.
       4. Rise of Nativism

2. Read 150 to 200 pages this week and create vocabulary cards.

3. Complete the speech assignment and have a teacher complete a speech evaluation (Appendix).

4. While preparing the warm-ups, pay particular attention to your writing style this week.

5. Meditate on 1 Kings 22. Reflect on the pattern created by King Ahaziah.

6. Write a warm-up essay every day.

RESEARCH PAPER BENCHMARK

Students should have their topic, thesis statement, and preliminary bibliography. During this lesson students will begin to take notes on their research paper topic.

WARM-UP ESSAYS:

	DAY 1	DAY 2	DAY 3	DAY 4	DAY 5
The student should solve these problems	You can find no books on your topic.	Your topic is too narrow.	Your topic is too broad.	You lost your preliminary bibliography two days before the paper was due.	You wish you had never enrolled in this course.

LESSON 26 TEST

TAKING NOTES (100 POINTS)

Take notes on the following passage from Edward Everett Hale's *The Life of Christopher Columbus:* (www.classicreader.com/read.php/sid.1/bookid.1293/sec.2/)

Christopher Columbus was born in the Republic of Genoa. The honor of his birth-place has been claimed by many villages in that Republic, and the house in which he was born cannot be now pointed out with certainty. But the best authorities agree that the children and the grown people of the world have never been mistaken when they have said: "America was discovered in 1492 by Christopher Columbus, a native of Genoa."

His name, and that of his family, is always written Colombo, in the Italian papers which refer to them, for more than one hundred years before his time. In Spain it was always written Colon; in France it is written as Colomb; while in England it has always kept its Latin form, Columbus. It has frequently been said that he himself assumed this form, because Columba is the Latin word for "Dove," with a fanciful feeling that, in carrying Christian light to the West, he had taken the mission of the dove. Thus, he had first found land where men thought there was ocean, and he was the messenger of the Holy Spirit to those who sat in darkness. It has also been assumed that he took the name of Christopher, "the Christ-bearer," for similar reasons. But there is no doubt that he was baptized "Christopher," and that the family name had long been Colombo. The coincidences of name are but two more in a calendar in which poetry delights, and of which history is full.

Christopher Columbus was the oldest son of Dominico Colombo and Suzanna Fontanarossa. This name means Red-fountain. He had two brothers, Bartholomew and Diego, whom we shall meet again. Diego is the Spanish way of writing the name which we call James.

It seems probable that Christopher was born in the year 1436, though some writers have said that he was older than this, and some that he was younger. The record of his birth and that of his baptism have not been found.

His father was not a rich man, but he was able to send Christopher, as a boy, to the University of Pavia, and here he studied grammar, geometry, geography and navigation, astronomy and the Latin language. But this was as a boy studies, for in his fourteenth year he left the university and entered, in hard work, on "the larger college of the world." If the date given above, of his birth, is correct, this was in the year 1450, a few years before the Turks took Constantinople, and, in their invasion of Europe, affected the daily life of everyone, young or old, who lived in the Mediterranean countries. From this time, for fifteen years, it is hard to trace along the life of Columbus. It was the life of an intelligent young seaman, going wherever there was a voyage for him. He says himself, "I passed twenty-three years on the sea. I have seen all the Levant, all the western coasts, and the North. I have seen England; I have often made the voyage from Lisbon to the Guinea coast." This he wrote in a letter to Ferdinand and Isabella. Again he says, "I went to sea from the most tender age and have continued in a sea life to this day. Whoever gives himself up to this art wants to know the secrets of Nature here below. It is more than forty years that I have been thus engaged. Wherever any one has sailed, there I have sailed."

Whoever goes into the detail of the history of that century will come upon the names of two relatives of his—Colon el Mozo (the Boy, or the Younger) and his uncle, Francesco Colon, both celebrated sailors. The latter of the two was a captain in the fleets of Louis XI of France, and imaginative students may represent him as meeting Quentin Durward at court. Christopher Columbus seems to have made several voyages under the command of the younger of these relatives. He commanded the Genoese galleys near Cyprus in a war which the Genoese had with the Venetians. Between the years 1461 and 1463 the Genoese were acting as allies with King John of Calabria, and Columbus had a command as captain in their navy at that time.

"In 1477," he says, in one of his letters, "in the month of February, I sailed more than a hundred leagues beyond Tile." By this he means Thule, or Iceland. "Of this island the southern part is seventy-three degrees from the equator, not sixty-three degrees, as some geographers pretend." But here he was wrong. The Southern part of Iceland is in the latitude of sixty-three and a half degrees. "The English, chiefly those of Bristol, carry their merchandise to this island, which is as large as England. When I was there the sea was not frozen, but the tides there are so strong that they rise and fall twenty-six cubits."

The order of his life, after his visit to Iceland, is better known. He was no longer an adventurous sailor-boy, glad of any voyage which offered; he was a man thirty years of age or more. He married in the city of

Lisbon and settled himself there. His wife was named Philippa. She was the daughter of an Italian gentleman named Bartolomeo Muniz de Perestrello, who was, like Columbus, a sailor, and was alive to all the new interests which geography then presented to all inquiring minds. This was in the year 1477, and the King of Portugal was pressing the expeditions which, before the end of the century, resulted in the discovery of the route to the Indies by the Cape of Good Hope.

The young couple had to live. Neither the bride nor her husband had any fortune, and Columbus occupied himself as a draftsman, illustrating books, making terrestrial globes, which must have been curiously inaccurate, since they had no Cape of Good Hope and no American Continent, drawing charts for sale, and collecting, where he could, the material for such study. Such charts and maps were beginning to assume new importance in those days of geographical discovery. The value attached to them may be judged from the statement that Vespucius paid one hundred and thirty ducats for one map. This sum would be more than five hundred dollars of our time.

Columbus did not give up his maritime enterprises. He made voyages to the coast of Guinea and in other directions.

LESSON 26 TEST ANSWER

TAKING NOTES (100 POINTS)

Take notes on the passage from Edward Everett Hale's *The Life of Christopher Columbus.*

ANSWER: *Notes would follow the chronology of Columbus' life: birth in Genoa, marriage in Portugal, and beginnings of sea exploration. Hale makes it clear that Columbus did not suddenly become interested in exploration — it was part of most of his adult life.*

LESSON 27

Goals/Objectives: What is the purpose of this lesson?	Strategies to meet these goals: How will I obtain these goals/objectives?	Evaluation: How will I know when I have met these goals/objectives?
Concept: debate case. (cognitive goal)	The parent/educator will engage students in discussions about ways to write and present speeches. In front of an audience, students will present a debate case on the assigned topic.	Students will be able to write and to present an inspired speech. Suggested evaluation sheet includes: Oratory Evaluation I. Poise: How does the student present himself/herself? Is the oratory/dramatic reading memorized? (25 points) II. Articulation: Does the student speak clearly, and slowly? (25 points) III. Presentation: What is the overall effect of the speech? Does it accomplish its purpose? (50 points)
Concept: improved writing skills. (cognitive goal)	Students will write five warm-up essays/week.	With minimal errors students will write these essays in 15-20 minutes.
Concept: increased vocabulary. (cognitive goal)	Students will collect at least five new vocabulary words and use these words in their warm-up essays.	Students will use five vocabulary words in conversation during the week, as well as use the words in their essays.

Goals/Objectives: What is the purpose of this lesson?	Strategies to meet these goals: How will I obtain these goals/objectives?	Evaluation: How will I know when I have met these goals/ objectives?
Concept: reflective writing. (affective/spiritual goal)	Using the Journal Guide Questions in the Appendices, students will record at least three entries this week. Suggested Scripture: 1 Kings 22.	Students will show evidence that they have reflected on this issue including informed discussions and written responses.
Concept: increased knowledge of the assigned essay. (cognitive goal)	Students will take Lesson 27 Test.	Students will score at least 80% on Lesson 27 Test.
Concept: preliminary outline and note-taking. (cognitive goal)	Students will create a preliminary outline and start taking notes.	Students will complete a workable preliminary outline and will continue to take notes.

SUGGESTED
Weekly *Implementation*

DAY 1	DAY 2	DAY 3	DAY 4	DAY 5
Write a Warm-up Essay.	Write a Warm-up Essay.	Write a Warm-up Essay.	Write a Warm-up Essay.	Write a Warm-up Essay.
Read 35-50 pages/day.	Read 35-50 pages/day.	Read 35-50 pages/day.	Read 35-50 pages/day.	Read 35-50 pages/day.
Find five new vocabulary words.	Find five new vocabulary words.	Find five new vocabulary words.	Find five new vocabulary words.	Find five new vocabulary words.
Reflect on the speech assignment for the week.	Compose a first draft of your speech.	Revise your speech and submit to your evaluator/ parent.	Prepare to present your speech tomorrow.	Present your speech to a live audience.
Create a preliminary outline and continue to take notes on your topic.	Create a preliminary outline and continue to take notes on your topic.	Create a preliminary outline and continue to take notes on your topic.	Create a preliminary outline and continue to take notes on your topic.	Submit your assignments to your evaluator/ parent.
Make a journal entry.	Make a journal entry.	Make a journal entry.	Make a journal entry.	Take Lesson 27 Test
				Make a journal entry.

ENRICHMENT ACTIVITIES/PROJECTS

Students should orally consider how to create a preliminary outline for a subject that interests them.

SPEECH ASSIGNMENT

Conduct some research and argue affirmatively about the following resolution: Resolved, whereas, in a time of national crisis, for the sake of national security, in the face of overwhelming danger, profiling of possible terrorists should be legal.

ANSWER: *The affirmative position would argue vigorously that public safety in this case, regrettably, was more important than individual rights of potential terrorists. The negative position, of course, would argue the opposite position.*

WRITING ASSIGNMENTS

1. Create a preliminary outline and continue to take notes on your topic. Create note cards or you use files created on your computer word-processing software.

NOTES: *Answers will vary.*

2. Read 200-250 pages this week and create vocabulary cards.

3. Create speech assignment and have a teacher complete a speech evaluation (Appendix).

4. While preparing the warm-ups, pay particular attention to your writing style this week.

5. Meditate on 1 Kings 22. Reflect on the difference between King Jehoshaphat and King Ahaziah's characters and explain the source of this difference.

6. Write a warm-up essay every day.

RESEARCH PAPER BENCHMARK

Students should have their topic, thesis statement, preliminary bibliography, and some notes. During this lesson students will create a preliminary outline and continue to take notes on their research paper topic.

WARM-UP ESSAYS:

	DAY 1	DAY 2	DAY 3	DAY 4	DAY 5
Summarize these topics	Happiness.	Warmth.	Trepidation.	Coldness.	Jealousy.

LESSON 27 TEST

TAKING NOTES (100 POINTS)

Using the following portion of a research project, speculate on what notes and outline underlie this paper. Research Note: This student sample of a researched paper does not provide here the references to the sources used in its compilation as your research will.

THREE RESULTS OF THE FRENCH REVOLUTION

The year 1989 marked the 200th anniversary of the French Revolution. To celebrate, the French government threw its biggest party in at least 100 years. It was to last all year. In the United States, an American Committee on the French Revolution was set up to coordinate programs on this side of the Atlantic, emphasizing the theme, "France and America: Partners in Liberty." The French, however, should be uneasy about their Revolution: whereas the American Revolution brought forth a relatively free economy and limited government, the French Revolution brought forth first anarchy, then dictatorship. The French Revolution brought forth the reign of terror, the guillotine, and the tyrant Napoléon Bonaparte. The results of this great war were chaos and disorder. Nothing good came out of this disgrace to France. *Three results came from this revolution that still haunts the memories of people today.* (Thesis statement)

First, the French Revolution marked the end of the French aristocracy. July 14, 1789, marked a day that France will not soon forget. The mobs flocked to the Bastille Prison to free their friends and neighbors. Screaming. Threatening. They did whatever they could to inflict fear on the soldiers guarding this prison. At first, the officer in charge, Monsieur de Launay, refused to negotiate, refused to surrender. Soon, though, Luanay saw he had no choice but to surrender. He did so but only after the mob promised to let his troops go free.

However, the mob could not be stopped, could not be controlled, could not be satisfied until they had their revenge. They stormed the Bastille, killing, looting, and destroying Launay and his troops, whose heads were carried on pikes in the streets of Paris. Throughout the next few years this slaughter was repeated.

The French Revolution had begun. Even the King was killed.

The French Revolution began as an aristocratic revolution, a revolt of the nobility against the king when he was forced to call a meeting of the Estates-General in 1789. In 1789–91, a comparatively peaceful period, the National Assembly did much to modernize France. Despite the Declaration of Rights, the reformed franchise which promoted free trade still excluded the poor; but the public maintained its faith in freedom and unity, as shown in the first Festival of Federation, a celebration of national unity on July 14, 1790. However, the groundwork was laid for the secularization and tragedy that was to fall on France in later years. Power and special interests joined together in the bloodbath called the French Revolution, and they were not going to step apart easily. Already French leadership was turning its back on centuries of Judeo-Christian morality and tradition.

By 1791 radical Jacobins had taken over the government. Louis XVI, because he had escaped and invited foreign intervention, was beheaded. A few years later his wife, the infamous Marie Antoinette, joined him at the guillotine. To repress counterrevolutionary movements, the community of public safety, under Robespierre's leadership, instituted what was called the Reign of Terror. In that bloodbath, about 40,000 Frenchman lost their lives, executed in many different ways, but mostly by the guillotine. This count does not include the 2,000 people who were loaded onto a boat that sank with the people in it near the city of Nantes. In addition, 100,000 people were taken captive. The Reign of Terror ended with the death of Robespierre.

Finally, the French Revolution helped Napoléon rise to power. The young 30-year-old Napoléon was a member of the Jacobins. At this point the soon-to-be dictator entered the story.

Napoléon Bonaparte, also known as the "little Corsican," was born August 15, 1769, in Ajaccio, Corsica. His original [Italian] name was Napoleone. He had seven brothers and sisters. His original nationality was Corsican-Italian. He despised the French. He thought they were oppressors of his native land. His father was a lawyer and was also anti-French. One reason Napoléon may have been such a conqueror was that he was reared in a family of radicals. When Napoléon was nine, his father sent him to a French military government school. He attended Brienne in Paris. While there, he was constantly teased by the French students. Because of this treatment, Napoléon started having dreams of personal glory and triumph.

In France, for at least a generation, the democratic republic government disappeared, and Napoléon came to power. (Timothy Stobaugh)

LESSON 27 TEST ANSWER

TAKING NOTES (100 POINTS)

Using the following portion of a research project, speculate on what notes and outline underlie this paper. Research Note: This student sample of a researched paper does not provide here the references to the sources used in its compilation as your research will.

ANSWER: *The title "Three Results of the French Revolution" tells it all. This is often the case in essay outlining and notetaking.*

LESSON 28

Goals/Objectives: What is the purpose of this lesson?	Strategies to meet these goals: How will I obtain these goals/objectives?	Evaluation: How will I know when I have met these goals/objectives?
Concept: debate case. (cognitive goal)	The parent/educator will engage students in discussions about ways to write and present speeches. In front of an audience, students will present debate case—affirmative and negative—on the efficacy of capital punishment.	Students will be able to write and to present an inspired speech. Suggested evaluation sheet includes: Oratory Evaluation I. Poise: How does the student present himself/herself? Is the oratory/dramatic reading memorized? (25 points) II. Articulation: Does the student speak clearly, and slowly? (25 points) III. Presentation: What is the overall effect of the speech? Does it accomplish its purpose? (50 points)
Concept: improved writing skills. (cognitive goal)	Students will write five warm-up essays/week.	With minimal errors students will write these essays in 15-20 minutes.
Concept: increased vocabulary. (cognitive goal)	Students will collect at least five new vocabulary words and use these words in their warm-up essays.	Students will use five vocabulary words in conversation during the week, as well as use the words in their essays.
Concept: reflective writing. (affective/spiritual goal)	Using the Journal Guide Questions in the Appendices, students will record at least three entries this week. Suggested Scripture: 2 Kings 2.	Students will show evidence that they have reflected on this issue including informed discussions and written responses.

Goals/Objectives: What is the purpose of this lesson?	Strategies to meet these goals: How will I obtain these goals/objectives?	Evaluation: How will I know when I have met these goals/objectives?
Concept: increased knowledge of the assigned essay. (cognitive goal)	Students will take Lesson 28 Test.	Students will score at least 80% on Lesson 28 Test.
Concept: outline. (cognitive goal)	Students will create an outline for their research paper.	Students, with minimal errors, will create a workable outline that is thorough enough to cover the subject and precise enough to keep the subject manageable.

SUGGESTED
Weekly *Implementation*

DAY 1	DAY 2	DAY 3	DAY 4	DAY 5
Write a Warm-up Essay.	Write a Warm-up Essay.	Write a Warm-up Essay.	Write a Warm-up Essay.	Write a Warm-up Essay.
Read 35-50 pages/day.	Read 35-50 pages/day.	Read 35-50 pages/day.	Read 35-50 pages/day.	Read 35-50 pages/day.
Find five new vocabulary words.	Find five new vocabulary words.	Find five new vocabulary words.	Find five new vocabulary words.	Find five new vocabulary words.
Reflect on the speech assignment for the week.	Compose a first draft of your speech.	Revise your speech and submit to your evaluator/ parent.	Prepare to present your speech tomorrow.	Present your speech to a live audience.
Create an outline.	Create an outline.	Create an outline.	Create an outline.	Submit your assignments to your evaluator/ parent.
Make a journal entry.	Make a journal entry.	Make a journal entry.	Make a journal entry.	Take Lesson 28 Test
				Make a journal entry.

ENRICHMENT ACTIVITIES/PROJECTS

Students should outline their pastor's sermons for several weeks.

SPEECH ASSIGNMENT

Students should outline and present an affirmative speech and then a negative speech for the following resolution: Resolved, capital punishment should be banned.

ANSWER: *The affirmative speech would develop the moral certitude of capital punishment and would also establish capital punishment as a deterrent to criminal activity. The negative position would try to argue an opposite position.*

WRITING ASSIGNMENTS

1. Write your outline for your research paper.

ANSWER: *Answers will vary according to the title and content of the research paper.*

2. Read 200-250 pages this week and create vocabulary cards.

3. Complete the speech assignment and have a teacher complete a speech evaluation (Appendix).

4. While preparing the warm-ups, pay particular attention to your writing style this week.

5. Meditate on 2 Kings 1. What is the mistake that Ahaziah makes?

6. Write a warm-up essay every day. Over the next few weeks, you will gradually be developing a "practice" paper on each topic. Add to the same topic each week as you build the paper. For instance: On Day 1, Lesson 28, you will compare a research paper with a cold shower. On Day 1, Lesson 29, you will continue writing on the same topic but will add more information. On Day 1, Lesson 30, you will add even more information to the same topic. On Day 1, Lesson 31, you will add even more information to the same topic. On Day 1, Lesson 32, you continue adding information to the growing paper. On Day 1, Lesson 33, conclude the paper. You have completed five "practice" papers on five topics

RESEARCH PAPER BENCHMARK

Student should have his/her topic, thesis statement, preliminary bibliography, a preliminary outline to guide student in his/her note-taking, and many notes. During this lesson student will create an outline.

WARM-UP ESSAYS:

	DAY I	DAY 2	DAY 3	DAY 4	DAY 5
Comparison/ Contrast	Compare a research paper with a cold shower.	Compare a research paper with your favorite CD.	Compare a footnote and an endnote. Which do you prefer? Why?	Compare a question mark with a colon.	Compare active voice with passive voice writing.

LESSON 28 TEST

OUTLINE (100 POINTS)

Critique the following outline:

MARIE ANTOINETTE: VICTIM OR CAUSE OF THE FRENCH REVOLUTION

The purpose of my paper is to show how an historical person—like Marie Antoinette—can be both the cause and victim of a significant historical event.

I. Introduction
A. Background to the French Revolution
B. Antoinette's early life

II. Antoinette as Cause of the French Revolution
A. She was living a selfish, lavish life
B She and her husband were unwilling to share power

III. Antoinette as victim of The French Revolution
A. She was only the partner of the King and did not make many decisions.
B. She was like every other monarch in Europe, but she happened to be in the wrong place at the wrong time.

IV. Conclusion

LESSON 28 TEST ANSWER

OUTLINE (100 POINTS)

Critique the outline.

ANSWER: *The thesis statement is not identified, does not clarify exactly what the paper will entail, and should not begin with "The purpose of my paper . . . ." The outline has sufficient content but is not parallel in form, does not have proper capitalization, and has an inappropriate mixture of phrases and sentences (consult a writing manual such as* Bedford's Handbook for Writers, Harbrace College Handbook, *or* MLA Handbook for Writers of Research Papers*).*

LESSON 29

Goals/Objectives: What is the purpose of this lesson?	Strategies to meet these goals: How will I obtain these goals/objectives?	Evaluation: How will I know when I have met these goals/objectives?
Concept: Speech Introduction. (cognitive goal)	The parent/educator will engage students in discussions about ways to write and present speeches. In front of an audience, students, giving particular attention to the introduction, will present a speech.	Students will be able to write and to present an inspired speech. Suggested evaluation sheet includes: Oratory Evaluation I. Poise: How does the student present himself/herself? Is the oratory/dramatic reading memorized? (25 points) II. Articulation: Does the student speak clearly, and slowly? (25 points) III. Presentation: What is the overall effect of the speech? Does it accomplish its purpose? (50 points)
Concept: improved writing skills. (cognitive goal)	Students will write five warm-up essays/week.	With minimal errors students will write these essays in 15-20 minutes.
Concept: increased vocabulary. (cognitive goal)	Students will collect at least five new vocabulary words and use these words in their warm-up essays	Students will use five vocabulary words in conversation during the week, as well as use the words in their essays.
Concept: reflective writing. (affective/spiritual goal)	Using the Journal Guide Questions in the Appendices, students will record at least three entries this week. Suggested Scripture: 2 Kings 2.	Students will show evidence that they have reflected on this issue including informed discussions and written responses.

Goals/Objectives: What is the purpose of this lesson?	Strategies to meet these goals: How will I obtain these goals/objectives?	Evaluation: How will I know when I have met these goals/ objectives?
Concept: increased knowledge of the assigned essay. (cognitive goal) Concept: introduction. (cognitive goal)	Students will take Lesson 29 Test. Students will begin the introduction to their research paper.	Students will score at least 80% on Lesson 29 Test. Students, with minimal errors, will write an introduction that is inspiring and informative.

SUGGESTED
Weekly *Implementation*

DAY 1	DAY 2	DAY 3	DAY 4	DAY 5
Write a Warm-up Essay.	Write a Warm-up Essay.	Write a Warm-up Essay.	Write a Warm-up Essay.	Write a Warm-up Essay.
Read 35-50 pages/day.	Read 35-50 pages/day.	Read 35-50 pages/day.	Read 35-50 pages/day.	Read 35-50 pages/day.
Find five new vocabulary words.	Find five new vocabulary words.	Find five new vocabulary words.	Find five new vocabulary words.	Find five new vocabulary words.
Reflect on the speech assignment for the week.	Compose a first draft of your speech.	Revise your speech and submit to your evaluator/ parent.	Prepare to present your speech tomorrow.	Present your speech to a live audience.
Start the introduction of your research paper.	Start the introduction of your research paper.	Start the introduction of your research paper.	Start the introduction of your research paper.	Submit your assignments to your evaluator/ parent.
Make a journal entry.	Make a journal entry.	Make a journal entry.	Make a journal entry.	Take Lesson 29 Test
				Make a journal entry.

ENRICHMENT ACTIVITIES/PROJECTS

Analyze the introduction to several book, movies, and television shows. Which ones are effective? Why? Why not?

SPEECH ASSIGNMENT

Write and then present a persuasive speech pro or con on this resolution: Resolved: homeschoolers should be allowed to participate in local school athletic events.

ANSWER: *The following is the famous eulogy by Mark Antony:*

(http://www.classicreader.com/read.php/sid.1/book id.155/sec.10/)

Friends, Romans, countrymen, lend me your ears!
I come to bury Caesar, not to praise him.
The evil that men do lives after them,
The good is oft interred with their bones;
So let it be with Caesar. The noble Brutus
Hath told you Caesar was ambitious;
If it were so, it was a grievous fault,
And grievously hath Caesar answer'd it.
Here, under leave of Brutus and the rest-
For Brutus is an honorable man;
So are they all, all honorable men-
Come I to speak in Caesar's funeral.
He was my friend, faithful and just to me;
But Brutus says he was ambitious,
And Brutus is an honorable man.
He hath brought many captives home to Rome,
Whose ransoms did the general coffers fill.
Did this in Caesar seem ambitious?
When that the poor have cried, Caesar hath wept;
Ambition should be made of sterner stuff:
Yet Brutus says he was ambitious,
And Brutus is an honorable man.
You all did see that on the Lupercal
I thrice presented him a kingly crown,
Which he did thrice refuse. Was this ambition?
Yet Brutus says he was ambitious,
And sure he is an honorable man.
I speak not to disprove what Brutus spoke,
But here I am to speak what I do know.
You all did love him once, not without cause;
What cause withholds you then to mourn for him?
O judgment, thou art fled to brutish beasts,
And men have lost their reason. Bear with me;
My heart is in the coffin there with Caesar,
And I must pause till it come back to me.

(Act III, Scene ii)

WRITING ASSIGNMENTS

1. Write the introduction to your research paper.

ANSWER: *The following is an effective introduction to a sermon entitled "Grieving for Lost Opportunities" based on 1 Samuel 1:17-27:*

Today we hear another cry of pain. David's cry of pain. And we grieve with David. The lesson from 2 Samuel is a scream of pain, and David will not be quieted, he will not be comforted, and he will not be ignored.

A messenger has come to David with the news that King Saul and Jonathan, who is Saul's son and David's best friend have been killed fighting the Philistines on Mount Gilboa. The messenger clearly believes that he is bringing good news to David. For years Saul has been a threat to David. Now, with the deaths of Saul the King and Jonathan, the heir to the throne, the obstacles that prevented David from becoming king have been cleared. David is now free to be who he is meant to be. It is time for rejoicing . . . but David does not rejoice. From somewhere deep within him, something boils up inside him. David aches with loss.

Your glory, O Israel, lies
slain upon your high places!
How the mighty have fallen!
Tell it not in Gath, proclaim it not
in the streets of
Ashkelon; or the daughters of the
Philistines will rejoice.

Among yourselves, and in our community, weep as you remember all that has been and that will be no more. (James P. Stobaugh)

2. Read 150 to 200 pages this week and create vocabulary cards.

3. Complete the speech assignment and have a teacher complete a speech evaluation of your speech (Appendix).

4. While preparing the warm-ups, pay particular attention to your writing style this week.

5. Meditate on 2 Kings 2, the story of Elijah and Elisha.

6. Write a warm-up essay every day. Over the next few weeks, you will gradually be developing a "practice" paper on each topic. Add to the same topic each week as you build the paper. For instance: On Day 1, Lesson 28, you will compare a research paper with a cold shower. On Day 1, Lesson 29, you will continue writing on the same topic but will add more information. On Day 1, Lesson 30, you will add even more information to the same topic. On Day 1, Lesson 31, you will add even more information to the same topic. On Day 1, Lesson 32, you continue adding information to the growing paper. On Day 1, Lesson 33, conclude the paper. You have now completed five "practice" papers on five topics

Research Paper Benchmark

Student should have his/her topic, thesis statement, preliminary bibliography, a preliminary outline to guide student in his/her note-taking, many notes, and an outline. During this lesson, student will begin the introduction to his/her research paper.

Warm-up Essays:

	DAY 1	DAY 2	DAY 3	DAY 4	DAY 5
Comparison/ Contrast	Compare a research paper with a cold shower.	Compare a research paper with your favorite CD.	Compare a foot-note and an end-note. Which do you prefer? Why?	Compare a ques-tion mark with a colon.	Compare active voice with pas-sive voice writ-ing.

LESSON 29 TEST

INTRODUCTION (100 POINTS)

Create an introduction to the following essay entitled "Uninvited Guests."

We go to football games with lots of people; we take communion only with other believers. During communion there should be a level of intensity present that far surpasses the ambiance of an ordinary social gathering.

This intensity arises out of a mutual openness to one another, a mutual submission to one another. We reveal ourselves to one another; we share perhaps the deepest form of revelation available to humankind. Luke gives testimony to the power of the fellowship meal in his account of the journey to Emmaus (Luke 24:13-25). The risen Jesus meets two of his disciples on the road, and they discuss what had happened over the last few days. They did not recognize Him, even though they had walked with him almost three years. Now keep in mind that they did not know who He was—even after He had revealed Scripture to them. No, their eyes were still closed even after the Word had been shared. Only at table, at the Lord's table, so to speak, did they recognize Him. Luke is speaking, surely, to the human fact that sharing a meal, especially the Communion meal, is itself revelatory; but even more decisively, it becomes our means of disclosure, of sharing ourselves with one another in a safe environment.

This self-disclosure element of the Communion meal, this *agape* love, this ability to be vulnerable, is vitally necessary to normal, healthy Christian growth. Its absence insures unhealthiness. This partially explains why Paul found the Corinthian practices so objectionable.

The sacrament of the Lord's Supper at Corinth was associated with a common meal which could be attended by all the members of the Christian community. This sacred rite, the Eucharist, thanksgiving meal, a forerunner of our communion meal, took place at the end of the agape feast. The love feast, agape meal, is similar to our once-a-month Fellowship lunch.

Everyone shared on a basis of equal fellowship in the food that was provided. Unfortunately, the mood and temper of elitism had invaded this gathering. The art of sharing had been lost. The delicate balance of trust had been broken. The fragile air of openness had disappeared. The rich had stopped sharing their food, but they ate it in little exclusive groups by themselves, hurrying through it in case they had to share, while the poor had almost nothing. Instead of being a sacred ritual, the so-called Lord's Supper had become a microcosm of the problems, prejudices, and preoccupations of the world—not of the Body of Christ.

Furthermore, other divisions arose. Differences of opinions—theological or otherwise—had created divisions that were undermining the whole basis of fellowship in this Christian community. The Corinthians had forgotten a most important Christian truth: our fellowship and community is based upon a mutual commitment to, and a mutual love for, Jesus Christ. We will never agree one hundred percent with anyone, but that is not important in this context. What is important is that we can sublimate our petty differences and instead love each other for what we are, not for what we do or don't do, for what we believe or don't believe.

A woman discovers her husband is unfaithful. Where can she find help where she's secure with her secret?

Someone has a problem with gossiping. Is there anyone who can in love hold this person accountable?

Your daughter is pregnant, and she's run away—for the third time. She's no longer listening to you. Who can you talk to?

You lost your job, and it was your fault. You blew it, so there's shame mixed with unemployment. How do you react?

The Corinthian Church, today's church, has become a severe, condemning, judgmental, guilt-giving people, and we claim it's in the name of Jesus Christ. The Corinthian Church, and perhaps some of us, had begun to partake of the elements with no forgiveness in their hearts, with a judgmental attitude and no repentance. We have perverted the deep purposes of this most sacred of Christian celebrations. (James P. Stobaugh)

LESSON 29 TEST ANSWER

INTRODUCTION (100 POINTS)

Create an introduction to the essay entitled "Uninvited Guests."

ANSWER SAMPLE: *Eating and drinking are the simplest requisites for survival. No needs are simpler. Indeed, in most cultures, clothes and shelter are sheer luxuries compared to the need for food and drink; starvation is after all the cruelest form of death.*

Nevertheless, eating and drinking are not simply biological occurrences. They are human occasions. We are tacitly committed to rules and regulations that govern our behavior. Everyone knows that one does not eat with elbows resting on the table—although one may wink if an occasional naughty appendage is surreptitiously placed on the edge. Knives are placed to the right of the plate and, once used, they should be placed on the right upper edge of the plate on a 45 degree angle (so as not to soil the host/hostess's table cloth). These simple, at times picayune, rules govern our social lives. We judge each other's worth and conduct the shank of our social interaction according to these spoken and unspoken customs.

At its most basic level the Lord's Supper is a meal, pure and simple. As in other meals and social gatherings, there are certain rules that we observe. The violation of these rules is exactly what Paul is discussing in this scripture reading. Just as we feel violated and disgusted if a friend violates our choice of table ethics—eg., sneezing all over our dinner—likewise Paul is offended by the Corinthian disregard for the rules surrounding this most sacred event: the Lord's Supper.

LESSON 30

Goals/Objectives: What is the purpose of this lesson?	Strategies to meet these goals: How will I obtain these goals/objectives?	Evaluation: How will I know when I have met these goals/objectives?
Concept: Impromptu Speech (cognitive goal)	The parent/educator will engage students in discussions about ways to write and present speeches. In front of an audience, students will present a impromptu speech on the assigned topic.	Students will be able to write and to present an inspired speech. Suggested evaluation sheet includes: Oratory Evaluation I. Poise: How does the student present himself/herself? Is the oratory/dramatic reading memorized? (25 points) II. Articulation: Does the student speak clearly, and slowly? (25 points) III. Presentation: What is the overall effect of the speech? Does it accomplish its purpose? (50 points)
Concept: improved writing skills. (cognitive goal)	Students will write five warm-up essays/week.	With minimal errors students will write these essays in 15-20 minutes.
Concept: increased vocabulary. (cognitive goal)	Students will collect at least five new vocabulary words and use these words in their warm-up essays.	Students will use five vocabulary words in conversation during the week, as well as use the words in their essays.
Concept: reflective writing. (affective/spiritual goal)	Using the Journal Guide Questions in the Appendices, students will record at least three entries this week. Suggested Scripture: 2 Kings 2:23.	Students will show evidence that they have reflected on this issue including informed discussions and written responses.

Goals/Objectives: What is the purpose of this lesson?	Strategies to meet these goals: How will I obtain these goals/objectives?	Evaluation: How will I know when I have met these goals/objectives?
Concept: increased knowledge of the assigned essay. (cognitive goal)	Students will take Lesson 30 Test.	Students will score at least 80% on Lesson 30 Test.
Concept: effective introduction. (cognitive goal)	Students will finish the introduction to their research paper.	Students, with minimal errors, will clearly write an effective introduction.

SUGGESTED
Weekly *Implementation*

DAY 1	DAY 2	DAY 3	DAY 4	DAY 5
Write a Warm-up Essay.	Write a Warm-up Essay.	Write a Warm-up Essay.	Write a Warm-up Essay.	Write a Warm-up Essay.
Read 35-50 pages/day.	Read 35-50 pages/day.	Read 35-50 pages/day.	Read 35-50 pages/day.	Read 35-50 pages/day.
Find five new vocabulary words.	Find five new vocabulary words.	Find five new vocabulary words.	Find five new vocabulary words.	Find five new vocabulary words.
Reflect on the speech assignment for the week.	Compose a first draft of your speech.	Revise your speech and submit to your evaluator/ parent.	Prepare to present your speech tomorrow.	Present your speech to a live audience.
Finish the introduction of your research paper.	Finish the introduction of your research paper.	Finish the introduction of your research paper.	Finish the introduction of your research paper.	Submit your assignments to your evaluator/ parent.
Make a journal entry.	Make a journal entry.	Make a journal entry.	Make a journal entry.	Take Lesson 30 Test
				Make a journal entry.

ENRICHMENT ACTIVITIES/PROJECTS

Students will identify the introduction in several newspaper articles.

SPEECH ASSIGNMENT

Deliver a 2-3 minute impromptu speech on the following topic: In a three-point argumentative speech, persuade a friend of yours that he/she should not date but should practice courtship.

ANSWER: *Reasons for courtship: biblical reasons, socio-economic reasons, maturity reasons.*

WRITING ASSIGNMENTS

1. Finish your introduction.

ANSWER SAMPLE: *The following is an introduction to a sermon entitled "The Way of Peace They do not Know" based on Isaiah 59:1-8. It begins with a quote—along with a rhetorical question. This method is one of the best ways to begin an essay/speech/novel.*

After the seas are all cross'd, (as they seem already cross'd)

After the great captains and engineers have accomplish'd their work,

After the noble inventors, after the scientists, the chemist, the geologist, the ethnologist,

Finally comes the poet worthy of that name,

The true son of God shall come singing his songs.

—Walt Whitman, Leaves of Grass (www.bartleby.com/142/)

Some people claim that Isaiah was the greatest of the Old Testament prophets. His career spanned the turbulent period from King Isaiah's death, about 740 B.C. to the end of Sennaacherib's siege of Jerusalem in 701 B.C. Judah's kings, especially timid and shaky Ahaz, persistently wanted to rely on political deals with foreign powers, usually Assyria or Egypt, to save the country. But Isaiah would not hear of it—"Tremble, you women who are at ease . . . (32:11a)."

Isaiah's ministry began with the famous "call" in chapter 6. Theologian and writer Fred Buechner, taking substantial liberty with Scripture, paraphrases Isaiah's call (chapter 6) this way:

There were banks of candles flickering in the distance and clouds of incense thickening the air with holiness and stinging his eyes, and high above him (Isaiah), as if it had always been there but was only now seen for what it was (like a face in the leaves of a tree or a bear among the stars), there was the Mystery Itself whose gown was the incense and the candles, a dusting of gold at the hem. There were winged creatures shouting back and forth . . . and

Isaiah responding, "O God, I am done for! I am foul of mouth and the member of a foul-mouthed race. . . I am a goner . . ." And God said, "Go give the deaf Hell till you're blue in the face and go show the blind Heaven till you drop in your tracks, because they'd sooner eat ground glass than swallow the bitter pill that puts roses in the cheeks and a gleam in the eye. Go do it." (Peculiar Treasures).

"That is what a prophet does," Buechner ends. "And Isaiah went and did it."

The word given to Isaiah rings true for his generation and for ours.

2. Read 150 to 200 pages this week and create vocabulary cards.

3. Complete the speech assignment and have a teacher complete a speech evaluation of your speech (Appendix).

4. While preparing the warm-ups, pay particular attention to your writing style this week.

5. Meditate on 2 Kings 2:23-25. What are the consequences for a person who mocks God's authority?

6. Write a warm-up essay every day. Over the next few weeks, you will gradually be developing a "practice" paper on each topic. Add to the same topic each week as you build the paper. For instance: On Day 1, Lesson 28, you will compare a research paper with a cold shower. On Day 1, Lesson 29, you will continue writing on the same topic but will add more information. On Day 1, Lesson 30, you will add even more information to the same topic. On Day 1, Lesson 31, you will add even more information to the same topic. On Day 1, Lesson 32, you continue adding information to the growing paper. On Day 1, Lesson 33, conclude the paper. You have now completed five "practice" papers on five topics.

WARM-UP ESSAYS:

	DAY 1	DAY 2	DAY 3	DAY 4	DAY 5
Comparison/ Contrast	Compare a research paper with a cold shower.	Compare a research paper with your favorite CD.	Compare a foot-note and an end-note. Which do you prefer? Why?	Compare a ques-tion mark with a colon.	Compare active voice with pas-sive voice writ-ing.

RESEARCH PAPER BENCHMARK

Student should have his/her topic, thesis statement, preliminary bibliography, a preliminary outline to guide student in his/her note-taking, many notes, and an out-line. During this lesson student will finish the introduction to his/her research paper.

LESSON 30 TEST

INTRODUCTION (100 POINTS)

Write an appropriate introduction to this essay:

The Gilgamesh text says, "Once upon a time the gods destroyed the city of Shuruppah in a great flood." (www.ancienttexts.org) At about the same time, Moses was writing the book of Genesis, in which he likewise described a flood. These two similar testimonies were written by different people at different places on the globe. Even if a person did not believe that the Bible is inspired, this is powerful evidence that the flood was a historical event.

Even the stories are similar. The protagonists in the two flood stories were given grace by their God, or gods, to make it through the flood alive. In the Gilgamesh text it was the god Ea that forewarned Utnapishtim about the flood. Likewise Utnapishtim, the man in the Gilgamesh flood, built a great boat. In the Bible, Noah did the same thing and was also fore-warned by God about the flood. Both men were told to bring animals on the ship. Could Utnapishtim be the Babylonian name for Noah? With their embellished stories, are the Babylonians telling the same story from their perspective? (Timothy Stobaugh)

LESSON 30 TEST ANSWER

INTRODUCTION (100 POINTS)

Write and appropriate introduction to this essay:

ANSWER: *What if there is independent testimony of an event by someone completely unconnected to a particular event? Would that provide credence to the event? Certainly, separate accounts of the same event would afford further investigation. The Gilgamesh Epic is an independent testimony completely unconnected to the event of Noah's Flood.*

LESSON 31

Writing Skill: Research Paper: Body (A)
Style (Writing and Speaking): Avoid Sexist Language
Public Speaking Skill: Didactic Speech
Looking Ahead: Body (B)

Goals/Objectives: What is the purpose of this lesson?	Strategies to meet these goals: How will I obtain these goals/objectives?	Evaluation: How will I know when I have met these goals/ objectives?
Concept: didactic speech. (cognitive goal)	The parent/educator will engage students in discussions about ways to write and present speeches. In front of an audience, students will present a didactic speech.	Students will be able to write and to present an inspired speech. Suggested evaluation sheet includes: Oratory Evaluation I. Poise: How does the student present himself/herself? Is the oratory/dramatic reading memorized? (25 points) II. Articulation: Does the student speak clearly, and slowly? (25 points) III. Presentation: What is the overall effect of the speech? Does it accomplish its purpose? (50 points)
Concept: improved writing skills. (cognitive goal)	Students will write five warm-up essays/week.	With minimal errors students will write these essays in 15-20 minutes.
Concept: increased vocabulary. (cognitive goal)	Students will collect at least five new vocabulary words and use these words in their warm-up essays.	Students will use five vocabulary words in conversation during the week, as well as use the words in their essays.
Concept: reflective writing. (affective/spiritual goal)	Using the Journal Guide Questions in the Appendices, students will record at least three entries this week. Suggested Scripture: 2 Kings 3.	Students will show evidence that they have reflected on this issue including informed discussions and written responses.

Goals/Objectives: What is the purpose of this lesson?	Strategies to meet these goals: How will I obtain these goals/objectives?	Evaluation: How will I know when I have met these goals/objectives?
Concept: increased knowledge of the assigned essay. (cognitive goal)	Students will take Lesson 31 Test.	Students will score at least 80% on Lesson 31 Test.
Concept: first draft of a research paper. (cognitive goal)	Students will begin the first draft of their paper.	Students, with minimal errors, will write the first draft of their research paper.

SUGGESTED
Weekly *Implementation*

DAY 1	DAY 2	DAY 3	DAY 4	DAY 5
Write a Warm-up Essay.	Write a Warm-up Essay.	Write a Warm-up Essay.	Write a Warm-up Essay.	Write a Warm-up Essay
Read 35-50 pages/day.	Read 35-50 pages/day.	Read 35-50 pages/day.	Read 35-50 pages/day.	Read 35-50 pages/day.
Find five new vocabulary words.	Find five new vocabulary words.	Find five new vocabulary words.	Find five new vocabulary words.	Find five new vocabulary words.
Reflect on your speech assignment for the week.	Compose a first draft of your speech.	Revise your speech and submit to your evaluator/ parent.	Prepare to present your speech tomorrow.	Present your speech to a live audience.
Begin the main body of your research paper.	Begin the main body of your research paper.	Begin the main body of your research paper.	Begin the main body of your research paper.	Submit your rough draft to your instructor/ guardian/ parent.
Make a journal entry.	Make a journal entry.	Make a journal entry.	Make a journal entry.	Take Lesson 31 Test
				Make a journal entry.

ENRICHMENT ACTIVITIES/PROJECT

Students should identify the main body of a newspaper article.

SPEECH ASSIGNMENT

Write a 2-3 minute didactic speech highlighting the main points of your research paper. Normally the didactic speech is greatly informed by the outline and thesis statement.

ANSWER: *The didactic speech should follow approximately the outline of the student's research paper.*

WRITING ASSIGNMENTS

1. Write the first-draft body of your research paper.

ANSWER: *Students should write the first draft of their research paper (minus the conclusion) and submit to their evaluator.*

2. Read 200-250 pages this week and create vocabulary cards.

3. Complete the speech assignment and have a teacher complete a speech evaluation of your speech (Appendix).

4. While preparing the warm-ups, pay particular attention to your writing style this week.

5. Meditate on 2 Kings 3 (the Moabite revolt).

6. Write a warm-up essay every day. Over the next few weeks, you will gradually be developing a "practice" paper on each topic. Add to the same topic each week as you build the paper. For instance: On Day 1, Lesson 28, you will compare a research paper with a cold shower. On Day 1, Lesson 29, you will continue writing on the same topic but will add more information. On Day 1, Lesson 30, you will add even more information to the same topic. On Day 1, Lesson 31, you will add even more information to the same topic. On Day 1, Lesson 32, you continue adding information to the growing paper. On Day 1, Lesson 33, conclude the paper. You have now completed five "practice" papers on five topics

RESEARCH PAPER BENCHMARK

Student should have his/her topic, thesis statement, preliminary bibliography, a preliminary outline to guide student in his/her note-taking, many notes, the outline, and the introduction to his/her research paper. During this lesson student will begin the main body of his/her research paper.

WARM-UP ESSAYS:

	DAY 1	DAY 2	DAY 3	DAY 4	DAY 5
Comparison/ Contrast	Compare a research paper with a cold shower.	Compare a research paper with your favorite CD.	Compare a foot-note and an end-note. Which do you prefer? Why?	Compare a question mark with a colon.	Compare active voice with passive voice writing.

LESSON 31 TEST

MAIN BODY (100 POINTS)

Write a main body to this introduction of an essay/sermon entitled "Hope Whispered in Every Ear":

Jesus really died on the cross.

This was not some metaphorical event, some dramatic hoax. No, He really died.

Today, it seems to me, we have as much a problem believing that Jesus died as we do that He arose from the grave. Our ubiquitous media promises us eternal bliss and immortality—just put this cream on and the wrinkles will go away. Take these vitamins, and you will live forever and so on.

It was not always so. Death was something our parents and grandparents had to face with more finality and frequency. The average life span was less than it is now. Medical science was not as successful with saving human life as now. Infant mortality was higher. Since there were fewer hospitals and no nursing homes, sick and dying relatives died at home. It was the custom years ago for the wake to be held in the family's living room. Then family members were buried in a local church cemetery. Every Sunday when our grandparents went to church, they were reminded of the reality of death as they passed the marble grave markers of their loved ones.

And so Jesus Christ was dead, really dead—He did not die quietly in bed with all His friends surrounding Him. No, He died a humiliating, messy, public death. And the world had no doubt of one salient fact on that first Easter morning: Jesus bar Joseph was very, very dead. (James P. Stobaugh)

LESSON 31 TEST ANSWERS

MAIN BODY (100 POINTS)

Write a main body to this introduction of an essay/sermon entitled "Hope Whispered in Every Ear":

ANSWER SAMPLE: *That Jesus was definitely dead explains why the disciples at first did not believe the women rushing from the tomb. In Luke's Gospel, when the women rushed back to the room where the terrified apostles had gathered in fear of being arrested, those who had been to the tomb early that morning gleefully announced that their crucified master had been raised from the dead. The eleven men listened in disbelief to the women.*

In his testimony, the renowned Christian thinker C. S. Lewis says that his conversion to the Christian faith was impeded as much by his lack of imagination as anything. Lewis agreed with Chesterton (another Christian thinker) who argued that in claiming to be the Son of God, Jesus was either a lunatic and a dishonest fraud, or He was speaking the truth. Lewis began to move toward Christ when his imagination was stimulated by the biblical stories—especially the story concerning a God whose dying could transform all those who believed in Him. In this critical phase of Lewis' faith journey, he wrote the famous Narnia Chronicles. He entered the imagination of little children whose playful antics in a wardrobe transported them into the realm of a strange, new reality. It is the child in Lewis—in us all—that most profoundly knows that this tangible world of death and dying and heartbreak is not our only reality.

It is into this world that the early disciples—and you and I—are invited to enter by the Apostle Paul.

Where Paul moves in I Cor. 15 is beyond logic: He moves into faith. "Lo! I tell you a mystery. . ." he says. His assertion of resurrection faith takes us considerably further than human logic. Reason may take us to the tomb and cause us to probe inside. Reason will cause us to accept His death—but only faith will cause us to believe in the resurrection. And faith alone will mend a broken heart, will save a lost soul.

Paul's understanding of the resurrection in 1 Cor. 15 defied prevailing ideas about the afterlife. To the Greek mind, death released a person's spirit form the prison of the body. The last thing, then, a Greek would want was to be reunited with a corruptible body. So, these questions were more than academic for Paul's audience—they really wanted to know what Paul meant when he said "we are crucified with Christ" (Gals. 2:20). They really were concerned about the afterlife. Are we?

The Easter story will not be proven empirically. Our reason will take us to Saturday evening, but only our faith will take us through Sunday. This Easter story seems like fiction: the American fiction writer, Kurt Vonnegut, Jr. argues that the truth can sometimes be so utterly fantastic that it seems like fiction. I would argue that the resurrection of Jesus Christ is so wonderful that its reality completely changes our world.

Easter faith invites the most significant leap of trust that one will ever make. There is a yearning deep inside us to do so.

Well, Easter morning reminds us that eternal life comes with knowing Jesus Christ as Lord and Savior.

We have pursued immortality with courage and fortitude. We have sought to preserve ourselves in the land of the living. But none of it really works. Sooner or later we will die. But the Easter hope is a message that leads us home to God our Father.
(James Stobaugh)

LESSON 32

Goals/Objectives: What is the purpose of this lesson?	Strategies to meet these goals: How will I obtain these goals/objectives?	Evaluation: How will I know when I have met these goals/ objectives?
Concept: summary (cognitive goal)	The parent/educator will engage students in discussions about ways to write and present speeches. Students will carefully present a speech on their research paper subject.	Students will be able to write and to present an inspired speech. Suggested evaluation sheet includes: Oratory Evaluation I. Poise: How does the student present himself/herself? Is the oratory/dramatic reading memorized? (25 points) II. Articulation: Does the student speak clearly, and slowly? (25 points) III. Presentation: What is the overall effect of the speech? Does it accomplish its purpose? (50 points)
Concept: improved writing skills. (cognitive goal)	Students will write five warm-up essays/week.	With minimal errors students will write these essays in 15-20 minutes.
Concept: increased vocabulary. (cognitive goal)	Students will collect at least five new vocabulary words and use these words in their warm-up essays.	Students will use five vocabulary words in conversation during the week, as well as use the words in their essays.

Goals/Objectives: What is the purpose of this lesson?	Strategies to meet these goals: How will I obtain these goals/objectives?	Evaluation: How will I know when I have met these goals/ objectives?
Concept: reflective writing. (affective/spiritual goal)	Using the Journal Guide Questions in the Appendices, students will record at least three entries this week. Suggested Scripture: 2 Kings 4.	Students will show evidence that they have reflected on this issue including informed discussions and written responses.
Concept: increased knowledge of the assigned essay. (cognitive goal)	Students will take Lesson 32 Test.	Students will score at least 80% on Lesson 32 Test.
Concept: illustration essay. (cognitive goal)	Students will continue to work the first draft of their paper.	Students, with minimal errors, will work on the first draft of their paper.

SUGGESTED
Weekly *Implementation*

DAY 1	DAY 2	DAY 3	DAY 4	DAY 5
Write a Warm-up Essay.	Write a Warm-up Essay.	Write a Warm-up Essay.	Write a Warm-up Essay.	Write a Warm-up Essay.
Read 35-50 pages/day.	Read 35-50 pages/day.	Read 35-50 pages/day.	Read 35-50 pages/day.	Read 35-50 pages/day.
Find five new vocabulary words.	Find five new vocabulary words.	Find five new vocabulary words.	Find five new vocabulary words.	Find five new vocabulary words.
Reflect on your speech assignment for the week.	Compose a first draft of your speech.	Revise your speech and submit to your evaluator/ parent.	Prepare to present your speech tomorrow.	Present your speech to a live audience.
Finish the main body of your research paper.	Finish the main body of your research paper.	Finish the main body of your research paper.	Finish the main body of your research paper.	Submit your rough draft to your instructor/ guardian/ parent.
Make a journal entry.	Make a journal entry.	Make a journal entry.	Make a journal entry.	Take Lesson 32 Test
				Make a journal entry.

Enrichment Activities/Project

Students will critique a paper written by a sibling or other student.

Speech Assignment

Present a 2-3 minute speech on your research paper topic. Memorize the introduction and give particular attention to your main body.

ANSWER: *Answers will vary.*

Writing Assignments

1. Write the first draft body of your research paper.

ANSWER: See the example above.

2. Read 200-250 pages this week and create vocabulary cards.

3. Complete the speech assignment and have a teacher complete a speech evaluation (Appendix).

4. While preparing the warm-ups, pay particular attention to your writing style this week.

5. Meditate on 2 Kings 4 (the Shunammite's son).

6. Write a warm-up essay every day. Over the past few weeks, you have been gradually developing a "practice" paper on each topic. Add to the same topic each week as you build the paper. For instance: On Day 1, Lesson 28, you compared a research paper with a cold shower. On Day 1, Lesson 29, you continued writing on the same topic but added more information. On Day 1, Lesson 30, you added even more information to the same topic. On Day 1, Lesson 31, you added even more information to the same topic. On Day 1, Lesson 32, you continue adding information to the growing paper. On Day 1, Lesson 33, conclude the paper. You have now completed five "practice" papers on five topics

Research Paper Benchmark

Students should have their topic, thesis statement, preliminary bibliography, a preliminary outline to guide students in their note-taking, many notes, the outline, the introduction, and students have begun the main body of their research paper. During this lesson students will finish the main body to their research paper.

Warm-up Essays:

	DAY 1	DAY 2	DAY 3	DAY 4	DAY 5
Comparison/ Contrast	Compare a research paper with a cold shower.	Compare a research paper with your favorite CD.	Compare a footnote and an endnote. Which do you prefer? Why?	Compare a question mark with a colon.	Compare active voice with passive voice writing.

LESSON 32 TEST

MAIN BODY (100 POINTS)

Write a main body to this introduction of an essay/sermon entitled "We Were Hoping that He was the Man."

""Moreover, some women from our group astounded us. They arrived early at the tomb, and when they didn't find His body, they came and reported that they had seen a vision of angels who said He was alive."
—Luke 24:22-23

This extraordinary rendition of a conversation by Luke is a marvelous insight into the confusion that occurred on that first Easter afternoon.

How does the church in our day, and in Luke's day, encounter and know the risen Christ? Or, more pointedly, why do we not know Him? Why are we right in our assessments of our life situations, but terribly wrong in our conclusions? How can we be right and blind at the same time?

"Are You the only visitor in Jerusalem who doesn't know the things that happened there in these days?" Cleopas and an unidentified disciple sarcastically ask this stranger. However, in spite of this stranger's obvious sheltered life, or stupidity, the disciples were desperate to tell someone—anyone—about their plight. "Jesus is dead!" They cried. "But we were hoping that He was the One who was about to redeem Israel."

Cleopas and his friend were on a trip to Emmaus. They just had to get away from Jerusalem. From those crazy women and their sensationalistic rumors. From Peter who denied the Lord and now confessed a cock and bull story about a resurrection.

No, Jesus was dead. They had seen it with their own eyes. He was dead. Dead as a door nail. Finished. Oh, they had once hoped. In the exciting days when He was performing miracle after miracle. But that all ended on the previous Friday. No, Jesus was dead. And, while they did not believe two crazy women, a fair weather friend [Peter], and a young disciple prone to exaggeration [John], they certainly understood the pain they felt in their hearts. They certainly believed in many things. They believed the picture of Christ's hands bleeding profusely upon the garbage lying on Golgotha hill. They believed in the sounds of Him gasping for breath as He painfully pushed up on his pain ridden feet, trying to survive in the hell that was a crucifixion. Oh, yes, they knew what to believe. They knew that they were in trouble—no doubt Caiaphas and his henchmen would be rounding up all the disciples of Christ they could find.

T. S. Eliot writes in his poem "The Hollow Men": "Between the idea/And the reality/Between the motion/And the act/Falls the shadow." http://www.cs.umbc.edu/~evans/hollow.html

Cleophas and his friend (whom some scholars think may have been Cleophas' wife) had run into the shadow. Theology and ideas and abstractions belong to others. They had no dreams left—only a Roman Empire and a Jewish state that wanted their blood.

For small griefs you shout, but for big griefs you whisper or say nothing. The big griefs must be borne alone, inside. Or so these two travelers thought, anyway. They resented the stranger's ignorance, but, like a survivor of a terrible accident or ordeal, they were grateful for the chance to tell him their story.

But the stranger was unflappable. He compounded their bewilderment by brilliantly expounding Scripture to them. Nothing impresses a religious person more than a thorough knowledge of his corpus. Furthermore, and this was quite disconcerting; this stranger was speaking as if he were present in the aforementioned events. He presumed to know their motivations and their minds! Did he dare suggest that they misunderstood the mission of their Lord!

Nevertheless, this stranger intrigued them enough that they invited him to supper. Mellowed somewhat, they asked the stranger to give the blessing. In a Galilean accent, he recited the Hallel. Suddenly, in the candle light, they saw that the stranger had nail-scarred hands, a thorn scarred brow: He is the Christ!

The meal was not finished before they ran seven miles back to Jerusalem. Bursting in to the disciples, they excitedly proclaimed what everyone else already knew: He is indeed risen!

What amazes me about this story is not that Christ ate with them, nor that they recognized him at this point. What truly bothers me is why they did not recognize Him from the beginning. We are given no indication in the text that the stranger did not look like Jesus. In fact, the implication is that the stranger looked like Jesus from the very beginning—after all he should—He was Jesus! Why did they not recognize Him? How often do we miss Jesus' presence in our lives?

On the road to Emmaus, we may be right and blind at the same time.

LESSON 32 TEST ANSWER

MAIN BODY (100 POINTS)

Write a main body to this introduction of an essay/sermon entitled "We Were Hoping that He was the Man."

ANSWER SAMPLE:

Doubt can lead us down a road of confusion and blindness. True, the Emmaus travelers were heavy with the bad news of life, but their reaction to that news blinded them to their salvation which walked with them on that road in those same bad times. He was there, and they did not know it.

We only can see what we imagine to be true. And what is happening—admittedly—is very new. A resurrection! Christ, too, did not evolve out of history: He created a new history.

This theme is orchestrated by earlier Jewish writers: notably Jeremiah and Isaiah. In Isaiah 42, for instance, we see the nation of Israel being liberated from bondage in Babylon. After two hundred years of slavery, the remnant nation is going home. Going home! And God has some very exciting news for this beleaguered people: "I have called you by name and you are my own./When you pass through deep waters, I am with you,/when you pass through rivers,/they will not sweep you away . . ." God is bringing His people home. He will sweep clean the record. The sins of their fathers and mothers are forgiven. The captivity is over. They are free. And, not only will the future be different, but so will the past. He has rewritten their history. What was meant for bad for them now has become good . . .

That is the incredibly good news—the Jesus—that the Emmaus travelers could not see. Their despairing doubt had blinded them to the truth.

Doubt, by the way, is not all bad. Their doubt was debilitating: it was doubt based on angry disappointment. Time and time again, they had been hurt, so much, in fact, that they could not imagine that life as they knew it was now ending.

I am truly shocked at how much despair there is in America.

At the end of World War II, many of the victims of Nazi atrocities—concentration inmates for instance—would not leave the camps. In spite of horrible conditions, and terrible memories, the victims preferred the familiarity of bondage rather than being free. The same is true in Numbers 11. Israel rebelled against Moses because they missed "onions and spices of Egypt." Again, they preferred the familiarity of bondage to the uncertainty of freedom. The good news of the Resurrection and of Isaiah (42) is that we can be healed by our remembrances.

Thus, these Emmaus road travelers have a real crisis on their hands: the one whom they loved and by whom they were loved has deeply disappointed them. Thus, as we see above, they do not see Him even when He is right before their eyes.

In effect, their theology has failed them. Based on their own sacred journeys, based on their experiences, they drew conclusions from Scripture. They found a way to justify a belief in a dead Savior, and incredibly they were not able to see the live one right in front of them.

What sort of theologies do we have? Are we walking around with our own maudlin theories of God based on years and years of disappointments? The theology of the Emmaus travelers was divorced from the Word (of their Lord) because their experience demanded the self-same response. Their high views of Scripture ended on Friday afternoon. From that point on they made things up as they went along.

How many of us found truth in Sunday school as a child and now reject it? Was life so hard on us that we simply gave up believing?

I met such a man during college days. Although he was a brilliant man, one of the greatest American Church Historians alive today, he had no faith. He had Bible knowledge but no faith. He stopped believing in God's Word when his retarded younger brother was born to his parents. As he watched his brother struggle and finally die when he was five, this professor—in spite of his great knowledge of the Bible—had no Scripture. Bible as the Word of God ceased to exist the day they put his brother in that cold grave.

In spite of Jesus' skillful explanation of Scripture, they still did not recognize Him. True, their hearts were on fire Luke says, but exegesis—no matter how inspired—will not remove our doubt, will not lead us into correct relationship with God. They did not recognize Christ until they had a meal with Him—were reacquainted with Him on a personal basis.

LESSON 33

Goals/Objectives: What is the purpose of this lesson?	Strategies to meet these goals: How will I obtain these goals/objectives?	Evaluation: How will I know when I have met these goals/ objectives?
Concept: enunciation of words in a speech. (cognitive goal)	The parent/educator will engage students in discussions about ways to write and present speeches. In front of an audience, students will present a speech that requires enunciation of every word.	Students will be able to write and to present an inspired speech. Suggested evaluation sheet includes: Oratory Evaluation I. Poise: How does the student present himself/herself? Is the oratory/dramatic reading memorized? (25 points) II. Articulation: Does the student speak clearly, and slowly? (25 points) III. Presentation: What is the overall effect of the speech? Does it accomplish its purpose? (50 points)
Concept: improved writing skills. (cognitive goal)	Students will write five warm-up essays/week.	With minimal errors students will write these essays in 15-20 minutes.
Concept: increased vocabulary. (cognitive goal)	Students will collect at least five new vocabulary words and use these words in their warm-up essays.	Students will use five vocabulary words in conversation during the week, as well as use the words in their essays.
Concept: reflective writing. (affective/spiritual goal)	Using the Journal Guide Questions in the Appendices, students will record at least three entries this week. Suggested Scripture: 2 Kings 5.	Students will show evidence that they have reflected on this issue including informed discussions and written responses.

Goals/Objectives: What is the purpose of this lesson?	Strategies to meet these goals: How will I obtain these goals/objectives?	Evaluation: How will I know when I have met these goals/objectives?
Concept: increased knowledge of the assigned essay. (cognitive goal)	Students will take Lesson 33 Test.	Students will score at least 80% on Lesson 33 Test.
Concept: conclusion. (cognitive goal)	Students will write an effective conclusion and thereby finish the first draft of their research paper.	Students, with minimal errors, will write an effective conclusion to their research paper.

SUGGESTED

Weekly *Implementation*

DAY 1	DAY 2	DAY 3	DAY 4	DAY 5
Write a Warm-up Essay.	Write a Warm-up Essay.	Write a Warm-up Essay.	Write a Warm-up Essay.	Write a Warm-up Essay.
Read 35-50 pages/day.	Read 35-50 pages/day.	Read 35-50 pages/day.	Read 35-50 pages/day.	Read 35-50 pages/day.
Find five new vocabulary words.	Find five new vocabulary words.	Find five new vocabulary words.	Find five new vocabulary words.	Find five new vocabulary words.
Reflect on your speech assignment for the week.	Compose a first draft of your speech.	Revise your speech and submit to your evaluator/ parent.	Prepare to present your speech tomorrow.	Present your speech to a live audience.
Finish the conclusion of your research paper.	Finish the conclusion of your research paper.	Finish the conclusion of your research paper.	Finish the conclusion of your research paper.	Submit your rough draft to your instructor/ guardian/ parent.
Make a journal entry.	Make a journal entry.	Make a journal entry.	Make a journal entry.	Take Lesson 33 Test
				Make a journal entry.

ENRICHMENT ACTIVITIES/PROJECT

Students will evaluate the conclusion of their pastor's sermons. Are they effective conclusions?

SPEECH ASSIGNMENT

Compose a speech with the following words: *tongue, fang, harangue, prong, anger, hunger, bungle,* and *jungle.* Then present it to an audience.

ANSWER: *Answers will vary.*

WRITING ASSIGNMENTS

1. Finish your paper with an inspiring conclusion. You are now ready to correct your paper, wait a few days, and then rewrite the paper.

ANSWER SAMPLE: *The following is the conclusion of a sermon entitled "The Deep Share" based on John 14:*

Where, then, when we feel abandoned, is the courage we need to go on? Simply put, we learn in John 14 that it is not what we know but who we know that counts. Faith is trust, not exact knowledge. Thomas wants to know more—so do we. Philip wants to know more, too, and feels abandoned when he realizes Christ will be leaving them. But Christ is leaving the Holy Spirit with them to comfort them—small comfort until they meet Him (i.e., the Holy Spirit) at Pentecost. But for now Christ is asking for a personal response—not a theological one. And, so, today, we are asked for the same. If we want to have a life that grows out of a deep share, then we need to have faith in Him, and in Him alone.

"Show us the father," Philip blurts out; "Why doesn't God say something, do something?" another asks. Jesus' answer is that in His life, as God's only Son, God has shown something and done something. This good news needs telling and retelling. That is where we come in; however, the task is not ours alone, and that is where the Holy Spirit comes in.

And, yet, the "Holy Spirit" is an unknown quantity. The Jewish mind had a very rudimentary concept of the Holy Spirit. Christ's promise, therefore, that He—the Spirit—is coming is

an invitation of faith. An invitation, again, to relate to God as a being rather than as information.

The invitation to you, and to me, is a deep share, an invitation to trust in God without anything but a profound and abiding belief in God's love . . . (James P. Stobaugh)

2. Read 200-250 pages this week and create vocabulary cards.

3. Complete the speech assignment and have a teacher complete a speech evaluation of your speech (Appendix).

4. While preparing the warm-ups, pay particular attention to your writing style this week.

5. Meditate on 2 Kings 5: Naaman is healed of leprosy.

6. Write a warm-up essay every day. Over the past few weeks, you gradually developed a "practice" paper on each topic, adding to the same topic each week as you built the paper. For instance: On Day 1, Lesson 28, you compared a research paper with a cold shower. On Day 1, Lesson 29, you continued writing on the same topic but added more information. On Day 1, Lesson 30, you added even more information to the same topic. On Day 1, Lesson 31, you added even more information to the same topic. On Day 1, Lesson 32, you continued adding information to the growing paper. On Day 1, Lesson 33, conclude the paper. You have now completed five "practice" papers on five topics.

RESEARCH PAPER BENCHMARK

Student should have his/her topic, thesis statement, preliminary bibliography, a preliminary outline to guide student in his/her note-taking, many notes, the outline, the introduction, and now student has even finished the main body of his/her research paper. During this lesson student will write a conclusion to his/her research paper.

WARM-UP ESSAYS:

	DAY 1	DAY 2	DAY 3	DAY 4	DAY 5
Comparison/ Contrast	Compare a research paper with a cold shower.	Compare a research paper with your favorite CD.	Compare a foot-note and an end-note. Which do you prefer? Why?	Compare a ques-tion mark with a colon.	Compare active voice with pas-sive voice writ-ing.

LESSON 33 TEST

CONCLUSION (100 POINTS)

Write a conclusion to this essay/sermon entitled "Uninvited Guests":

Eating and drinking are the simplest requisites for survival. No needs are simpler. Indeed, in most cultures, clothes and shelter are sheer luxuries compared to the need for food and drink; after all, starvation is one of the cruelest form of death.

Nevertheless, eating and drinking are not simply biological occurrences. They are human occasions. We are tacitly committed to rules and regulations that govern our behavior. Everyone knows that one does not eat with elbows resting on the table although one may wink if an occasional naughty appendage is surreptitiously placed on the edge. Knives are placed to the right of the plate and, once used, they should be placed on the right upper edge of the plate on a 45 degree angle (so as not to soil the host/hostess's table cloth). These simple, at times picayune rules govern our social lives. We judge the worth of each other and conduct the shank of our social interaction according to these spoken and unspoken customs.

The Lord's Supper at its most basic level is a meal, pure and simple. As in other meals and social gatherings, there are certain rules that we observe. The violation of these rules is exactly what Paul is discussing in this scripture reading. Just as we feel violated and disgusted if a friend violates our choice of table ethics—e.g., sneezing all over our dinner, Paul is offended by the Corinthian disregard for the rules surrounding this most sacred event: the Lord's Supper.

LESSON 33 TEST ANSWER

CONCLUSION (100 POINTS)

Write a conclusion to this essay/sermon entitled "Uninvited Guests":

ANSWER SAMPLE:

We must forgive one another. Communion is a celebration of that act—a celebration of the reconciling presence of Jesus Christ. The sort of forgiveness that the communion event demands is not easy though.

Professor G. Johnstone Ross tells of an incident that occurred years ago during the celebration of the Lord's Supper in a little mission church in New Zealand. A line of worshippers had just knelt at the altar rail when suddenly from among them a young native arose and returned to his pew. Some minutes later, however, he returned to his place at the rail. Afterward, a friend inquired why he had done this, and he replied:

When I went forward and knelt, I found myself side by side with a man who some years ago had slain my father and whom I had vowed to kill. I felt I could not partake with him, so I returned to my pew. But as I sat there, my mind went back to a picture of the Upper Room, with its table set, and I heard a voice saying, "By this shall all persons know that you are my disciples, if you have loved one to another." And then I saw a Cross with a man nailed upon it and the same voice saying, "Father, forgive them for they know not what they do." It was then I arose and returned to the altar rail. (Macleod, <u>Presbyterian Worship</u>)

There is nothing magical about the Lord's Supper. Behind magic is the belief that if a certain act is correctly performed, it will produce certain consequences automatically (Macleod, p. 61). It is an operation in which human technique is everything and belief in a divine will is nonexistence. The Lord's Supper was instituted with the painful suffering of our Lord. Neither is

it intellectualism. It is not an academic endeavor open only to the elite, to the favored, to the healthy. It is not a memorial service for a dead Savior. It is done in remembrance of our risen Lord. As Calvin said, the Lord's Supper is a "Spiritual communion with the Risen Lord." Here, as nowhere else, God gives himself to us through Christ. It is the supreme act of Grace. We respond by giving ourselves to one another, by surrendering in trust to one another.

There are a few uncomfortable footnotes, though, that must be mentioned. Every Christian is welcome to the table, <u>but</u> Paul warns "anyone who eats and drinks without discerning the body, eats and drinks judgment upon himself."

If you are out of fellowship with your brother or sister; if you cannot love every saint in this body, then you come to this table uninvited.

If you have wronged your neighbor, if you have harmed your brother or sister and you have not asked his/her forgiveness, you come to this table uninvited.

If you have sinned and you have not confessed this sin before Almighty God and received His forgiveness, you come to this table uninvited.

And most important, if you do not have Jesus Christ as your personal Lord and Savior—it does not matter whether you are Methodist, Baptist, or Evangelical Free—if you have not committed your whole being to Christ, then, you come to this table uninvited, and you bring judgment on us all.

The Lord's Supper is a time of thanksgiving and celebration, but it is also a time of serious reflection. Do not play around with God. Communion is a divine encounter with the Almighty, not a mindless chance encounter with an unknown deity. God means business in the communion meal. It is easy enough to hide behind our hallelujahs and Amens (even though they are necessary), but in the Lord's Supper, God flushes us out of our secret hiding places and demands that we be serious. Be an invited guest at this table.

LESSON 34

Writing Skill: Research Paper: Rewriting and Submission
Style (Writing and Speaking): Summary
Public Speaking Skill: Summary
Looking Ahead: Research Paper is due

Goals/Objectives: What is the purpose of this lesson?	Strategies to meet these goals: How will I obtain these goals/objectives?	Evaluation: How will I know when I have met these goals/objectives?
Concept: enunciation of words in speech (cognitive goal)	The parent/educator will engage students in discussions about ways to write and present speeches. In front of an audience, students will enunciate all the words in a speech.	Students will be able to write and to present an inspired speech. Suggested evaluation sheet includes: Oratory Evaluation I. Poise: How does the student present himself/herself? Is the oratory/dramatic reading memorized? (25 points) II. Articulation: Does the student speak clearly, and slowly? (25 points) III. Presentation: What is the overall effect of the speech? Does it accomplish its purpose? (50 points)
Concept: improved writing skills. (cognitive goal)	Students will write five warm-up essays/week.	With minimal errors students will write these essays in 15-20 minutes.
Concept: increased vocabulary. (cognitive goal)	Students will collect at least five new vocabulary words and use these words in their warm-up essays.	Students will use five vocabulary words in conversation during the week, as well as use the words in their essays.
Concept: reflective writing. (affective/spiritual goal)	Using the Journal Guide Questions in the Appendices, students will record at least three entries this week. Suggested Scripture: 2 Kings 6.	Students will show evidence that they have reflected on this issue including informed discussions and written responses.

Goals/Objectives: What is the purpose of this lesson?	Strategies to meet these goals: How will I obtain these goals/objectives?	Evaluation: How will I know when I have met these goals/objectives?
Concept: increased knowledge of the assigned essay. (cognitive goal)	Students will take Lesson 34 Test.	Students will score at least 80% on Lesson 34 Test.
Concept: illustration essay. (cognitive goal)	Students will rewrite their research paper.	Students, with minimal errors, will rewrite their research paper.

SUGGESTED

Weekly *Implementation*

DAY 1	DAY 2	DAY 3	DAY 4	DAY 5
Rewrite your paper and submit it to your teacher/ guardian/ parents. Make a journal entry.	Rewrite your paper and submit it to your teacher/ guardian/ parents. Make a journal entry.	Rewrite your paper and submit it to your teacher/ guardian/ parents. Make a journal entry.	Rewrite your paper and submit it to your teacher/ guardian/ parents. Make a journal entry.	Submit your rough draft to your instructor/ guardian/ parent. Take Lesson 34 Test Make a journal entry.

ENRICHMENT ACTIVITIES/PROJECT

Students will rewrite a warm-up exercise.

SPEECH ASSIGNMENT

The student should practice saying the following phrases aloud in a speech.

Loose lips sink ships.

The sixth soldier sold his soul to the shepherd.

The big black bug bit the bitter bright burglar.

Round and round the rugged rocks the ragged rascals ran.

ANSWER: *Answers will vary.*

WRITING ASSIGNMENTS

1. Rewrite your entire paper.

2. Read 150 to 200 pages this week and create vocabulary cards.

3. Complete the speech assignment and have a teacher complete a speech evaluation (Appendix).

4. While preparing the warm-ups, pay particular attention to your writing style this week.

5. Meditate on 2 Kings 6.

RESEARCH PAPER BENCHMARK

The first draft of student research paper is finished! Now, during this lesson, student will revise/rewrite his/her entire paper. Once the rewrite is complete, submit the entire project to student evaluator/parent/teacher. Student paper will include: a cover sheet (example below), outline, the paper itself, and a bibliography (see Lesson 25).

Title
Author

Address
Date

LESSON 34 TEST

REWRITE (100 POINTS)

Revise and rewrite the following essay.

In James Fenimore Cooper's *Deerslayer* (www.4literature.net/James_Fenimore_Cooper/Deerslayer/), Hetty Hutter symbolized religion and morality. In the whole book she is the only character who showed an understanding of God's word. Cooper used her to symbolize not just religion and morality but also humility and peace. Though at times she was referred to as "feeble minded," she was clear-minded about God and her faith.

When Hetty gave herself over to the Iroquois, she did so with the attitude of a missionary. Willing to give her life for the sake of sharing the Word of God and rescuing her father and Hurry Harry showed her courage and selflessness. They listen to her, but their lives were not changed by what she said. In other words they were not affected by Hetty.

Hetty saw God as the Creator and the Lord of all, but she did not and probably could not change anyone's life with her knowledge of Him [God]. In a way it seems Cooper is making fun of Christians by using a feeble-minded girl who could not convert anyone to Christ. However, even though people around her respected and loved her, they never took her seriously. (Jessica Stobaugh)

LESSON 34 TEST ANSWER

REWRITE (100 POINTS)

Revise and rewrite the following essay.

SAMPLE ANSWER: rewrites will vary; check student rewrites for mechanics, punctuation, and structure:

Hetty Hutter, one of the main characters in James Fennimore Cooper's Deerslayer (www.4literature.net/ James_Fenimore_Cooper/Deerslayer/), symbolizes religion and morality. She is the only character who understands God's Word. Hetty symbolizes not just religion and morality but also the virtues of humility and peace. In fact, though she was referred to as "feeble-minded" in one way, in other ways she was clear-minded. She alone understood about God and her faith.

For example, when Hetty gave herself over to the Iroquois, she did so with the attitude of a missionary. Willing to give her life for the sake of sharing the Word of God and rescuing her father, her sacrifice showed courage and selflessness, Christ-like qualities.

Ironically, Cooper is trying to belittle Hetty by making her feeble-minded. In fact, though, she is the strongest moral character in this novel.

SKILLS OF RHETORIC

ENCOURAGING THOUGHTFUL CHRISTIANS
TO BE WORLD CHANGERS

APPENDICES

APPENDIX A

Writing Tips

How do students produce concise, well-written essays?

GENERAL STATEMENTS

• Essays should be written in the context of the other social sciences. This means that essays should be written on all topics: science topics, history topics, social science topics, etc.

• Some essays should be rewritten, depending on the assignment and the purpose of the writing; definitely those essays which are to be presented to various readers or a public audience should be rewritten for their best presentation. Parents and other educators should discuss with their students which and how many essays will be rewritten. Generally speaking, I suggest that students rewrite at least one essay per week.

• Students should write something every day and read something every day. Students will be prompted to read assigned whole books before they are due. It is imperative that students read ahead as they write present essays or they will not be able to read all the material. Remember this too: students tend to write what they read. Poor material—material that is too juvenile—will be echoed in the vocabulary and syntax of student essays.

• Students should begin writing assignments immediately after they are assigned. A suggested implementation schedule is provided. Generally speaking, students will write about one hour per day to accomplish the writing component of this course.

• Students should revise their papers as soon as they are evaluated. Follow the implementation schedule at the end of each course.

Every essay includes a *prewriting phase, an outlining phase, a writing phase, a revision phase,* and for the purposes of this course, *a publishing phase.*

PRE-WRITING THINKING CHALLENGE

ISSUE
State problem/issue in five sentences.

State problem/issue in two sentences.

State problem/issue in one sentence.

NAME THREE OR MORE SUBTOPICS OF PROBLEM.

NAME THREE OR MORE SUBTOPICS OF THE SUBTOPICS.

WHAT INFORMATION MUST BE KNOWN TO SOLVE THE PROBLEM OR TO ANSWER THE QUESTION?

STATE THE ANSWER TO THE QUESTION/
PROBLEM
—In five sentences.

—In two sentences.

—In one sentence.

STATED IN TERMS OF OUTCOMES, WHAT
EVIDENCES DO I SEE THAT CONFIRM THAT I
HAVE MADE THE RIGHT DECISION?

ONCE THE PROBLEM/QUESTION IS
ANSWERED/SOLVED, WHAT ONE OR TWO
NEW PROBLEMS/ANSWERS MAY ARISE?

ABBREVIATED PRE-WRITING THINKING CHALLENGE

What is the issue?
State problem/issue in five sentences.
State problem/issue in two sentences.
State problem/issue in one sentence.
Name three or more subtopics of problem.
Name three or more subtopics of the subtopics.
What information must be known to solve the problem
or to answer the question?
State the answer to the question/problem
—in five sentences —in two sentences —in one sentence.
Stated in terms of outcomes, what evidences do I see
that confirm that I have made the right decision?

Once the problem or question is answered or solved,
what are one or two new problems or answers that
could arise?

PRE-WRITING PHASE

Often called the brainstorming phase, the pre-writing
phase is the time you decide on exactly what your topic

is. What questions must you answer? You should articulate a thesis (a one sentence statement of purpose for
why you are writing about this topic. The thesis typically has two to four specific points contained within
it). You should decide what sort of essay this is—for
instance, a definition, an exposition, a persuasive argument—and then design a strategy. For example, a
clearly persuasive essay will demand that you state the
issue and give your opinion in the opening paragraph.

Next, after a thesis statement, you will write an outline. *No matter what length the essay may be, 20 pages or one
paragraph, you should create an outline.*

Outline
Thesis: In his poem *The Raven*, Edgar Allan Poe
uses literary devices to describe such weighty topics as
death and *unrequited love*, which draw the reader to an
insightful and many times emotional moment. (Note
that this thesis informs the reader that the author will
be exploring *death* and *unrequited love*.)

   I.   Introduction (Opens to the reader the exploration of the writing and tells the reader what
to expect.)
  II.   Body (This particular essay will include two
main points developed in two main paragraphs, one paragraph about death and one
paragraph about emotions. The second paragraph will be introduced by means of a transition word or phrase or sentence.)
     A. Imagining Death
     B. Feeling Emotions
 III. Conclusions (A paragraph which draws conclusions or solves the problem mentioned in
the thesis statement.)

One of the best ways to organize your thoughts is
to spend time in concentrated thinking, what some call
brainstorming. Thinking through what you want to
write is a way to narrow your topic.

Sample Outline:
Persuasive Paper with Three Major Points (Arguments)

I. Introduction: <u>Thesis statement</u> includes a listing or a summary of the three supportive arguments and introduces the paper.

II. Body
A. Argument 1
   Evidence
   (transition words or phrases or sentences to the next topic)
B. Argument 2
   Evidence
   (transition words or phrases or sentences to the next topic)
C. Argument 3
   Evidence
   (transition words or phrases or sentences to the conclusion)

III. Conclusion: Restatement of arguments and evidence used throughout the paper (do not use the words *in conclusion*—just conclude).

NOTE: For greater detail and explanation of outlining, refer to a composition handbook. Careful attention should be paid to parallel structure with words or phrases, to correct form with headings and subheadings, to punctuation, and to pairing of information. Correct outline structure will greatly enhance the writing of any paper.

Sample Outline:
Expository Essay with Four Major Points

I. Introduction: <u>Thesis statement</u> includes a listing or mention of four examples or supports and introduces the paper; use transitional words or phrases at the end of the paragraph.

II. Body
A. Example 1
   Application
   (transition words or phrases or sentences to the next topic)
B. Example 2
   Application
   (transition words or phrases or sentences to the next topic)
C. Example 3
   Application
   (transition words or phrases or sentences to the next topic)
D. Example 4
   Application
   (transition words or phrases or sentences to the conclusion)

III. Conclusion: Restatement of thesis, drawing from the evidence or applications used in the paper (do not use the words *in conclusion*—just conclude).

NOTE: For greater detail and explanation of outlining, refer to a composition handbook. Careful attention should be paid to parallel structure with words or phrases, to correct form with headings and subheadings, to punctuation, and to pairing of information. Correct outline structure will greatly enhance the writing of any paper.

The Thinking Challenge

The following is an example of a Thinking Challenge approach to Mark Twain's *The Adventures of Huckleberry Finn*:

The Problem or The Issue or The Question:

Should Huck turn in his escaped slave-friend Jim to the authorities?

State problem/issue in five sentences, then in two sentences, and, finally, in one sentence.

Five Sentences:
Huck runs away with Jim. He does so knowing that he is breaking the law. However, the lure of friendship overrides the perfidy he knows he is committing. As he floats down the Mississippi River, he finds it increasingly difficult to hide his friend from the authorities and to hide his feelings of ambivalence. Finally he manages to satisfy both ambiguities.

Two Sentences:
Huck intentionally helps his slave friend Jim escape from servitude. As Huck floats down the Mississippi River, he finds it increasingly difficult to hide his friend from the authorities and at the same time to hide his own feelings of ambivalence.

One Sentence:
After escaping with his slave-friend Jim and floating down the Mississippi River, Huck finds it increasingly difficult to hide his friend from the authorities and at the same time to hide his own feelings of ambivalence.

Name three or more subtopics of problem.
Are there times when we should disobey the law?
What responsibilities does Huck have to his family?
What should Huck do?

Name three or more subtopics of the subtopics.
Are there times when we should disobey the law?
Who determines what laws are unjust?
Should the law be disobeyed publicly?
Who is injured when we disobey the law?
What responsibilities does Huck have to his family?
Who is his family? Jim? His dad?
Is allegiance to them secondary to Jim's needs?
Should his family support his civil disobedience?

What should Huck do?
Turn in Jim?
Escape with Jim?
Both?

What information must be known?
Laws? Jim's character? If he is bad, then should Huck save him?

State the answer to the question/problem in five, two, and one sentence(s).

Five Sentences:
Huck can escape with Jim with profound feelings of guilt. After all, he is helping a slave escape. This is important because it shows that Huck is still a moral, if flawed, character. Jim's freedom does outweigh any other consideration—including the laws of the land and his family's wishes. As the story unfolds the reader sees that Huck is indeed a reluctant criminal, and the reader takes comfort in that fact.

Two Sentences:
Showing reluctance and ambivalence, Huck embarks on an arduous but moral adventure. Jim's freedom outweighs any other need or consideration.

One Sentence:
Putting Jim's freedom above all other considerations, Huck, the reluctant criminal, embarks on an arduous but moral adventure.

Once the Problem or Issue or Question is solved, what are one or two new problems that may arise? What if Huck is wrong? What consequences could Huck face?

Every essay has a beginning (introduction), a middle part (body), and an ending (conclusion). The introduction must draw the reader into the topic and usually presents the thesis to the reader. The body organizes the material and expounds on the thesis (a one sentence statement of purpose) in a cogent and inspiring way. The conclusion generally is a solution to the problem or issue or question or is sometimes a summary. Paragraphs in the body are connected with transitional words or phrases: *furthermore, therefore, in spite of.* Another effective transition technique is to mention in the first sentence of a new paragraph a thought or word that occurs in the last sentence of the previous paragraph. In any event, the body should be intentionally organized to advance the purposes of the paper. A disciplined writer *always* writes a rough draft. Using the well-thought-out outline composed during the pre-writing phase is an excellent way to begin the actual writing. The paper has already been processed mentally and only lacks the writing.

WRITING PHASE

The writer must make the first paragraph grab the reader's attention enough that the reader will want to continue reading.

The writer should write naturally, but not colloquially. In other words, the writer should not use clichés and everyday coded language. *The football players blew it* is too colloquial.

The writer should use as much visual imagery and precise detail as possible, should assume nothing, and should explain everything.

REWRITING PHASE

Despite however many rewrites are necessary, when the writer has effectively communicated the subject and corrected grammar and usage problems, she is ready to write the final copy.

Top Ten Most Frequent Essay Problems

Agreement between the Subject and Verb: Use singular forms of verbs with singular subjects and use plural forms of verbs with plural subjects.
WRONG: Everyone finished their homework.
RIGHT: Everyone finished his homework (*Everyone* is an indefinite singular pronoun.)

Using the Second Person Pronoun—"you," "your" should rarely, if ever, be used in a formal essay.
WRONG: You know what I mean (Too informal).

Redundancy: Never use "I think" or "It seems to me"
WRONG: I think that is true.
RIGHT: That is true (We know you think it, or you would not write it!)

Tense consistency: Use the same tense (usually present) throughout the paper.
WRONG: I was ready to go, but my friend is tired.
RIGHT: I am ready to go but my friend is tired.

Misplaced Modifiers: Place the phrase or clause close to its modifier.
WRONG: The man drove the car with a bright smile into the garage.
RIGHT: The man with a bright smile drove the car into the garage.

Antecedent Pronoun Problems: Make sure pronouns match (agree) in number and gender with their antecedents.
WRONG: Mary and Susan both enjoyed her dinner.
RIGHT: Mary and Susan both enjoyed their dinners.

Parallelism: Make certain that your list/sentence includes similar phrase types.
WRONG: I like to take a walk and swimming.
RIGHT: I like walking and swimming

Affect vs. Effect: Affect is a verb; Effect is a noun unless it means to achieve.

WRONG: His mood effects me negatively.

RIGHT: His mood affects me negatively.

RIGHT: The effects of his mood are devastating.

Dangling Prepositions: Rarely end a sentence with an unmodified preposition.

WRONG: Who were you speaking to?

RIGHT: To whom were you speaking?

Transitions: Make certain that paragraphs are connected with transitions (e.g., furthermore, therefore, in spite of).

RIGHT: Furthermore, Jack London loves to describe animal behavior.

APPENDIX B

PEER EVALUATION CHECKLIST

I. Organization

___ Is the writer's purpose clearly introduced? What is it?

___ Does the organization of the paper coincide with the outline?

___ Does the writer answer the assignment?

___ Does the introduction grab the reader's attention?

___ Is the purpose advanced by each sentence and paragraph? (Are there sentences which don't seem to belong in the paragraphs?)

___ Does the body (middle) of the paper advance the purpose?

___ Does the conclusion solve the purpose of the paper?

Comments regarding organization:

II. Mechanics

___ Does the writer use active voice?

___ Does the writer use the appropriate verb tense throughout the paper?

___ Is there agreement between all pronouns and antecedents?

___ Are there effective and appropriately used transitions?

Comments regarding other mechanical problems:

III. Argument

___ Are you persuaded by the arguments?

___ Does the author need stronger arguments? More arguments?

Other helpful comments:

COMPOSITION EVALUATION
TECHNIQUE I

Based on 100 points: 95/A

I. Grammar and Syntax: Is the composition grammatically correct?
(25 points) 20/25
   Comments: See Corrections. Watch Agreement. Your verb usage could be a lot more precise. Look up "Subject/Verb Agreement" in your grammar test, read about it, write the grammar rule, and then correct this part of your essay.

II. Organization: Does this composition exhibit well considered organization? Does it flow? Transitions? Introduction and a conclusion?
(25 points) 25/25
Comments: Good job with transitional phrases and with having a strong introduction. Your thesis statement gives me a clear idea about the content of your paper. Your conclusion explains your thesis very thoroughly.

III. Content: Does this composition answer the question, argue the point well, and/or persuade the reader?
(50 points) 50/50
Comments: Excellent insights. I was fully persuaded to your point of view. You supported your thesis well with strong arguments. I especially was impressed with _____

COMPOSITION EVALUATION
TECHNIQUE 2

I. Organization

___ Is the writer's purpose stated clearly in the introduction? Is there a thesis sentence? What is it?

___ Does the writer answer the assignment?

___ Does the introduction grab the reader's attention?

___ Is the purpose advanced by each sentence and
paragraph?

___ Does the body (middle) of the paper advance the
purpose?

___ Does the conclusion accomplish its purpose?

Other helpful comments for the writer:

II. Mechanics

___ Does the writer use active voice?

___ Does the writer use the appropriate verb tense
throughout the paper?

___ Is there agreement between all pronouns and
antecedents?

___ Is there appropriately subject/verb agreement?

___ Are the transitions effective and appropriate?

Other mechanical trouble spots:

III. Argument

___ Are you persuaded by the arguments?

Other helpful comments for the writer:

If the parent/educator does not wish to evaluate a student with a number grade, another option is to use a
checklist:

EVALUATION: SPEECH CHECKLIST

I. Poise
___ How does the student present him/herself? (10 points)
___ Is the oratory/dramatic reaading memorized? (10 points)

II. Articulation:
___ Does the student speak clearly? (20 points)
___ Does the student speak with appropriate volume? (20 points)

III. Presentation:
___ Does the speech accomplish its purpose? (40 points)

SAMPLE STUDENT ESSAY WITH EVALUATOR'S COMMENTS

Telling The Bees

Whittier was excellent at taking real life situations and turning them into poetry. He writes in such a way as to make the **reader** feel as though **he** | Sexist language: use plural form of nouns and pronouns to avoid this kind of discrimination. ie. readers feel as though they are there... | **is** there, experiencing **it** | indefinite pronoun: experiencing *what*? | with Whittier. He creates this effect by employing powerful imagery.

In his poem," Telling the Bees," | Good use of textual evidence—direct quotations. |

Whittier **takes** a life situation that actually happened in his life and **turned** | Verb tense change: takes—-turned | it into a poem. The poem is about the death of "Mistress Mary's." He begins with a description of the farm on which Mary and her bees live. **"There is the house, with the gate red-barred/ And the popular tall;/and the barns brown length, and the cattle yard,/And the white horns tossing above the wall."(lines 5-8)** The reader can see the farm and all its buildings. **He** feels as if **he** is there. | Use of sexist language; change nouns and pronouns to plural to avoid this type of discrimination. ie. Readers can see the farm and all its buildings. They feel as if they are there. |

The imagery only gets better. In lines 17-20 Whittier describes well the smells and feeling of the farmyard. "There's the same sweet clover-smell in the breeze;/ And the June sun warm/ Tangle his wings of fire in the trees,/Setting as then, over Fernside farm." Now the reader feels and even smells | Effective comparison to another poem. |

the farmyard. Whittier definitely has fond feeling for this place of | The word "This" needs something to modify. This *what*? |

peace and solitude. The language is similar to a poem a lover would write to his mistress. This imagery is nothing like the imagery one would read in a Robert Frost poem. In Frost's poem "Home Burial" a couple is struggling to overcome the grief of the loss of their baby. Nature, as described in the farmyard is alien, bitter, even dangerous. **This** is not the farmyard that Whittier describes. In "Home Burial" one sees a winter day; "Telling the Bees" describes a June day. The farmyard, nature, in Whittier is a place of life and hope.

It | Indefinite pronoun | is a place he knows well and enjoys visiting. Once again **he** | Whittier | draws the **reader** in taking **us** | who? reader = singular; who is **us**? | on a tour of the farm telling **us** about every little detail as a tour guide would for a tourist. **Now** | Next = a good transition word | he leads us to the bee hive where the **scene** of peace and servitude, **is** | Subject is separated from its predicate with a comma | suddenly **dash** | incorrect verb tense | by the "dearily singing" of "the chore- girl small,/ Draping each hive with a shred of black" (lines 39-40). **This** | Indefinite; This what? | is signaling a death. The happy, jolly feeling the reader felt just moments before is no longer **there, Whittier** has taken us on an unexpected turn," Run-on sentences Trembling, I [we] listened : the summer sun/ Had the chill of snow ;/ For I [we] knew she was telling the bee of one/ Gone on the journey we all must go!" **This** is not the care free guide who **had lead** incorrect verb tense us through the barn yard telling us of each land mark **he know** incorrect verb form so well. We can feel the "The fret and the pain" Whittier **most** spelling have gone through upon the death of this Mary. "And the song she was singing ever since/ In my ear sounds on:-/" Stay at home pretty bees, fly not hence!/ Mistress Mary is dead and gone!" (lines 53-56) The unbridled power in the chaos of the bee hive causes the reader to be uncomfortable. Mistress Mary, the bee keeper is dead. However, **they** indefinite: who is *they*? **drap** spelling the hive with black cloth and sing to the bees. Presumably now the chaos is controlled and order is returned. Again, returning to the Naturalistic writer Robert Frost, Nature is never controlled, never an altruistic presence in the world. Nature is impersonal.

Through effective imagery, Whittier succeeds in having his reader feel what he feels. **Not so much by telling us how he feels, but by his powerful descriptions of the farm and all its wonders.** Fragment By drawing the **reader** into the poem and making **us** pronoun/antecedent disagreement feel the same emotions he does, **we** are able to better understand the poem as well as the poet. We are left with a sense of hope.

Note: There are several other unmarked errors in this essay.

Can you find some of them?

What is your opinion of this essay?

What criteria would you use to evaluate it?

How can you make it into a stronger essay?

APPENDIX C

NOVEL REVIEW

BOOK _____ STUDENT _____

AUTHOR _____ DATE OF READING _____

I. BRIEFLY DESCRIBE:
PROTAGONIST—

ANTAGONIST—

OTHER CHARACTERS USED TO DEVELOP PROTAGONIST—

IF APPLICABLE, STATE WHY ANY OF THE BOOK'S CHARACTERS REMIND YOU OF SPECIFIC BIBLE CHARACTERS.

II. SETTING:

III. POINT OF VIEW: (CIRCLE ONE) FIRST PERSON, THIRD PERSON, THIRD PERSON OMNISCIENT

IV. BRIEF SUMMARY OF THE PLOT:

V. THEME (THE QUINTESSENTIAL MEANING/PURPOSE OF THE BOOK IN ONE OR TWO SENTENCES):

VI. AUTHOR'S WORLDVIEW: HOW DO YOU KNOW? WHAT BEHAVIORS DO(ES) THE CHARACTER(S) MANIFEST THAT LEAD YOU TO THIS CONCLUSION?

VII. WHY DID YOU LIKE/DISLIKE THIS BOOK?

VIII. THE NEXT LITERARY WORK I READ WILL BE . . .

SHORT STORY REVIEW

SHORT STORY _____ STUDENT _____

AUTHOR _____ DATE OF READING _____

I. BRIEFLY DESCRIBE
PROTAGONIST—

ANTAGONIST—

OTHER CHARACTERS USED TO DEVELOP PROTAGONIST—

IF APPLICABLE, STATE WHY ANY OF THE STORY'S CHARACTERS REMIND YOU OF SPECIFIC
BIBLE CHARACTERS.

II. SETTING

III. POINT OF VIEW: (CIRCLE ONE) FIRST PERSON, THIRD PERSON, THIRD PERSON OMNISCIENT

IV. BRIEF SUMMARY OF THE PLOT

IDENTIFY THE CLIMAX OF THE SHORT STORY.

V. THEME (THE QUINTESSENTIAL MEANING/PURPOSE OF THE STORY IN ONE OR TWO SENTENCES):

VI. AUTHOR'S WORLDVIEW:
HOW DO YOU KNOW THIS? WHAT BEHAVIORS DO(ES) THE CHARACTER(S) MANIFEST THAT LEAD YOU TO THIS CONCLUSION?

VII. WHY DID YOU LIKE/DISLIKE THIS SHORT STORY?

VIII. THE NEXT LITERARY WORK I READ WILL BE . . .

DRAMA REVIEW

PLAY _____ STUDENT _____

AUTHOR _____ DATE OF READING _____

I. BRIEFLY DESCRIBE
PROTAGONIST—

ANTAGONIST—

IF APPLICABLE, STATE WHY ANY OF THE PLAY'S CHARACTERS REMIND YOU OF SPECIFIC BIBLE CHARACTERS.

II. SETTING

III. POINT OF VIEW: (CIRCLE ONE) FIRST PERSON, THIRD PERSON, THIRD PERSON OMNISCIENT

IV. BRIEF SUMMARY OF THE PLOT

IDENTIFY THE CLIMAX OF THE PLAY.

V. THEME (THE QUINTESSENTIAL MEANING/PURPOSE OF THE PLAY IN ONE OR TWO SENTENCES)

VI. AUTHOR'S WORLDVIEW
HOW DO YOU KNOW THIS? WHAT BEHAVIORS DO(ES) THE CHARACTER(S) MANIFEST THAT LEAD YOU TO THIS CONCLUSION?

VII. WHY DID YOU LIKE/DISLIKE THIS PLAY?

VIII. THE NEXT LITERARY WORK I WILL READ WILL BE . . .

NON-FICTION REVIEW

LITERARY WORK _____ STUDENT _____

AUTHOR _____ DATE OF READING _____

I. WRITE A PRÉCIS OF THIS BOOK. IN YOUR PRÉCIS, CLEARLY STATE THE AUTHOR'S THESIS AND SUPPORTING ARGUMENTS.

II. ARE YOU PERSUADED? WHY OR WHY NOT?

III. WHY DID YOU LIKE/DISLIKE THIS BOOK?

IV. THE NEXT LITERARY WORK I READ WILL BE . . .

APPENDIX D

PRAYER JOURNAL GUIDE

Journal Guide Questions

Bible Passage(s): _____

_____

_____

1. Centering Time (a list of those things that I must do later):

2. Discipline of Silence (remain absolutely still and quiet).

3. Reading Scripture Passage (with notes on text):

4. Living in Scripture:

A. How does the passage affect the person mentioned in the passage? How does he/she feel?

B. How does the passage affect my life? What is the Lord saying to me through this passage?

5. Prayers of Adoration and Thanksgiving, Intercession, and Future Prayer Targets:

6. Discipline of Silence

APPENDIX E

BOOK LIST FOR SUPPLEMENTAL READING

Note:
Not all literature is suitable for all students; educators and students should choose literature appropriate to students' age, maturity, interests, and abilities.

Jane Austen, EMMA

Charlotte Brontë, JANE EYRE

Thomas Bulfinch, THE AGE OF FABLE

Pearl S. Buck, THE GOOD EARTH

John Bunyan, PILGRIM'S PROGRESS

Agatha Christie, AND THEN THERE WERE NONE

Samuel T. Coleridge, RIME OF THE ANCIENT MARINER

Jospeh Conrad, HEART OF DARKNESS, LORD JIM

James F. Cooper, THE LAST OF THE MOHICANS, DEERSLAYER

Stephen Crane, THE RED BADGE OF COURAGE

Clarence Day, LIFE WITH FATHER

Daniel Defoe, ROBINSON CRUSOE

Charles Dickens, GREAT EXPECTATIONS, A CHRISTMAS CAROL, A TALE OF TWO CITIES, OLIVER TWIST, NICHOLAS NICKLEBY

Arthur C. Doyle, THE ADVENTURES OF SHERLOCK HOLMES

Alexander Dumas, THE THREE MUSKETEERS

George Eliot, SILAS MARNER

T.S. Eliot, MURDER IN THE CATHEDRAL, SILAS MARNER

Anne Frank, THE DIARY OF ANNE FRANK

Oliver Goldsmith, THE VICAR OF WAKEFIELD

Edith Hamilton, MYTHOLOGY

Nathaniel Hawthorne, THE SCARLET LETTER, THE HOUSE OF THE SEVEN GABLES

Thor Heyerdahl, KON-TIKI

J. Hilton, LOST HORIZON, GOODBYE, MR. CHIPS

Homer, THE ODYSSEY, THE ILIAD

W. H. Hudson, GREEN MANSIONS

Victor Hugo, LES MISERABLES, THE HUNCHBACK OF NOTRE DAME

Zora Neale Hurston, THEIR EYES WERE WATCHING GOD

Washington Irving, THE SKETCH BOOK

Rudyard Kipling, CAPTAINS COURAGEOUS

Harper Lee, TO KILL A MOCKINGBIRD

Madeline L'Engle, A CIRCLE OF QUIET, THE SUMMER OF THE GREAT GRANDMOTHER, A WRINKLE IN TIME

C. S. Lewis, THE SCREWTAPE LETTERS, MERE CHRISTIANITY, CHRONICLES OF NARNIA

Jack London, THE CALL OF THE WILD, WHITE FANG

George MacDonald, CURATE'S AWAKENING, ETC.

Sir Thomas Malory, LE MORTE D'ARTHUR

Guy de Maupassant, SHORT STORIES

Herman Melville, BILLY BUDD, MOBY DICK

Monsarrat, THE CRUEL SEA

C. Nordhoff & Hall, MUTINY ON THE BOUNTY

Edgar Allen Poe, POEMS & SHORT STORIES

E. M. Remarque, ALL QUIET ON THE WESTERN FRONT

Anne Rinaldi, A BREAK WITH CHARITY: STORY OF THE SALEM WITCH TRIALS

Carl Sanburg, ABRAHAM LINCOLN

William Saroyan, THE HUMAN COMEDY

Sir Walter Scott, IVANHOE

William Shakespeare, HAMLET, MACBETH, JULIUS CAESAR, AS YOU LIKE IT, ROMEO AND JULIET, A MIDSUMMER NIGHT'S DREAM, ETC.

George Bernard Shaw, PYGMALION

Sophocles, ANTIGONE

Harriet Beecher Stowe, UNCLE TOM'S CABIN

John Steinbeck, OF MICE AND MEN, GRAPES OF WRATH

R.L. Stevenson, DR. JEKYLL AND MR. HYDE, TREASURE ISLAND, KIDNAPPED

Irving Stone, LUST FOR LIFE

Jonathan Swift, GULLIVER'S TRAVELS
Booth Tarkington, PENROD
J.R.R. Tolkien, THE LORD OF THE RINGS TRILOGY
Mark Twain, ADVENTURES OF HUCKLEBERRY FINN, THE ADVENTURES OF TOM SAWYER
Jules Verne, MASTER OF THE WORLD
Booker T. Washington, UP FROM SLAVERY
H. G. Wells, COLLECTED WORKS
Tennessee Williams, THE GLASS MENAGERIE

FOR OLDER STUDENTS

Chinua Achebe, THINGS FALL APART
Aristotle, POETICUS
Edward Bellamy, LOOKING BACKWARD
Jorge Luis Borges, (Colombia, Argentina) VARIOUS SHORT STORIES
Stephen V. Benet, JOHN BROWN'S BODY
Charlotte Brontë, WUTHERING HEIGHTS
Camus, THE STRANGER
Chaucer, THE CANTERBURY TALES, BEOWULF
Willa Cather, MY ANTONIA
Miguel de Cervantes, DON QUIXOTE
Fyodor Dostovesky, CRIME AND PUNISHMENT, THE IDIOT, THE BROTHERS KARAMAZOV
William Faulkner, THE HAMLET TRIOLOGY
F. Scott Fitzgerald, THE GREAT GATSBY
John Galsworthy, THE FORSYTHE SAGA
Lorraine Hansberry, RAISIN IN THE SUN
Thomas Hardy, THE RETURN OF THE NATIVE, THE MAYOR OF CASTERBRIDGE
A. E. Housman, A SHROPSHIRE LAD
Henrik Ibsen, A DOLL'S HOUSE
Charles Lamb THE ESSAYS OF ELIA
Sinclair Lewis, BABBITT, ARROWSMITH
Kamala Markandaya, NECTAR IN A SIEVE
Gabriel Barcia Marquez, 100 YEARS OF SOLITUDE
John P. Marquand, THE LATE GEORGE APLEY
E. Lee Masters, A SPOON RIVER ANTHOLOGY
Somerset Maugham, OF HUMAN BONDAGE
Arthur Miller, THE CRUCIBLE, DEATH OF A SALESMAN
Eugene O'Neill, THE EMPEROR JONES
George Orwell, ANIMAL FARM, 1984
Thomas Paine, THE RIGHTS OF MAN
Alan Paton, CRY THE BELOVED COUNTRY
Plato, THE REPUBLIC
Plutarch, LIVES
O. E. Rolvaag, GIANTS IN THE EARTH
Edmund Rostand, CYRANO DE BERGERAC
Mary Shelley, FRANKENSTEIN
Sophocles, OEDIPUS REX
John Steinbeck, THE PEARL
Ivan Turgenev, FATHERS AND SONS
William Thackeray, VANITY FAIR
Leo Tolstoy, WAR AND PEACE
Edith Wharton, ETHAN FROME
Walt Whitman, LEAVES OF GRASS
Thornton Wilder, OUR TOWN
Thomas Wolfe, LOOK HOMEWARD ANGEL

APPENDIX F

GLOSSARY OF LITERARY TERMS

Allegory A story or tale with two or more levels of meaning—a literal level and one or more symbolic levels. The events, setting, and characters in an allegory are symbols for ideas or qualities.

Alliteration The repetition of initial consonant sounds. The repetition can be juxtaposed (side by side; e.g., simply sad). An example:

I conceive therefore, as to the business of being profound, that it is with writers, as with wells; a person with good eyes may see to the bottom of the deepest, provided any water be there; and that often, when there is nothing in the world at the bottom, besides dryness and dirt, though it be but a yard and a half under ground, it shall pass, however, for wondrous deep, upon no wiser a reason than because it is wondrous dark. (Jonathan Swift)

Allusion A casual and brief reference to a famous historical or literary figure or event:

You must borrow me Gargantua's mouth first. 'Tis a word too great for any mouth of this age's size. (Shakespeare)

Analogy The process by which new or less familiar words, constructions, or pronunciations conform to the pattern of older or more familiar (and often unrelated) ones; a comparison between two unlike things. The purpose of an analogy is to describe something unfamiliar by pointing out its similarities to something that is familiar.

Antagonist In a narrative, the character with whom the main character has the most conflict. In Jack London's "To Build a Fire" the antagonist is the extreme cold of the Yukon rather than a person or animal.

Archetype The original pattern or model from which all other things of the same kind are made; a perfect example of a type or group. (e.g. The biblical character Joseph is often considered an archetype of Jesus Christ.)

Argumentation The discourse in which the writer presents and logically supports a particular view or opinion; sometimes used interchangeably with *persuasion*.

Aside In a play an aside is a speech delivered by an actor in such a way that other characters on the stage are presumed not to hear it; an aside generally reveals a character's inner thoughts.

Autobiography A form of nonfiction in which a person tells his/her own life story. Notable examples of autobiography include those by Benjamin Franklin and Frederick Douglass.

Ballad A song or poem that tells a story in short stanzas and simple words with repetition, refrain, etc.

Biography A form of nonfiction in which a writer tells the life story of another person.

Character A person or an animal who takes part in the action of a literary work. The *main character* is the one on whom the work focuses. The person with whom the main character has the most conflict is the *antagonist*. He is the enemy of the main character (*protagonist*). For instance, in *The Scarlet Letter*, by Nathaniel Hawthorne, Chillingsworth is the antagonist. Hester is the protagonist. Characters who appear in the story may perform actions, speak to other characters, be described by the narrator, or be remembered. Characters introduced whose sole purpose is to develop the main character are called *foils*.

Classicism An approach to literature and the other arts that stresses reason, balance, clarity, ideal beauty, and orderly form in imitation of the arts of Greece and Rome.

Conflict A struggle between opposing forces; can be internal or external; when occurring within a character is called *internal conflict*. An example of this occurs in Mark Twain's *Adventures of Huckleberry Finn*. In this novel Huck is struggling in his mind about whether to return an escaped slave, his good friend Jim, to the authorities. An *external conflict* is normally an obvious conflict between the protagonist and antagonist(s). London's "To Build a Fire" illustrates conflict between a character and an outside force. Most plots develop from conflict, making conflict one of the primary elements of narrative literature.

Crisis or *Climax* The moment or event in the *plot* in which the conflict is most directly addressed: the main character "wins" or "loses"; the secret is revealed. After the climax, the *denouement* or falling action occurs.

Dialectic Examining opinions or ideas logically, often by the method of question and answer

Discourse, Forms of Various modes into which writing can be classified; traditionally, writing has been divided into the following modes:
Exposition Writing which presents information
Narration Writing which tells a story
Description Writing which portrays people, places, or things
Persuasion (sometimes also called *Argumentation*) Writing which attempts to convince people to think or act in a certain way

Drama A story written to be performed by actors; the playwright supplies dialogue for the characters to speak and stage directions that give information about costumes, lighting, scenery, properties, the setting, and the character's movements and ways of speaking.

Dramatic monologue A poem or speech in which an imaginary character speaks to a silent listener. Eliot's "The Love Song of J. Alfred Prufrock" is a dramatic monologue.

Elegy A solemn and formal lyric poem about death, often one that mourns the passing of some particular person; Whitman's "When Lilacs Last in the Dooryard Bloom'd" is an elegy lamenting the death of President Lincoln.

Essay A short, nonfiction work about a particular subject; *essay* comes from the Old French word *essai*, meaning "a trial or attempt"; meant to be explanatory, an essay is not meant to be an exhaustive treatment of a subject; can be classified as formal or informal, personal or impersonal; can also be classified according to purpose as either expository, argumentative, descriptive, persuasive, or narrative.

Figurative Language See *metaphor, simile, analogy*

Foil A character who provides a contrast to another character and whose purpose is to develop the main character.

Genre A division or type of literature; commonly divided into three major divisions, literature is either poetry, prose, or drama; each major genre can then be divided into smaller genres: poetry can be divided into lyric, concrete, dramatic, narrative, and epic poetry; prose can be divided into fiction (novels and short stories) and nonfiction (biography, autobiography, letters, essays, and reports); drama can be divided into serious drama, tragedy, comic drama, melodrama, and farce.

Gothic The use of primitive, medieval, wild, or mysterious elements in literature; Gothic elements offended 18th century classical writers but appealed to the Romantic writers who followed them. Gothic novels feature writers who use places like mysterious castles where horrifying supernatural events take place; Poe's "The Fall of the House of Usher" illustrates the influence of Gothic elements.

Harlem Renaissance Occurring during the 1920s, a time of African American artistic creativity centered in Harlem in New York City; Langston Hughes was a Harlem Renaissance writer.

Hyperbole A deliberate exaggeration or overstatement; in Mark Twain's "The Notorious Jumping From of Calaveras County," the claim that Jim Smiley would follow a bug as far as Mexico to win a bet is hyperbolic.

Idyll A poem or part of a poem that describes and idealizes country life; Whittier's "Snowbound" is an idyll.

Irony A method of humorous or subtly sarcastic expression in which the intended meanings of the words used is the direct opposite of their usual sense.

Journal A daily autobiographical account of events and personal reactions.

Kenning Indirect way of naming people or things; knowledge or recognition; in Old English poetry, a metaphorical name for something.

Literature All writings in prose or verse, especially those of an imaginative or critical character, without regard to their excellence and/or writings considered as having permanent value, excellence of form, great emotional effect, etc.

Metaphor (Figure of speech) A comparison which creatively identifies one thing with another dissimilar thing and transfers or ascribes to the first thing some of the qualities of the second. Unlike a *simile* or *analogy*, metaphor asserts that one thing is another thing—not just that one is like another. Very frequently a metaphor is invoked by the verb *to be*:

Affliction then is ours;
We are the trees whom shaking fastens more. (George Herbert)

Then Jesus declared, "I am the bread of life." (John 6:35)
Jesus answered, "I am the Way and the truth and the life." (John 14:6)

Meter A poem's rhythmical pattern, determined by the number and types of stresses, or beats, in each line; a certain number of *metrical feet* make up a *line* of verse; (pentameter denotes a line containing five metrical feet); the act of describing the meter of a poem is called *scanning* which involves marking the stressed and unstressed syllables, as follows:
   iamb A foot with one unstressed syllable followed by one stressed syllable, as in the word *abound*.
   trochee A foot with one stressed syllable followed by one unstressed syllable, as in the word *spoken*.
   anapest A foot with two unstressed syllables followed by one stressed syllable, as in the word *interrupt*.

   dactyl A foot with a stressed syllable followed by two unstressed syllables, as in the word *accident*.
   spondee Two stressed feet: *quicksand, heartbeat*; occurs only occasionally in English.

Motif A main idea element, feature; a main theme or subject to be elaborated on.

Narration The way the author chooses to tell the story.
   First Person Narration: A character and refers to himself or herself, using "I." Example: Huck Finn in *The Adventures of Huckleberry Finn* tells the story from his perspective. This is a creative way to bring humor into the plot.
   Second Person Narration: Addresses the reader and/or the main character as "you" (and may also use first person narration, but not necessarily). One example is the opening of each of Rudyard Kipling's *Just So Stories*, in which the narrator refers to the child listener as "O Best Beloved."
   Third Person Narration: Not a character in the story; refers to the story's characters as "he" and "she." This is probably the most common form of narration.
   Limited Narration: Only able to tell what one person is thinking or feeling. Example: in *A Separate Peace*, by John Knowles, we only see the story from Gene's perspective.
   Omniscient Narration: Charles Dickens employs this narration in most of his novels.
   Reliable Narration: Everything this Narration says is true, and the Narrator knows everything that is necessary to the story.
   Unreliable Narrator: May not know all the relevant information; may be intoxicated or mentally ill; may lie to the audience. Example: Edgar Allan Poe's narrators are frequently unreliable. Think of the delusions that the narrator of "The Tell-Tale Heart" has about the old man.

Narrative In story form.

Onomatopoeia. Use of words which, in their pronunciation, suggest their meaning. "Hiss," for example, when spoken is intended to resemble the sound of steam or of a snake. Other examples include these: *slam, buzz, screech, whirr, crush, sizzle, crunch, wring, wrench, gouge, grind, mangle, bang, blam, pow, zap, fizz, urp, roar, growl, blip, click, whimper*, and, of course, *snap, crackle, and pop*.

255

Parallelism Two or more balancing statements with phrases, clauses, or paragraphs of similar length and grammatical structure.

Plot Arrangement of the action in fiction or drama— events of the story in the order the story gives them. A typical plot has five parts: *Exposition, Rising Action, Crisis* or *Climax, Falling Action,* and *Resolution* (sometimes called *Denouement).*

Précis Summary of the plot of a literary piece.

Protagonist The enemy of the main character (*antagonist*).

Rhetoric Using words effectively in writing and speaking.

Setting The place(s) and time(s) of a story, including the historical period, social milieu of the characters, geographical location, descriptions of indoor and outdoor locales.

Scop An Old English poet or bard.

Simile A figure of speech in which one thing is likened to another dissimilar thing by the use of *like, as,* etc.

Sonnet A poem normally of fourteen lines in any of several fixed verse and rhyme schemes, typically in rhymed iambic pentameter; sonnets characteristically express a single theme or idea.

Structure The arrangement of details and scenes that make up a literary work.

Style An author's characteristic arrangement of words. A style may be colloquial, formal, terse, wordy, theoretical, subdued, colorful, poetic, or highly individual. Style is the arrangement of words in groups and sentences; *diction* on the other hand refers to the choice of individual words; the arrangement of details and scenes make up the *structure* of a literary work; all combine to influence the tone of the work; thus, diction, style, and structure make up the *form* of the literary work.

Theme The one-sentence, major meaning of a literary piece, rarely stated but implied. The theme is not a moral, which is a statement of the author's didactic purpose of his literary piece. A thesis statement is very similar to the theme.

Tone The attitude the author takes toward his subject; author's attitude is revealed through choice of details, through diction and style, and through the emphasis and comments that are made; like theme and style, tone is sometimes difficult to describe with a single word or phrase; often it varies in the same literary piece to suit the moods of the characters and the situations. For instance, the tone or mood of Poe's "Annabel Lee" is very somber.

Credits, Permissions, and Sources

Efforts have been made to conform to US Copyright Law. Any infringement is unintentional, and any file which infringes copyright, and about which the copyright claimant informs me, will be removed pending resolution.

All graphics are copyrighted by Clipart.com unless otherwise noted.

Most of the literature cited in this book is in the public domain. Much of it is available on the Internet through the following sites:

Bartleby.com, Great Books Online
Aeschylus, *Oresteia*
Budda, *The Bhagavad-Gîtââ*
Confucius, *The Sayings of Confucius*
Epictetus, *The golden sayings of Epictetus*, with the Hymn of Cleanthes; translated and arranged by Hastings Crossley
Mohammed, *Koran*
Plato, *Apology*
Unknown, *The Song of Roland*

Susan Wise Bauer, *Writing The Short Story* (Charles City, VA)

Classical Short Stories: The Best of the Genre (http://www.geocities.com/short_stories_page/index.html)
Leo Tolstoy, The Death of Ivan Ilych, Translated by Louise and Aylmer Maude.

Early Christian Writings (http://www.earlychristianwritings.com/justin.html)
Writings, by Polycarp, Justin Martyr, and Clement

Enuma Elish translated by N. K. Sanders (http://www.piney.com/Enuma.html)

Everypoet.com
Dante, *Inferno*

Gilgamesh Epic, translated by E. A. Speiser, in *Ancient Near Eastern Texts* (Princeton, 1950), pp. 60-72, as reprinted in Isaac Mendelsohn (ed.), *Religions of the Ancient Near East*, Library of Religion paperbook series (New York, 1955). PP. 100-6; notes by Mendolenson (http://www-relg-studies.scu.edu/netcours/rs011/restrict/gilflood.htm).

Herodotus, *Histories*. Translated by Rawlinson. (http://www.concordance.com/)

Herodotus and the Bible, Wayne Jackson (http://www.christiancourier.com/archives/)

http://www.cyberhymnal.org/htm/m/i/mightyfo.htm
Martin Luther, *A Mighty Fortress is Our God*

Infomotions, Inc. The Alex Catalogue of Electronic Texts (http://www.infomotions.com/alex/).

Infoplease.com. 2002 Family Education Network. (http://aolsvc.aol.infoplease.com/ipa/A0874987.html)

The Internet Classics Archive (http://classics.mit.edu/Aristotle/poetics.1.1.html)

Aristotle, *Poetics*

Internet Applications Laboratory at the University of Evansville
Plato, *Symposium*

The Library of Congress Collection (http://www.loc.gov/exhibits/gadd/)

Lecture on Sor Juana Ines de la Cruz (http://www.latin_american.cam.ac.uk/SorJuana/)
Sor Juana Ines de la Cruz, "May Heaven Serve as Plate for the Engraving" and "Yet if, for Singing your Praise."

National Park Service (http://www.nps.gov/edal/index.htm)

The Pachomius Library (http://www.ocf.org/OrthodoxPage/reading/St.Pachomius/Liturgical/didache.html)
Unknown, *The Didache*, edited by Friar Martin Fontenot Gonzalez

Shinto Creation Stories (http://www.wsu.edu/~dee/ANCJAPAN/CREAT2.HTM)
The Creation of the gods (Translated by W.G. Aston, Nihongi (London: Kegan, Paul, Trench, Trüübner, 1896), 1-2

Stephane Theroux. Classic Reader (http://classicreader.com/)
Anton Chekov, *The Sea Gull*
Andrew Barton Paterson, The Man From Snowy River

University of Oregon. (http://www.uoregon.edu)
Iliad, Homer. Translated by Samuel Butler.

University of Pennsylvania (www.sas.upenn.edu/)
Author Unknown, *Ani Papyrus: Book of the Dead*

University of Virginia. Browse E-Books by Author (http://etext.lib.virginia.edu/ebooks/Wlist.html).

University of Wisconsin, Milwaukee. The Classic Text: Traditions and Interpretations (http://www.uwm.edu/Library/
    special/exhibits/clastext/clshome.htm)

NOTES

NOTES

NOTES

NOTES

NOTES

NOTES